Ethical Leadership for
School Administrators and Teachers

ALSO BY JOSEPH P. HESTER

*The Ten Commandments: A Handbook of
Religious, Legal and Social Issues*
(McFarland, 2003)

*Public School Safety:
A Handbook, with a Resource Guide*
(McFarland, 2003)

Ethical Leadership
for School
Administrators
and Teachers

JOSEPH P. HESTER

with a foreword by H. Darrell Young

McFarland & Company, Inc., Publishers
Jefferson, North Carolina, and London

LIBRARY OF CONGRESS ONLINE CATALOG

Hester, Joseph P.
    Ethical leadership for school administrators and teachers
/ Joseph P. Hester ; with a foreword by H. Darrell Young.
        p.   cm.
    Includes bibliographical reference and index.

    ISBN 0-7864-1715-3 (softcover : 50# alkaline paper)

    1. Educational leadership—Moral and ethical aspects—United
States.   2. School administrators—Professional ethics—United
States.   3. Teachers—Professional ethics—United States.   I. Title.
LB1779 .H47   2003
371.2'0122   2003016496

British Library cataloguing data are available

Manufactured in the United States of America

Cover image photograph ©2003 Comstock

McFarland & Company, Inc., Publishers
    Box 611, Jefferson, North Carolina 28640
        www.mcfarlandpub.com

This book is dedicated to two outstanding educational leaders.
First, to Dr. Robert Ayers,
Professor Emeritus at the University of Georgia,
who was instrumental in bringing the university's
Philosophy Department to national prominence
during the 1960s and 1970s, and who gave freely of his time and
finances at the end of his career to create and build
the university's Department of Religious Studies.

Second, to my wife Pat,
who was an exceptional leader for Park View Play School
in Athens, Georgia, from 1969 to 1972,
and who mentored and counseled young teachers
while teaching second grade at Balls Creek Elementary School
from 1975 to 2001.

Both of these individuals
have had a profound influence on my life and career,
and I am deeply indebted to them.

Acknowledgments

Many individuals helped make possible the writing of this book. The willingness of McFarland & Company to support this project and allow my creativity and ideas to flourish provided the needed motivation and enthusiasm for its accomplishment.

I would like to thank my wife, who put up with my many hours in front of a computer or curled up with several books only to ignore whatever chores awaited me around the house and in the yard. I also ask the pardon of my children and grandchildren, friends and relatives, whom I have in part neglected while researching and writing this manuscript. Although I did manage a short vacation with my wife and our friends, Rod and Joan Skaggs, in the fall of 2002, it was a much-needed reprieve from writing and gave me the added strength to generate new ideas, especially the Manifesto of Ethical Leadership for Educators.

Two principals and one assistant principal read the completed manuscript in January and February of 2003. Our discussions greatly improved the flow of my words as well as clarified what was then ambiguous and tentative. To Jeff Isenhour, Principal of Balls Creek Elementary School; Jerry Griffin, Principal of Oxford Elementary School; and Karen Hammett, Assistant Principal of Lyle Creek Elementary School—all in the Catawba County School System, Newton, North Carolina—I indeed am grateful that they took the time to read, edit, and comment about my ideas.

I would also like to thank the following individuals for adding some of their experiences and insights to the Manifesto: Robert Ayers, Professor Emeritus, Department of Religious Studies, University of Georgia; Donald R. Killian, Professor Emeritus, Gaston College, Gastonia, North Carolina; Philip F. Vincent, consultant and owner of the Character Development Group, Chapel Hill, North Carolina; Dr. Garnet Millar, Provincial Coordinator, Guidance and Counseling, Alberta Learning, Alberta, Canada, and Adjunct Professor with the Educational Psychology Department, Faculty of Education, University of Alberta, Edmonton, Alberta. Although now retired, Dr. Millar continues his work as a practicing psychologist and school counselor one day a week in Edmonton.

Finally, I would like to thank H. Darrell Young, without whose guidance and insights this book could not have been written. For the past five years Darrell and I have collaborated on several leadership projects. We began working together when he asked me to assist with his leadership training manual in 1998. From then until now we have worked to support each other's work in leadership development and hope to continue to do so into the foreseeable future. I am indeed indebted for his insights, ideas, and ability to mentor an old warhorse this late in his career.

Contents

Foreword
by H. Darrell Young

Scottish psychiatrist R. D. Lang once said, "We live in a moment in time where the rate of change is so speeded up, we see the future only as it is disappearing." External forces that we neither individually nor corporately have the influence to slow down drive the acceleration of these changes. Yet these forces are rewriting the rules of personal value creation and improvement. A good example is the transition into an age of information and knowledge workers in which information becomes valuable only if it is turned into knowledge and is used in the service of others. However, the more knowledge we create, the more specialized we become, and the more specialized we become, the greater our dependence on each other for increased and enhanced value. Individual knowledge, which often rewards only the individual is no longer acceptable. It is our ability to share and combine our knowledge with that of others, and apply it accurately to the needs and values of our society that develops and creates personal value. Built into the information age is the fact that we are dependent on each other for the creation and delivery of human value. As a result, the challenge of educating future generations of knowledge workers will be determined by our ability to balance intellectual and interpersonal capabilities and skills. The time has come to give up the individualism and selfishness that drives personal profit. Twenty-first-century leadership will be built on a solid foundation of dialogue and understanding, of relationships that bring together a respect and integrity for each others' collective abilities.

In order for us to deal with this environment, it becomes imperative that we know who we are, where we're going, and who will be going with us. Who we are determines our foundation and establishes our standards for accountability. Where we're going will demand continuous learning, improvement, and growth. Who will go with us becomes an indicator of the effectiveness of our influence and relationships. The need for ethical servant behaviors to ensure sustainable quality relationships in an environment of unpredictability, volatility, and uncertainty screams for ethical serving leaders. Dr. Joe Hester has explicitly issued the call in this book. He has defined the current realities of our educational environment and has painted a vision of a future, which is in sync with twenty-first-century requirements. He has issued the challenge of learning to love change and not to resist change or being changed. How can we say that as educators we love to learn and are committed to perpetual learning and not be willing to get out of the box in which we've lived for most of our careers? The very purpose of leadership is to transform cultures with a shared vision of the future that in some way makes things better than what presently exists. Personal transformation is not an option if we intend to create leadership environments that build community and continually improve value for the purpose of developing leaders. Dr. Hester points out that the greatest roadblock to transformation is an unwillingness to give up what we know in order to get what we need to learn. Past behaviors that honored position, stability, power, and control through systems and procedures must be balanced with a new set of behaviors and disciplines that are driven by an understanding of the concepts and interconnections of strategic/critical thinking, continuous improvement, divesting of self and investing in others. These are the global concepts of leadership.

Dr. Hester has summed up the twenty-first-century definition of leadership in two words: ethics and servanthood. Even though there have been libraries written on each of these two subjects, they cannot be separated in the context of leadership. Several years ago I was asked by a ninth grade student what happens when leaders stop following? I was so taken back by the depth and breath of the question that my answer was, "I don't know." I asked the class to give thought to the answer before our next class and to choose someone they considered to be a leader to compile the thoughts and present them at our next meeting. Here was their answer: "We believe that leaders who stop following become *dictators* because they no longer perceive the need for perpetual learning, self-development, and improvement." Great leadership is not about making the decision to lead, but about owning and holding onto the concepts, behaviors, and disciplines once they are understood. Dr. Hester has given us the model in this book.

H. Darrell Young is chairman and CEO of Transformance Concepts, president and CEO of HIE, and president and CEO of HBO & Company of Georgia.

Preface

A basic theme of my work as an administrator and teacher was "pushing the boundaries outward," or as one of my own teachers used to say, "Expand your horizons!" This theme makes the assumption that we lead most effectively from the inside out—from our values and beliefs and from internalized wisdom mediated through years of experience and commitment to lifelong learning. We are compelled, I believe, to always push, extend, serve, support, and grow our own value and the value of those whom we lead. What we are on the inside determines how we lead others—on the outside.

The basic premises of this book come from the theme of pushing outward, expanding, learning, and serving others as a fundamental part of leadership. It has been a model for me in the past, but one that I didn't always live up to. My workload, departmental responsibilities, commitments to curricula and program development, consulting, and developing materials in critical thinking and problem solving consumed much of my last decade of full-time employment. In 1999, H. Darrell Young asked me to assist with the writing of a training guide in leadership development. Once again, ideas about leadership began to occupy my thoughts and rekindled my interest is composing a book for educators which focused on ethical leadership.

Subsequent conversations with McFarland & Company brought encouragement for this project and well-founded advice to keep the material practical, add activities and exercises at the end of each chapter for training purposes, and further engage the mind of the reader. For this purpose, I asked several educators to read this manuscript and offer their own suggestions. I also asked them to put down actual accounts from their experiences that illustrate some of the major points of each chapter. I have tried to incorporate all of their ideas into this book. With any luck I have accomplished that task successfully.

3

Many stories from my personal experiences and the experiences of others are included to illustrate some of the major leadership concepts of this book. The actual times and situations of these stories have been altered so as not to bring attention to any particular school or school system. Having consulted with schools and school systems throughout the southeast and in other parts of the United States and Canada for nearly thirty years, I have witnessed many events and situations—some almost unbelievable—that have also been included. The purpose of using these stories is to illustrate and teach, not to point a finger or blame. I have been, since 1964, a teacher first. This is my intention.

The reader will notice in chapter 1 that I have responded quite negatively to the "testing culture" that began to redefine the environment of teaching and learning during the decades of the 1980s and 1990s. This in no way means that I am opposed to education accountability. Quite the contrary, accountability is what is needed, but the question must be asked, "Is the over-testing of students the only way to accomplish this task?" The obsessive testing of students at every grade level, using practice tests two or more times a year, narrowing the curriculum to what is being tested, and using "stem questions" from actual end-of-year tests and end-of-course tests to further redefine the content of what is taught, more and more puts educational results in the hands of a few test makers. Although student testing is only one accountability measure for schools, it has become the major focus of state legislatures and the federal government. Having worked in this environment for over half of my career, I have had first-hand knowledge of how it has affected teachers and students.

Finally, I have been fortunate throughout a long and successful career to have worked in many different places and capacities. I have served as a teaching assistant at two major universities, a minister with both small and large congregations, a college professor, a public school teacher, and a central office administrator. I have served in positions of leadership, and I have been led as I served. Throughout a career of over four decades, my daily notebooks became jam-packed with ideas, quotes, and notes about people, ideas, successes, failures, often-inarticulate ramblings, and leadership. During my last decade as a public school administrator, my focus was even more narrowed to thoughts about leadership. I hope that the insights I have gained will help other educators lead in more ethical ways.

Introduction

The reasons for writing this book come from many situations and sources in my thirty-eight years as an educator. If they could be boiled down to two, the first would be utilitarian and the second, personal. First, I wish to share what I have learned about leadership, with the hope that others will be able to learn from my own experiences and observations. Second, I would like to promote a particular kind of leadership, which has its roots in the history of ethical thought and has been brought forward in our time by those who wish to develop a community of learners, not only in educational organizations, but in businesses and industries as well.[1]

There is perhaps nothing more inspiring than a leader with vision and the commitment to see it through. Add to this leader the special traits of ethical leadership and the ability to recognize the value of nonpositional power, and we truly have a dynamic leadership core. Position is a crude and sad way of measuring power. Sally Hefgesen observes, "In order for an organization to operate with flexibility, power must derive from more than rank."[2] Peter Senge points out that leadership comes from many places within the organization and comments that we lead best by "developing new skills, capabilities and understandings."[3] Ethical conduct accompanied by effective leadership practices is the key to transforming organizations, especially schools.

Applying these observations to education and educational organizations, we discover that educators at every level of the school organization have opportunities to lead. At the most significant level in the system — the classroom — the teacher carries the responsibility of ethical leadership: the important mission of educating young leaders, leading them through their maturation years, and helping to grow them as leaders for the future. Everyone else in this community of learners, save the students, has the responsibility of supporting the teacher's mission—anything less misses the point of education, and anything more is perhaps superfluous. Every ounce of energy in a school system should be directed toward this primary mission. The theme of every school system should be, "everyone a leader," and part of its central mission should be to grow leadership, in personnel and in students.

For this to happen, ethical leadership must take root in schoolhouses and central offices across America. School systems and schools must move beyond traditional concepts of hierarchy and reach consensus that education and educational leadership are about serving—not about the persona of the chief educational executive. One of the chief purposes of education is developing environments that promote excellence and growth so that those who can lead, lead. William Bridges has commented, "If you have an organization full of job holders and a hierarchical framework to keep them in place, the traditional patriarchal leader works fine."[4] But, Bridges asks, what kind of leader does it take to lead a constantly shifting group of people, where people forget their job and do, instead, the work that needs doing? His answer is the "leader-as-servant." Concluding, he says, "Wherever they exist, the de-jobbed organization's leaders are responsible for generating and delivering the resources needed by working units in the organization."[5]

The purpose of ethical leadership is to transform the school culture. Educators, at all levels, can accomplish this goal by facilitating a shared vision where all employees understand and support the missions and goals of the school system, where ideas and curricular applications are generated from the classroom up, where there is a unity of purpose, and where all educators claim the school and systemic vision as their own. Implied in ethical leadership is, as indicated by William Bridges, servant leadership where growth is measured by how well educational leaders serve one another and the basic mission of educating all students.

The last quarter of the twentieth century witnessed a wide and extensive discussion of the nature of human organizations, especially about the nature and role of leadership. The focus was predominantly on business and management training, and it provided examples of leadership excellence, discussions of leadership characteristics, and a rich variety of books and articles on the subject. These reflective analyses have come as a response to a widespread feeling that today's business, industrial, and professional organizations—including educational bureaucracies—need to undergo fundamental transformations. During the last decade of the twentieth century, the transformations being called for were of the nature of both servant and ethical leadership. In this book "servant" and "ethical" leadership will not be used synonymously, but because they share many characteristics, they will be used conjunctively.

I have found that servant leadership and ethical leadership are closely aligned and that these kinds of leadership are needed for today's learning organizations such as schools. Both ethical and servant leadership rely on skillful decision-making and respect for moral principles. The ethical and the servant leader make it a point to listen, with mind and spirit, and utilize, to the advantage of all, useful intuitions, factual evidence, and their own growth experiences. The ethical leader exhibits, internally and externally, human integrity. The servant leader employs human integrity in the service of others, is a model of credibility, and creates positive images of what the future might become.

Learning organizations are populated by knowledge workers—teachers, students, principals, and educational specialists of all kinds—who work best in environments that support growth and productivity. Knowledge workers are a special breed who know more than their predecessors, are lifelong learners, and are not afraid to question authority or take risks. Ethical leaders who lead with integrity, inspire, challenge, energize, and support the knowledge workers in their care. The working units in a school system are its schools, and the working units of a school are its classrooms. Most who choose education as a career have the desire to make a contribution to their students and community. They also want to be appreciated and supported by administrators and parents. Nothing less than increasing the personal worth and dignity of the classroom and school leader should be the mission of the system's executive leadership. In doing this, they are increasing the value of the school system within its community of learners and within the community at large.

We have learned by experience that the basic desire to follow a leader comes not from the fear of retribution (although we may perform contracted duties based upon this particular motivation), but from a deep, often unspoken, conviction that our lives are special, our talents are valued, and that present leadership recognizes and honors them. In saying this, I am making the assumption that true leadership has to be earned, and the best way to earn this capacity is by serving others. An experienced teacher willingly assists and guides a first-year teacher with patience and wisdom. A central office specialist supports and helps maintain a principal's efforts to introduce innovative programs and methods in a school. A superintendent demonstrates respect for principals and other central office staff by listening, supporting, and giving special attention to their work. All educators are in a position to lead, and to lead ethically. When this happens, there is a certain dynamic spirit that begins to inhabit the school and school system which connects teacher with teacher, teacher with learner, and administrators with learning growth. When this begins to occur, there is an unusual feeling that something truly wonderful is happening as both individuals and the school system itself begin to move forward. When learning becomes contagious and there is an excitement among both teachers and students about learning and knowledge, the spirit of ethical leadership is taking hold of the educational organization.

Experience teaches us that those who lead by the command-and-control method are sometimes effective; especially if employees don't ask questions or buck the orders they are given. They can "make" their programs work by unifying methods, creating programs that meet their goals, and ordering others to remain loyal to those in top educational positions. All of us have worked for leaders like this. These leaders will be feared but seldom respected, and when no one is looking, employees will ignore their directives and move in the direction of their own personal commitments. Sadly, when these leaders move on they take their visions with them, and those who work in the school or school system breathe a sigh of relief and eventually return to the methods and programs their knowledge and experience tells them work best.

This is why this book is written to promote ethical leadership. Ethical leaders listen, learn, and praise others for their dedication and hard work. Ethical leaders recognize that schools and school systems are communities of learners and, therefore, encourage personal development, networking, and innovation. Ethical leaders are demanding but fair. Although recognized by the importance of their office and concomitant responsibilities, ethical leaders are admired because of their integrity and because they make others feel equally important and necessary to the health and vitality of the school system and school. And when they move—and they will eventually—they leave with their staffs a vision articulated, a mission shared, and the commitment and motivation to see it through. Max DePree says, "Without a clear moral purpose competence has no measure, and trust has no goal."[6] This is why ethical leadership that serves those who are led is so vital to schools today.

Although demanding and energizing, ethical leaders are not controlling, as one of their goals is the growing of future leaders. They are at ease in letting the expertise and skills of others take the lead in producing learning results. They are individuals of vision and give so that others are able to grow. They draw others into their vision, which is enriched and recreated by the individual visions of others. It goes without saying that ethical leaders are about people—working and networking; growing, sharing, and supporting; and caring and building. They give others opportunities to grow and, in growing, to discover their own leadership capabilities and personal strengths. John Burkhardt and Larry C. Spears, commenting about Greenleaf's conception of "servant leadership," said, "His [Greenleaf's] challenge to leaders was to put the needs of their followers first and to subject their leadership to this test: 'Do those served grow as persons; do they, while being served, become healthier, wiser, freer, more autonomous, more likely themselves to become servants?'"[7]

Experience teaches us that ethical leaders create ethical organizations. An ethical school organization is committed to improving student learning and character. It is also dedicated to its educational professionals and understands that their growth is of great value to the mission of the school system. Viewed in this way, ethical leaders have a moral calling: it is a call to moral unity, to all of those essential values that hold society together and allow us to think highly of others and ourselves. This is the fabric of our moral obligations, the fabric from which our leadership responsibility is woven. As John W. Work observes, "It may be fairly said that the *character* of a society's leadership may substantially determine how that society fares in an environment of change."[8] Commenting about the character of organizational leadership, Alfred Gottschalk comments, "Character is vital in a leader, the basis for everything else ... character, perseverance, and imagination are the sine qua non of leadership."[9]

As a former college/public schoolteacher and director/supervisor in the central office of a medium-sized school system, I have had the opportunity to experience many different kinds of management techniques and leadership dispositions. Early on I read Max DePree's *Leadership Is an* Art[10] and saw that the ethical principles espoused by DePree were consistent with my ideas about leadership and ethics. In 1990, while in Boston, I picked up Peter Senge's newest book, *The Fifth Discipline*,[11] and my excitement over his conceptualization of the "learning organization" became the dominant theme of my life and work. My work in curriculum development, teaching and learning styles, creativity, thinking skill infusion, and conflict management was now given a meaningful foundation in organizational theory and practice. I led off my 1994 *Teaching for Thinking*[12] by placing the infusion of thinking skills into the school curriculum as a vital part of making schools "learning organizations" in the sense that Senge had discussed. These experiences crystallized my vision of what our school system could become. I saw many useful applications for the ideas

and methods that were being developed in gifted education, especially at
the University of Georgia and the University of Connecticut. I engaged
in informal cross-departmental meetings, met informally with principals
and teachers, and began a decade-long journey of selling my vision of
ethical leadership to our school leaders. This vision touched not only the
top administrators in our school system, but included all teachers, students, and their parents. With retirements and transfers, new administrators, and new teachers, I discovered that this would be an on-going and
demanding task. The compartmentalization and departmentalization of
curriculum and technology from the central office level to the classroom
made the job of finding common ground and working as a team an arduous undertaking.

One thing that time teaches is that articulating and selling a vision
enlarges the horizon of what we believe to be significant, especially from
an ethical point of view. It is a continuous process and, when done from
the inside out, brings with it meaning and purpose, conviction and motivation. This is especially important in periods of value transition such as
the past fifteen years. So many times educators do not work at the high
level of which they are capable because they do not want to risk standing out or making a mistake; they are unable to judge the vision of the
top executive—the principal or the superintendent—and, therefore, sink
back into a comfort zone of mediocrity. When this happens, many sell
out to security and safety. These are values that characterize many principals and superintendent-level employees who have reached high levels
of income and now wish to protect what they have gained. In many situations, they gather around them people who will unthinkingly do their
jobs and remain relatively inert as they play the roles to which they have
been assigned.

In his book, *Leading from the Inside Out,* Kevin Cashman comments,
"Leadership is not simply something people do. It comes from somewhere
inside us. Leadership is a process, an intimate expression of who we are.
It is our being in action."[13] Who we are—our beliefs, purposes, and, yes,
hidden agendas—reveals our leadership potential just as much as the act
of leading itself. Cashman continues by quoting Paul Walsh, Chairman
and CEO of Pillsbury, who said, "The missing link in leadership development is growing the person to grow the leader." Cashman adds, "As we
grow, so shall we lead."

Perhaps the key to the development of meaning lies in the concept of
value structure. Each of us has a value hierarchy, a scale of values, which
we follow as a guide for ordering our behavior. Inside and outside of us,

the way our values have been configured determines what meaning there is. Here both mental structures and organizational structures are important. They order our environment, open us to future possibilities, and encapsulate us in ways of thinking and acting that are inflexible and limiting. This is our value structure, and however open and resourceful, it sets limits and parameters on our reasoning and our work. In this way, values can be paradoxical: setting limits, creating walls, and then daring us to break through and climb over; to take risks and be creative. The key to ethical and servant leadership is unlocking the creative forces in our values and in the values espoused by our school system. Overcoming the limiting structures of our environment will make possible larger visions. We need leaders who recognize that we lose personal integrity and wholeness unless we adhere to a value system which is consistent with individual uniqueness and that expands rather than limits creative choice. Only when we tap the creativity of each student, teacher, principal, and central office employee can we unlock the potential that lies within the school organization.

The idea of growing leaders is one of the themes of this book.[14] It takes as a major premise the ethical importance of not only the organization of schooling and its purposes, but of the individuals—administrators, teachers, staffs, students, and parents—who are directly involved with helping students learn. It is the dignity, worth, and growth of the people who are involved in education that is the concern of ethical leadership. They give meaning to education. In providing meaning, they excite and change the operative value base from which we work. Remaining open and flexible is essential. Working in cooperative relationships with other educational leaders unifies the vision and purpose of the school system. Unity implies that we are able to integrate the values and beliefs of all educational stakeholders into a harmonious, working whole. This requires, among other things, respecting and enhancing their self-esteem and value as human beings and their potential for improving human life through their own creative endeavors.

In their book, *The Art of Possibility,* Rosamund Stone Zander and Benjamin Zander provide a positive message and an invitation to possibility. Their book provides practical pathways for bringing possibility to life as it concentrates on the growth of persons, potentiality, and giving birth to new and innovative behaviors. Their premise is "that many of the circumstances that seem to block us in our daily lives may only appear to do so based on a framework of assumptions we carry with us. Draw a different frame around the same set of circumstances and new pathways come into view. Find the right framework and extraordinary accom-

plishment becomes an everyday experience."[15] Again, this framework of
assumptions reflects our value structures that either limit our growth and
openness to future possibilities or provide windows of opportunity and
expansion that compel us to change.

We have found that assumptions are arbitrary and usually authoritarian in nature. Assumptions also affect the values of the educational
organization. Their adequacy can only be judged, not by their point of
origin, but in terms of their consequences. Therefore, assumptions require
the fresh air of critical inspection. Their origin and promise compel continual recognition and evaluation. Self- and organizational-analysis are
the way we grow as leaders and the way leaders grow organizations. Bennis calls this "reflection and resolution,"[16] which seeks openness to individual differences and the creative input of others. It also requires that we
think about and analyze our own mistakes for they hold important lessons
for us. Most of us need to create more windows in our lives that permit
the light of new ideas to penetrate our opinions, judgments, and convictions. Putting ideas into context and adding perspective to organizational
purpose is a mark of effective leadership and a growth-oriented school
system.[17]

The Zanders' insights into the art of the possible are reminiscent of
those of psychologist E. Paul Torrance. Torrance's lifetime of research,
teaching, and writing about creative thinking saw him continually breaking the mold of traditional educational thinking and encouraging his students and colleagues to do the same. As early as 1963, Torrance was calling
for "a revision of the objectives of education." He said, "More and more
insistently, today's schools and colleges are being asked to produce men
and women who can think, who can make new scientific discoveries, who
can find more adequate solutions to impelling world problems, who cannot be brainwashed, men and women who can adapt to change and maintain sanity in this age of acceleration. This is the creative challenge to
education."[18] He continued by observing, "These facts, together with the
unprecedented needs of our society today for creative talent, call for some
truly revolutionary changes in educational objectives and in the retooling that must accompany such changes. What is called for is a far cry from
the model of the quiz-program champion of a few years ago."[19] The questions Torrance asked about educational objectives can also be asked about
educational leadership: What kind of leaders are our administrators
becoming? What kind of thinking do they do? How resourceful are they
becoming? Are they becoming more responsible? Do they provide
thoughtful explanations to what they see and do? Do they believe that

their ideas and those of their colleagues are of value? Are they willing and able to share ideas and opinions with others? Do they bring together and relate similar experiences in order to draw conclusions? Do they do some thinking for themselves?

What we learn from creativity research is that educating students is as much an art as it is technique and organization. The art of teaching is about leadership, and not only at the principal and superintendent levels. Also, the choice of approaches is important. One may be rational, intuitive, empirical, or authoritative in leadership and management style. Experience teaches us that using a combination of these approaches—perhaps letting circumstances dictate their congruence—serves us better. Manage this process too tightly and the art disappears along with the growth and creativity of teachers; and students suffer. Education is about growing teacher leaders, and it's about cultivating leadership in students as well. This book concentrates on helping leaders lead. It is a guidebook, a resource that provides an overview of the major research in leadership development with a focus on empowering leaders at all levels of educational organizations. It's also about infusing leadership with ethical principles and behaviors. This, we shall learn, is the heart of servant leadership. Ethical leadership puts value on treating others as having worth and intrinsic dignity. This means that students, teachers, principals, and central office administrators are required to view others and each other as "ends" and never as "means" to some unknown and preconceived end. They are not to be manipulated but allowed to grow value within themselves, a value that will enrich and bring to fruition the purposes and goals of the educational system.

Drawing energy and direction from the many who have written on this subject, as well as my association with H. Darrell Young,[20] whom I consider a model for servant leadership, I have extracted from my own experience a knowledge of leadership and leadership processes that I wish to pass on to others. Like Cashman, I believe that it is the character of the person that determines the quality of leadership brought to the central office, school, or classroom. And like the Zanders, I believe that individuals must be given a place of respect and treated with respect if they are to have the room to realize their potential selves. They call this giving a person an *A*. As the Zanders's say, "This *A* is not an expectation to live up to, but a possibility to live into."[21] I call this "ethical leadership."

My basic premise is that a leader, at any level, should serve others authentically. *Authenticity* means bringing life to the organization by empowering the community of educators to increase their personal flexibility, creativity, and learning potential. It also requires that leaders enhance the dignity and humanity of all whom they serve as they connect with these qualities of character within themselves. An ethic of authenticity does not only turn inward to examine beliefs, values, and missions, but outward, where it connects with others, builds relationships, and creates community within families, among friends, and in organizations. Fritjof Capra says that those leaders who facilitate emergence (of new personal and organizational structures) use their own power to empower others.[22] Authentic leadership creates an enabling environment, which makes possible the exercise of personal abilities and individual initiatives in the education of youth. Releasing such creative energy can impact the organization in both negative and positive ways. In the negative sense, it will be difficult to control the system from top to bottom—what was once a left-brain organization is today moving in many and different exciting directions. Control is perhaps a goal that needs reassessing. In the positive sense, new visions and new futures will begin to emerge at the grassroots level that pull the organization into many interesting ways. In this case, the role of leadership will be to harness this newfound energy, give it purpose and direction, and allow it to change the environment of learning.

As Cashman says, "Ultimately, a leader is not judged so much by how well he or she leads, but by how well he or she serves."[23] Servant leadership is an underlying theme closely connected to the idea of ethical leadership. Its foundation is the ethical treatment of coworkers—from the superintendent's office to the elementary school custodian. Cashman makes the point quite clearly in his chapter on personal mastery and growth toward wholeness. He says, "Beliefs literally create our reality; they are the lenses through which we interpret the world. Some of these 'lenses' focus and open up new horizons; others dim our view and limit possibilities. Beliefs are transformational. Every belief we have transforms our life in either a life-enriching or life-limiting way."[24]

Leaders whose major aim is to serve others and who recognize the worth and spiritual significance of others in every decision that is made are leaders whose ethical character is able to transform the workplace and open up possibilities, potentialities, and creativity. The authentic ethical character includes a vision and purpose that is organizational- and people-centered and not ego-centered. It is flexible and open to change and the ideas of others. The ethical character creates value—trust, congruence, and compassion—and is involved in empowering and strengthening the productivity and fortitude of others and of the workplace itself.

1

Leadership Needs:
A Focus on Requirements

Having retired from public education in 2001, I can only write this book retrospectively and bring to the reader my understanding of the role of the leader from current research and my own experiences. As I pulled my thoughts together, many events, personalities, and situations of my working years came to mind. Some of these were conversations, meetings, and discussions held with colleagues over how best to serve students and teachers. Putting both research and experience together, allowing former colleagues and associates to read this manuscript, and making many changes and additions suggested by them has helped me gain perspective and objectivity. Acknowledging their valuable assistance has helped me understand that not all who found themselves in positions of responsibility and authority were, at the same time, excellent leaders. Actually, some were stubborn, hardheaded, and unyielding in their approach to managing and leading others. Many were like me in my early years, struggling to find the ability to lead, the courage to make decisions, and the understanding that to lead best, one must serve.

The changes that began in the middle 1980s and reached their zenith in the 1990s profoundly affected the work of teachers and administrators in public education. These years will be looked upon as watershed years during which time great paradigm shifts were made in our way of educating children and training and evaluating teachers. These were days of value shifts where beliefs and purposes changed, but where the language of education the public heard was relatively unaltered. The public read about testing and scores, but few understood the statistical jargon used in their reporting. They knew that their children complained about tests, but they had complained when they were in school. Most trusted their public educators and did not question the shift that was occurring.

Parents and teachers experienced these great changes together. They reacted, as Zander and Zander have reflected about the changes that occur in our central selves, "like a stream under no illusion that it can control the movement of the river, it joins rather than resists its bountiful flow."[1] Many educators, including myself, have accepted movement after movement touted to increase student growth and make teaching more efficient only to regret the hours we spent preparing ourselves for programs designed solely for their ease of statistical analysis and evaluation. Educational leaders must learn to trust those within the system, at both the collegiate level and in their own schools, but they must always make it a point to verify the claims being make. Trust should not be rewarded that hasn't been earned! Under no illusion that this book will change education's direction or make servant leaders out of top-down autocrats, the readers are asked to listen for my passion and commitment and, from deep within, make commitments to elevate their leadership style, drop their hidden agendas and the masks they wear, and begin operating from "the inside out." When teachers and principals, central office supervisors, and superintendents recognize that they live in an arena of possibility—that our students are truly our future—and that everything occurs in that context, trust, openness, and a recognition of the worth and dignity of their colleagues will follow.

The Need for Ethical Leadership

During my last thirteen years of employment in the public schools (from 1988 to 2001), I worked as an administrator in what was the most challenging decade of my career, comparable only to the 1960s with the volatility and unpredictability of integration efforts in both the public and private sectors of education. This decade witnessed the politicalization of education with student/teacher/school accountability on both state and federal levels. With the dawning of the twenty-first century the effects of this process have intensified, and school superintendents and staffs have struggled to find ways to keep scores high despite research that demonstrates the relationship between high or low scores and economic/educational levels of parents.

Beginning at this time, under the auspices of "what gets tested gets taught," teachers were affected by curricular standardization as well as by the control placed on the techniques and methods they were permitted to use with children. In many instances, drill and practice, memorization and multiple-choice testing replaced research, report writing, and proven small-group learning techniques. Forgotten was the vision of educators like E. Paul Torrance who had said as far back as 1963, that schools needed to produce students who can do more than score well on quiz-bowl-type questions.[2]

Also replaced was a method known as "whole language" and its child-centered, developmental approach to reading and writing. Many curriculum and instructional leaders that I talked with wanted everyone on "the same page." This, they said, would make more efficient their control and assessment of instructional processes. Micromanagement soon became a preferred method of getting principals and teachers focused on what had become the bottom line of education—improved test scores. Parenthetically, although micro-management is, in the final analysis, an ineffective tool for building leadership among school employees, at all levels school leaders need to stay in touch with the heartbeat of the classroom, school, or educational system. Staying in tune means having microknowledge—shared information about every aspect of the educational process. Productive results were called for, meaning higher test scores in reading and mathematics. In many school systems, phonics and drill and practice were mandated as the surest and quickest means to this end. The arts, foreign languages, and social sciences suffered from this testing mania. Less time in the school day was being devoted to these so-called "periphery" subjects. Some of them were set aside entirely in elementary schools or the time for them was severely curtailed because they were not a part of the tested curriculum. At the grassroots level, those classroom teachers and principals who dared to venture out on their own or disagree entirely with the changes that were occurring in education were simply ignored. Curriculum mapping was commonly used to match curriculum with tests and keep teachers on track focusing on state mandated curricula and the limited content that was being evaluated. With this loss of classroom freedom, the rise in discipline problems, and the coefficient demands of increased paperwork and preparing students for tests, it was not surprising that a dramatic teacher and principal shortage began impacting schools in negative ways.

As a result of these practices, including the vast amount of training and clerical work required of educators—computer grading systems, attendance and grading programs, keeping up with exceptional children's records and requirements including Medicaid—many of our nation's brightest teachers have left and are leaving the classroom, and many more are changing their majors because of negative student teaching experiences, discipline issues, and the requirements of conformity. Philip C. Schlechty reports, "While once the common school was viewed as a community center where the young were sent to be socialized, as well as educated, the urban high school, junior high school, and, to a lesser extent, the elementary schools came to be viewed as institutions to be managed and a set of educational experiences to be organized…. School leaders, like the industrial leaders they looked to as models and guides, sought the Holy Grail of scientific management. Efficiency became the prime value; differentiation, standardization, control, and rationality became the operating guides."[3]

Not surprising, during the past decade, the theme "every child can learn" became the calling card of every forthright educator. School board members created their political agendas around this slogan. Superintendents turned it into a highly recognizable motto. Translated to the public this meant, "Every child can make at least one year of predetermined growth on end-of-grade and end-of-course tests." To teachers it meant, "get the scores up faster." The reality is that some students can achieve this predetermined goal — or even score more than one year's growth — and others cannot. Statistical average became the name of the game. In part, the Effective Schools Movement advertised itself as providing the means for the completion of this goal.[4] As more and more certified personnel were schooled in "effective teacher training," mission statements, school mottos, success parades, partial site-based decision-making, and commercial hype were used to disguise the seemingly total emphasis on testing and the lack of emphasis on creativity, a challenging curriculum, and the educational diversity that was impacting the classroom. Although meant to improve schools and teaching, the Effective Schools Movement soon became just another commercial adventure designed to focus teachers and principles on methods to improve test scores.

Larry Lezotte speaks positively about the Effective Schools Movement in his response to those who have criticized its applications in the "real" world of educating our nation's children. He says, "… researchers contend that 'the Effective Schools Movement, as currently promoted by consultants, is contaminated with a series of fallacies.' I don't know which consultants they had in mind, since they weren't required to document this or any of their other sweeping generalizations."[5] Lezotte provides what he calls "the true interpretation of these principles." His edited analysis of five fallacies follows:

1. *The fallacy that "all children can learn"* Lezotte maintains that while all children can learn at some level, children who come to school with environmental deficits cannot, as a rule, achieve at the same level as those who come to school with all the advantages of good nutrition and a stimulating environment. "To claim that 'all children can learn' is a fallacy invented by Effective Schools consultants is wrong on both counts and truly misrepresents the Effective Schools Movement and the writings of Ron Edmonds." The statement "all children can learn" does not mean that all children can learn at the same rate, on the same day, and in the same way. Instruction must be customized to meet each child's unique needs and strengths. The Effective Schools Movement correlate—"frequent monitoring of progress"—provides the foundation for customization.

2. *The fallacy of principal as instructional leader* Those who criticize the Effective Schools Movement assert that "instructional effectiveness is the responsibility of the teachers" and that principals have too many other things to do to also be the instructional leader. Lezotte says, "Have you ever heard of a world-class orchestra that didn't have a world-class conductor? Even if every individual musician were a virtuoso, the orchestra still needs the world-class conductor to be all that it can be. It seems that these authors have forgotten that a school is a complex, goal-oriented, resource-limited, social system. They have overlooked the fact that schools are being asked to accomplish something that they were not initially intended to do—successfully teach all the children. Leadership is needed, management alone will not assure success on the new mission." He continues by saying, "Ron Edmonds felt strongly about the principal as instructional leader. He used to say that there were schools with principals who were effective instructional leaders that were not yet effective schools (implying that leadership was necessary, but not sufficient). He would add, however, that he had never found an effective school that did not have an effective instructional leader as its principal. Contemporary research on leadership suggests that this statement is as true today as it was when Edmonds first said it."

3. *The fallacy of setting standards by exceptions* Those who criticize the Effective Schools Movement contend that holding up a poor child who has become successful or a school that is successfully teaching low-income children as an example of what can be accomplished is misleading and dangerous. Lezotte comments, "They also state that 'the hard truth is that exceptions occur under special circumstances that cannot be replicated or may be partially replicated only if sufficient resources are

available.' To quote Ron Edmonds: 'How many schools do you have to see where all children are successfully learning before you would believe that such is possible? If you need more than one you have reasons of your own for not believing that all children can learn.' Over the last quarter of a century, numerous studies have validated the basic concept of the effective school. Given the weight of the available evidence that has been accumulated, it is reasonable to believe that all children can indeed meet the standards."

4. *The fallacy of uniform academic standards for all children*   The detractors believe that disadvantaged children generally begin school with lower capacities for achievement and that it is patently unfair to hold them to the same achievement standards. Lezotte comments, "They assert that 'the idea that children and schools should be evaluated by a uniform criterion ... is ignorance at best and criminal at worst.'" Lezotte supports the idea "that the curriculum and instructional program ought to be different for different students. Academic standards should not be based on what we think is possible. They should not change depending on who you are, where you live, or how much money you make. Rather, the standards must be based on what children need to be prepared for success in our society. I deeply believe that the concept of 'common learning for all' is the right and proper educational goal for a democracy that wishes to remain a democracy. We all agree that the system-in-place does not work for large numbers of these disadvantaged children. But the solution to the challenge of successfully teaching poor children is not to lower expectations. The proper response is to modify the system so that these children can succeed."

5. *The fallacy of work smarter, not harder*   Those who criticize the Effective Schools Movement interpret this statement as suggesting that teachers are not too bright and it is demeaning to them. Lezotte responds, "This is simply nonsense. I am one of those consultants who encourage teachers to work smarter, not harder. Most teachers are working as hard as they can. Therefore, working harder is not the answer. Working differently (smarter) would seem to be the teachers' best hope. This requires both new knowledge and a climate conducive to its implementation. To say that teachers and schools, as learning communities, need to be committed to continuous lifelong learning in no way suggests or implies that they are not bright, hard working people."

I will give Larry Lezotte and Rod Edmonds credit for pinpointing the essential elements of effective schooling. On the other hand, as the age of accountability began to exert itself on public education, Effective Schools Movement consultants frequently ignored the details of Edmonds's research as they added to his basic principles: What gets tested gets taught. Soon this became their dominating theme, and test scores—not children with real social, cultural, and educational needs—won the day. At the same time the character education movement climbed on board the testing train with its list of politically correct values and emphasis on following school rules. Not to be completely washed away, character education consultants claimed that by following rules, improving school discipline, and developing character, achievement scores would be improved. So far, no data has been developed which supports this claim.

Trying not to belabor the accountability movement, with its emphasis on testing, incentives, top-down management, and central control of teaching, or to kick the Effective Schools Movement and character education, the purpose here is to point to a method of leadership that is antithetical to the premises of servant/ethical leadership. There is a great need for creative leadership in public schooling. We need to find ways to expand—not limit—the curriculum, teach more creatively, and engage the hearts and the minds of both teachers and students even when faced with the negative aspects of accountability. Having worked as a teacher and as an administrator, I found it interesting, but not surprising, that many of these highly paid consultants turned from their greatly advertised primary missions—developing character, improving the school climate, and focusing teachers on student academic growth—to support the schools with their testing efforts, as if learning improvement and improvement on standardized tests are equivalent. Suffice it to say, accountability and the exaggerated emphasis being placed on testing, dominates American schooling today. Schlechty makes this clear by pointing out how schools are designed[6]:

1. Schools designed to select and sort begin with the assumption that standards must be established and then maintained.

2. The school as factory model was put in place in the latter part of the nineteenth century and reached full flower by the end of the twentieth century. "In this image," Schlechty says, "the curriculum is an assembly line for students: a fast curriculum for fast students, a modified curriculum for the not so fast, and a vocational curriculum for others."

3. In this vision, students are thought of as products to be molded, tested by means of common standards, and inspected carefully before being passed on to the next benchmark for further processing.

4. Given the environment of testing and pressure to make all students fit a common ideal, curriculum design and curriculum supervision became focal points in the control structure of schools. Not coincidentally, there was a quest for "the" right method of instruction, "tight supervision, and production inspection." This also meant teacher accountability and measures were designed to sort and evaluate new teachers just as their students were being judged.

5. "Above all," Schlechty observes, "The curriculum must be articulated with the tests that will be used to inspect the students who are the products of this controlled and rational process."

All of these practices are not necessarily a cancer eating the substance out of educators of children. Schools have always had the responsibility of passing on the commonalities of the dominant culture to its students and making sure the curriculum is being taught and students are learning. This is the heart of the common school movement in the nineteenth century. Accountability is needed for maintaining consistency and focus. Accountability is needed for making sure that standards are being met, standards that began to disappear during years of educational experimentation in the 1960s and 1970s.

Perhaps the pendulum has swung too far today as testing dominates every aspect of schooling. Another outgrowth of this emphasis on testing has been the creation of testing departments in school systems, further burdening school and district budgets. These departments not only administer state and federally mandated tests, but they have found ways of teaching the tests to students, often under the pseudo-name of "criterion reference testing." From previous test databases, test questions are created and shared. Faux tests are then fashioned from these databases and administered to students—sometimes three or more times a year. Testing departments have begun to take on a life of their own, and certified teachers, who are needed for classroom teaching, are increasingly employed as testing watchdogs. Now more and more "teaching days" are being devoted to testing. This also means a more narrowed curriculum as test item banks have come to dominate teaching content. And when teacher, principal, and superintendent bonuses were attached to reaching certain score plateaus, the race to improve test scores began to overshadow all other needs of teachers and pupils. Only recently several teachers in an elementary school were overheard complaining about the low scores their students had received the previous year and the fact that the teachers missed out on the financial bonuses that came with test score improvement. One teacher said, "We failed to get a bonus last year, but we're going to get one this year even if we have to beat the information into the heads of our students." The motivation of expanding and enriching student learning has effectively been replaced by the motivation of financial reward for increased student testing performance. Of course, due to the generally low pay for teachers, this attitude is not surprising.

Competency tests, writing tests, aptitude tests, math and language assessment procedures, in-course tests, and year-end tests now dominate the work of teachers from kindergarten through the twelfth grade. Although recommended for only benchmark grade levels, more and more school districts—following the lead of testing administrators—have begun creating their own tests and testing every grade level from kindergarten through the eighth grade. It is believed that test familiarity and test preparation lead to higher scores, which in turn lead to positive state and local recognition and additional incentive money.

During the 1990s, curriculum discussions soon gave way to testing discussions, with some of the most intensified debates over how to test students with learning disabilities or those who were identified as having a mental or physical disability. Because some schools have higher percentages of these exceptional children, ways of balancing these percentages have been developed. Teachers in schools with larger numbers of exceptional children say it's only fair. Without some kind of balance, they would be unable to receive their share of incentive money for improved test scores. But fair to whom is the question. Surely testing students with mental disadvantages is unfair to the students! The question of fairness has been selectively applied as students are more and more thought of in terms of numbers and statistical averages.

Lost in this spectacle of trying to increase student and school average scores has been both the child and the love of learning, and the teacher and the love of teaching. My interview with school administers in preparing this manuscript found that many schools are adjusting to the testing environment and are turning, once again, to more creative teaching practices. Perhaps the pendulum is beginning to swing back, or just maybe educators are learning how to focus on the child while preparing them for state tests. Teaching styles and creativity, which lost their emphasis in the later part of the 1990s, along with learning styles, cooperative learning, and a focus on student differences—such as giftedness, retardation, and learning disabilities—are once again finding their place. It still remains a struggle for many teachers. Over fifty years of research on creativity, problem solving, learning styles, and methods of teaching critical thinking skills has generally been replaced by standardized curricula and synchronized teaching. More and more we should worry about the effect this is having on young teachers. The fear is that the creativity of teachers and what we have learned about cognitive growth and development has been buried under the avalanche of drill and practice and of "what gets tested gets taught."

As scores began to level off at the end of the 1990s, many educators were left scratching their heads. At a time when educational research was at its zenith, at a time when teachers had discovered "whole language," "teaching and learning styles," "cooperative learning," and techniques for "infusing reasoning and problem solving skills" into their bank of methods, preparing to take standardized tests became the leading raison d'être of education. While teachers were being prepared with knowledge in content and technique, in how students learn best, and in the differences among their students, the politicians took over the classroom and forever changed the face of education. Educational leadership soon became educational management, which had one purpose: improving tests scores. Teaching "to the test" and "practice tests" can improve test scores, but there are limits. Hopefully, in the future, teaching will return to what it does best—educate students in content and skills and with knowledge, wisdom, and understanding that are consistent with student ability and need, subject matter, and teacher maturity.

What happened to our leaders? Why didn't they speak up? And in our colleges, why didn't the Ph.D.s of education voice their opinion? Those scholars who had concentrated upon statistical methods and testing were now the advisors to politicians and superintendents. In only a decade, Frederick Taylor's industrial assembly line model with its sameness, interchangeable parts, and timed (time on task) production measurements replaced the 1970s and 1980s emphasis on individual learning styles, cooperative learning, and a focus on genuine student differences.[7] What was once herald as a calculus of possibility was now turned on its head to become one of probability—a statistical map on a bell-shaped curve. Differentiated teaching and learning soon collapsed into a process of rote drill and memorization, and students were classified—not by type, but by number—a statistical spread over a bell-shaped curve.

It was not that schools lacked direction, but that the new direction of education and the methods of arriving at satisfactory preset educational goals did not originate within educational theory, knowledge about child cognitive development, or the vast knowledge that experienced teachers possess about teaching and learning. At a time when business and industry were turning from their nineteenth-century origins and top-down models to site-based management and problem solving, schools were becoming entrenched in those nineteenth-century procedures. School boards began hiring superintendents to manage the processes of "learning" and testing, and, in turn, superintendents began hiring principals who could effectively manage this process in their schools. Thus, where education is being managed only, there is a perceived need for leadership—at the school board, superintendent, principal, and teacher levels.

My last decade in public education were years during which leadership at every level was challenged by the pressures associated with testing and accountability. I saw the disapproval given to those administrators and teachers who had the courage to question the testing mania that has captivated public education. Those who have spoken out have been warned to keep quiet about their feelings. Being a leader in such an environment is difficult. Being an "ethical" leader in this environment is even more challenging.

One incident may illustrate this point. In the early 1990s, the year-round school concept was being publicized as a change that would produce higher test scores or what was spoken of publicly as "student success." A school system with which I was acquainted moved cautiously in the year-round direction. Several principals and their staffs had taken workshops in the year-round concept, and some had visited schools in other states that were built on the year-round model. Excited by a "we were first" mentality, they lobbied the superintendent and school board for a chance to try it. The administration decided that three schools would be allowed to create a year-round program, but they had to keep a traditional schedule in their schools for those students whose parents did not like the idea. This school-within-a-school model was going to be a very expensive undertaking with duplicate bus routes requiring additional buses and drivers, staff duplication, and the opening of schools in the summer, which meant employing some teachers, staffs, and cafeteria workers for longer periods of time.

A curriculum supervisor had made it her responsibility to research the year-round concept and the improvements it promised. She found that there was no hard data to support the expenditure of the extra dollars, which would eventually run into the millions. At a summer staff meeting, the superintendent called for the central office staff to support his venture into this area. All the central office staff except this one curriculum specialist voiced their support of the superintendent. While no other staff members were asked to share their reasons for supporting the experiment, the specialist was singled out and asked why she had not voted. Her response was that the idea lacked concrete evidence that it could deliver the results it promised. She also said that she would not speak negatively to others about the experiment, that she felt it was okay to be innovative and creative, but that the administration should be honest about the results they were promising.

When the meeting was over, several supervisors told her, "You had better get with the program or else." They left a package of "research" for her to read. She found this "research" to be surveys, statements, and reports from teachers where the year-round concept had been implemented. They were, as she said, "feel-good" surveys in which teachers told how they felt about the projects in which they were involved. No hard data was evident to support the claims of year-round schooling. She predicted that when test data were available for these schools, she would be surprised if there were any perceivable differences from the present situation. She also anticipated that the project would be dropped in three years or less, and it was.

In the situation described above, the top-down model of management is evident. I hesitate to call it "leadership." The superintendent had made up his mind and did not want, nor did he solicit, input from his entire staff of educational professionals. He emphatically did not want to hear a view that was significantly different from his. Thomas Sowel, in his book, *The Vision of the Anointed*, labels leaders who use the top-down model, give lip service to facts, and continually berate their subordinates as "the anointed." He says, "Factual evidence and logical arguments are often not merely lacking but ignored in many discussion of those with the vision of the anointed. Much that is said by the anointed in the outward form of an argument turns out not to be an argument at all. Often the logical structure of argument is replaced by preemptive rhetoric or, where an argument is made, its validity remains unchecked against any evidence, even when such evidence is abundant."[8] Sowell quotes John Adams who said, "Facts are stubborn things; and whatever may be our wishes, our inclinations, or the dictates of our passions, they cannot alter the state of facts and evidence."

Referring to top-down managers, Sowell also points out that those at the top of organizations—the anointed—are usually concerned with "the maintenance of their reputations in the face of repeated predictions that proved to be wrong by miles." He labels these persons as "Teflon prophets." He says, "In each case, the utter certainty of their predictions has been matched by the utter failure of the real world to cooperate—and by the utter invulnerability of their reputations." He comments that more often than not, "they look through statistics until they find some numbers that fit their preconceptions, and then cry, 'Aha!'"[9] This is not an uncommon practice in education, where top-down administrators have placed blame on others when their pet programs did not meet with their expectations.

Obviously, when schools are organized on a top-down model, there is a need for a change in leadership style—at the top and in all levels of school operation. Even in these situations there are some supervisors, teachers, and principals who continue to function as objective, intellectual leaders rather than as technocrats. Schlechty points out, "There are superintendents who view their job as creating conditions in which others make good decisions rather than reserving all decision making to themselves. But such superintendents are all too rare."[10] There is a need, therefore, for reinventing our schools, for creating a new model for school leadership—at all levels—that breaks through fear, ignorance, and misperception to create possibility rather than the sameness and status quo of predictable probability. And there is a need for superintendents and principals who do not want just "yes men or women" in their core of advisors and teachers. Like teachers who would rather have students who sit quietly at their desks and never ask questions are superintendents and principals who would rather command than lead and force compliance to their demands rather than serve the diversity, creativity, and professional expertise of their staffs.

We all perceive the world differently. When we imposed a statistical model for judging student and teacher production, our projected "real world" corresponds to the way it is measured and observed. But schools are made up of individuals—most of whom rigorously resist being sorted and classified and typecast. The world of people is a world where everyone has a different way of seeing, which entails the ability to develop fresh and original ideas and then to incorporate with these, those of many others. When we standardize the curriculum (and teacher) and student assessment, when we treat all of our students the same, we are in fact treating them unequally. All of us are unique and have different strengths and weaknesses and ways of understanding and applying our knowledge.

Developing alternative beliefs and understanding the ideas of others are the roots of both creativity and objectivity. As Christopher Hoenig observes, "A problem solving journey is the sum of many different points of view." He comments that "problem solving needs to be looked at as opportunity-oriented, strategic, and nonlinear to be effective."[11] This is the essence of "servant leadership." This idea, says Dee Hock, the man who turned Visa into a $1 trillion-plus corporation, is "like a diamond in the dirt." It encompasses the need for a new concept of organization, which can become a precarious toehold from which to make it happen. Hock understands the creative leader as one who has the following five characteristics.

1. Turns problems into opportunities and sees larger fields of possibilities for positive change;
2. Commits to new journeys by moving from a sense of possibility to a visceral personal choice to strike out on a new path;
3. Creates strength out of vulnerability and develops confidence through shared awareness, knowledge, and struggle;
4. Moves from a confident pursuit of an opportunity to a stubborn refusal to settle for half measures or compromises; and
5. Transcends limits to create breakthrough solutions that lie in the path of an organization's future.

Likewise, former mayor of New York Rudolph W. Giuliani encourages leaders "to do what's possible and try what's not."[13] He says, "A leader must manage not only results but expectations."[14]

Building a Leadership Culture

Most books on the topic of leadership devote the bulk of their attention to executive leadership: that is, to the CEO as leader. Little has been written about leadership in the middle, meaning for the middle manager, lead employee, principal, or teacher. Those books that have been written about school leadership, like those for business and industry, skew their attention to the top—the superintendent, or to principals at the school level. Few books on leadership have been developed for the central office supervisor/director or with the teacher-as-leader in mind. The fact is, all who are leaders sometimes find themselves in the so-called middle and must learn to follow as well as lead. Always, getting attention for our ideas takes patience and persistence. If the leader to whom we are responsible ignores us in order to follow his or her own agenda, our following this leader becomes much more difficult. In my experience, the leader who continues to drain his or her account with employees—who doesn't make deposits by listening to and utilizing the expertise within the organization—will soon suck the life out of employees, and those employees will soon become a discombobulation of disinterested workers.

As we unravel the concept of leadership, we join core ethical and servant leadership criteria, demonstrate their applications in school settings, and provide activity suggestions that will allow school personnel to use this material in training situations. Several years ago I cooperated with H. Darrell Young, a former CEO of a major computer software company specializing in developing software for the healthcare industry (HBO), in writing a training manual on leadership. This manual, Leadership under Construction: Bridge to the Next Century: A Training Manual Focusing on Unity of Vision, Transformance of the Workplace, and Developing Leadership, is used in his training of teachers, coaches, and students in the Atlanta, Georgia, area including the Cobb County Leadership Academy and various leadership programs at the University of Georgia.[15] While working on this book with Mr. Young, I was able to develop activities and exercises which enable organizations to provide hands-on training in leadership development. These leadership exercises and activities utilize thinking and reasoning and conflict resolution and problem solving. Like the activities developed for Mr. Young's book, those in this book will assist young and experienced leaders alike to clarify their vision, build strategies for success, and grow new leaders for their school organizations. The emphasis is not on being theoretical or philosophical and not on being super critical of present-day practices, but on providing a practical means for changing old ways of leading with methods of servant/ethical leadership.

A major theme of servant leadership is that leaders are followers. Effective leaders must learn to follow before they can lead, and once one is in a position of leadership, serving and following are dominate characteristics that propel problematic situations into solution alternatives and possibilities. It's about building relationships and providing for human growth. It's about harvesting the expertise and ideas of teachers and other educational leaders and following their lead as well. Therefore, all leaders must learn to follow, and followers should be trained as leaders. This is the way we grow leadership in our schools, but I'm not so sure how much of this is being practiced today. It was my experience as a central office supervisor/director that many who made the transition from the classroom to the ranks of administration may have taken the requisite college courses to become administrators and supervisors but were hired not only for their knowledge but because of their demonstrated willingness to perform certain assigned duties without question or discussion.

The top-down model of leadership was poignantly illustrated to me as I consulted school systems during the 1980s and 1990s. Decisions were usually made by top administrators, while those central office staffs, on the front line of delivering new ideas and training to teachers, many times had to sit and wait for answers that should have been made well in advance of my coming to their school system. My experience was that a "power" mentality had taken hold of many of these administrators as they spent much of their time consolidating both their position and control and following—unquestionably—whatever those above them said. In many of these school systems the behavior of a servant leader was seldom displayed while precious manpower and time were lost as departmental heads and curriculum specialists were left idle.

My own frustrations came to bear on this issue as I assisted H. Darrell Young with the development and writing of his leadership training manual and participant activity book for school leaders. The purpose of this project was "building a leadership culture," and the focus was on "leadership under construction." My role was to translate excellent material, which had been written for the business sector, into educational vernacular and provide appropriate applications. We developed this material for educators at all levels with the intention that they would use it to educate student leaders parallel to their own development as leaders. We were continually stymied on several fronts—namely, the public school and the college levels—by those in positions of leadership and by those engaged in leadership training who either failed to recognized the importance of servant leadership or were unwilling to give up perceived "power" to engage in serving others and growing leaders who would eventually replace them.

In 1998, Mr. Young and I were engaged to offer assistance to a well-known leadership institute. At that time the institute was struggling with its own identity, and we spent two days with them discussing practical situations and problems and offering our assistance in redefining their vision, purpose, and beliefs. But we were met with resistance by several of the dozen consultants attached to the institute. Leadership was apparently nonexistent as the institute was being managed but not led with vision and commitment, beliefs that would sustain its activities, and a clearly articulated purpose. Many of the consultants were actually operating independently of the institute's director, and their coworkers had little knowledge of what each other was doing or why. Some had carved out some areas of work that provided what they deemed as job and financial security for themselves. Although several of the consultants, who were working with student leadership in area public schools, responded positively to our ideas, overall, it was a very frustrating experience. I felt then as I do today that leaders, especially those in education, have a responsibility to perform honestly and effectively. In his book *Leadership*, Rudolph W. Giuliani advises:

1. Point out underachievement because it gives others a chance to ask for help;
2. Evaluate how others accept responsibility because it tells us about their commitment and accountability;
3. Everyone is accountable;
4. For any system to be effective, it must continually challenge itself;
5. Learn from great teams; and
6. Develop and communicate strong beliefs, communicate them — being direct and unfiltered — and take action.[16]

This is good advice for any organization, especially one that specializes in leadership development. Today the leadership that was at the institute has been replaced, and it is slowly being forced to change — something they could have done as a group if only their mindset had been focused on the possibilities that lay before them. In doing what they had always done, in maintaining the status quo, and in using the strategies of the past, the institute had grown stale and ineffective.

Leadership Roles

The leadership roles of educators at all levels will be discussed in this book. Although it is not written as a training manual, each chapter provides examples and activities for leadership development. It especially concentrates on principals and teachers and includes central office personnel and superintendents. This chapter focuses on the need for ethical and servant leadership. The remainder of this book concentrates on five areas of leadership:

1. principles
2. characteristics
3. skills
4. climate
5. performance standards

The chapter on leadership performance standards is particularly important. Here, a basic model of leadership is developed that encompasses the concepts voiced in this book. This chapter also outlines performance standards and provides a checklist of leadership skills as a self-checking assessment or an assessment that can be used by a supervising evaluator. It can also become a resource for future leadership training and evaluation.

The assumption is made that leadership and management are two separate, but closely related, skill sets. Using the work of Peter Drucker[17] as a guide, another assumption is made that to be effective, leaders must possess solid management skills. For example, a young teacher fresh out of college must first develop strong and efficient management and organizational skills. This is a given in education. Without these skills, the role of this person as teacher will continually be frustrated and the patience of those who work with this young person will also be tried and aggravated. Exasperation will set in if this condition continues. Only when management skills are mastered will the young teacher mature in his or her profession. This is the first step in becoming a useful and efficient leader.

In chapter five the climate of leadership addresses the responsibility of leaders growing leaders. Part of this responsibility is providing inexperienced personnel with opportunities for growth, including leadership responsibilities. Counseling, coaching, and feedback are necessary tools for that development. Some paideia-type discussions about leadership should be included in their developmental package. Three areas will be addressed in leadership climate assessment:

1. how to empower others
2. how to enable and enhance the performance of others
3. how to serve others

A story may help illustrate the responsibility of leaders growing leaders. In 1969, I enrolled at the University of Georgia's Franklin College of Arts and Sciences to pursue the doctorate of philosophy. I was intent on majoring in philosophy, having earned an undergraduate degree in history and two graduate degrees in theology. I had taken only a couple of required undergraduate courses in philosophy but felt that this area was missing from the humanities background that I was trying to develop for myself. While at the university, I became a teaching assistant and fellow working under the guidance of Dr. Tony Nemitz. Tony was demanding, but fair. Understanding our need to "practice-teach" in philosophy under the guidance of a master teacher, he set up large classes and employed graduate students such as myself to team-teach with him. He lectured alone on Mondays, Wednesdays, and Fridays, and we taught smaller groups on Tuesdays and Thursdays with Tony sitting in and evaluating our performance. His lectures were masterful and dramatically delivered, engaging student interest and dialogue. In our feedback sessions he gave reasons for every movement and every gesture that he had made during his lecture. We even graded student essays in a group setting with Tony sitting in to watch and give advice. He asked each of us to verbally justify each grade we gave. This was an arduous task. Tony was teaching us how to separate "fluff" from "content" and content that mattered from answers that were immaterial. We were beginning to learn about teaching as an art, and he was an unusually gifted model for us.

Tony was an excellent teacher and mentor. He gave of his time freely and taught us how to lecture, discuss ideas, and effectively dialogue with our students. In the truest sense, he was a servant leader who enabled our performance and empowered us with knowledge and technique. On the night before my exit oral examination from the university, Tony dropped by my house for a casual visit. During the evening we talked and reminisced about my three years at the university and the courses that I had taken with him. As we said our goodbyes, I will never forget Tony's parting words to me. He said, "As a teacher, never forget that your role is to serve your students, to make them better than you have been, and to inspire them to excellence." This is the ethical responsibility of the educational leader.

In the chapters that follow, the idea of ethical leadership will be developed and applied to educational organizations, schools, and classrooms for the purpose of calling educators to a more human and moral approach to their work. Appendixes added to this material are designed to provide school leaders with the most recent information on servant leadership, ethical leadership, and educational leadership. The organizations, centers, and institutes that provide information and training in these areas will be appropriately mentioned, and the services and information that they provide will be described and explained. Hopefully, school administrators and teachers alike will find this book an invaluable tool in their quest to fulfill their servant leadership responsibilities.

Activities That Promote
Ethical Leadership

1. Describe the leadership style that you use, either in the classroom or as an administrator. Do you think you would be more effective by adopting the principles of ethical and servant leadership?

2. Do you agree or disagree with Schlechty's five points on how schools are managed today? Read each of them again and illustrate them using examples from your own experience.

3. If you could change one thing about your school or school system to make it more "student friendly," what would it be? Give reasons for making this change.

4. Hoenig says, "A problem solving journey is the sum of many different points of view." In your school, school system, or classroom are many different points of view openly and willingly invited? If so, how is this process managed? If not, how can this situation be improved? Explain.

5. Explain how ethical and servant leadership are interconnected.

6. "A major theme of ethical and servant leadership is that leaders are followers." Do you agree with this statement? How is this put into action where you work? Give several examples.

7. Do you agree with the idea that a leader must meet the needs of those whom she or he serves? Explain and give several examples that support your explanation.

8. Dee Hock gave five qualities of the creative leader. In groups of three or four, discuss each of these characteristics and provide concrete examples for each of them. Be prepared to share your examples and understanding of these qualities with the entire group.

2

Leadership Principles: A Focus on Foundations

Leadership Foundations

In the year 2000, along with scholars from the United States and several foreign countries, I was invited by the Torrance Center for Creative Studies at the University of Georgia to speak on the subject, "The Future of Creativity."[1] These lectures and discussions were a part of the Dr. E. Paul Torrance Annual Lectures on Creativity. I had given a major presentation about my research and writing at the Center in 1995,[2] and the scholars who delivered Torrance Lectures in the 1990s had been invited back to the Torrance Center to present their thoughts on the future of creative thinking and creativity, especially as it is applied to the public schools. There was a inspiring exchange of ideas among those who attended this gathering; the audience participated by asking questions and providing insights about their work, and each scholar was given time to deliver a short summary address.

My topic focused on educational leadership and creativity as "thinking outside the boundaries." I pointed to some of the major ideas and strategies I had learned in my attempt to use creativity in my work over the course of my career. These are summarized in the twelve axioms below. Although this list doesn't exhaust the fundamental principles of creative or ethical leadership, they do point us in that direction. They are gems of wisdom drawn from my daily journal and represent insights from experience, from reading, and from my own mentors. They are the following:

AXIOM #1: Don't be coerced by your environment; instead, become a positive force that incorporates within itself quality, value, and self-awareness.

AXIOM #2: Don't swim in the same ocean over and over again; rather, re-create yourself and your world through imagination, caring for others, and happiness in your life.

AXIOM #3: There is no such place as "somewhere else." This moment is the most important time of your life.

AXIOM #4: As Wittgenstein said, "One keeps forgetting to go right down to the foundations. One doesn't put the question marks deep enough down." Living on the surface often leaves us empty, without meaning and value.

AXIOM #5: Our character is revealed in our actions. Therefore, we have to go deep and pull out who we are by its roots.

AXIOM #6: Let go of the old and live on the edge of possibility.

AXIOM #7: We can't move or grow without friction; creative thinkers are always needed.

AXIOM #8: Questions open new worlds and expand possibilities, as those who answer them provide ideas, opinions, and challenges to our old ways of thinking.

AXIOM #9: Dialogue is exhilarating!

AXIOM #10: Confidence and self-respect are necessary for self-improvement and for helping to change the world for the better. We need to protect and encourage our creative children.

AXIOM #11: Creativity requires commitment. When you are committed, there is boldness, genius, and magic in what you do.

AXIOM #12: When creative change becomes the norm, routine will become boring and mindless. Give yourself permission to change!

These axioms can be combined into the following six basic principles for ethical leadership for educators.

PRINCIPLE #1: Caring for others is the first step toward ethical leadership.

PRINCIPLE #2: Recognize the dignity and worth of those with whom you work and serve by putting every educator, student, and staff member on an equal human level.

PRINCIPLE #3: Become a positive force for improving the human value within your school system.

PRINCIPLE #4: Lead from character and with confidence and self-respect, which are the necessary first steps for personal and organizational improvement.

PRINCIPLE #5: Make creative change the norm by letting go of the old and leading on the edge of possibility.

PRINCIPLE #6: Commit yourself to open communication and dialogue by including others in planning, initiating, and decision-making processes.

As this chapter unfolds, these twelve principles will be further developed, elaborated upon, and expanded as the model of ethical leadership is more completely explained and illustrated. I concluded my remarks at the Torrance Center with the following words[3]:

> With the wave of accountability moving through public education, we find that the curriculum has become increasingly narrowed (what gets tested gets taught) and that many states are developing their own standardized curriculum with testing to match what state boards of education deem important. Recent books such as Peter Sacks's *Standardized Minds* and Alfie Kohn's soon to be released *The Case Against Standardized Testing* have a common theme: standardized testing leads to standardized thinking. And that's not all, it seems that with these new accountability procedures we have replaced an emphasis on creative thinking (a calculus of possibility) with one of probability (a statistical calculus) and more active ways of thinking and learning with teaching to the test and the limited goal of becoming efficient at correctly answering short-answer, multiple-choice questions. Research studies need to be initiated to support the claims made by Sacks and Kohn as well as to discover the effects of the accountability movement on programs that have been developed to promote creative thinking and decision making.
>
> Finally, in the past few years, many books and articles have been written about "leadership" and "management." Although these two functions have been separated in theory, most believe that a person cannot be an effective leader if he or she lacks the ability to manage. What role does creativity play in these two functions? Does leadership require a different type of creativity than management, or do they both require creative thinking, although applying it to different functions? Leadership seems to require vision, purpose, and values. Can the Future Problem Solving Program and Incubation Model Program help develop leadership abilities?[4] These areas need to be fully explored, not only by educational departments but by business departments and leadership institutes as well. A cross-departmental ingathering of those concerned with developing future leaders needs to occur so that all their insights and abilities can be applied to this project.

Leadership Principles

*Principle #1: Caring for others is
the first step toward ethical leadership.*

Associated actions:

1. Acknowledge the strengths of employees by garnishing their input into important decision-making and problem-solving groups.
2. Increase the staff's repertoire of curricular interests and instructional strategies through professional growth activities.
3. Be inclusive and encourage the sharing of curricular interests and instructional strengths.
4. In small groups and at staff meetings, promote reflection about teaching, mentoring, and supervisory practices.
5. Strive to be impartial, and exercise observable care for the welfare and growth of all employees.

Without question, the school, like any other workplace, needs a grass-roots model of leadership. We can envision a "Field of Dreams" where the name of the game is education, where students are successful, teachers are treated as professional classroom leaders, and the community also provides leadership and accepts the school system as its partner and responsibility. Kay McSpadden, a high school English teacher writing in the *Charlotte Observer*, develops this metaphor as her ideal educational world and then says, "School districts that are planning to address the requirements of 'No Child Left Behind' [the "No Child Left Behind" Act signed by President Bush in January 2002] had better give serious thought to how to attract—and keep—qualified teachers, and they can't pretend that education reform can be bought with stopgap gimmicks such as subsidized housing or hiring bonuses."[5] McSpadden continues by observing that school districts and states need to spend the money to treat teachers as professionals. The bottom line, she says, is that other professionals are paid competitively, are able to advance in their careers, and are encouraged to search for personal growth in their areas of expertise. But this is not the case for teachers who are generally underpaid, overworked, and underappreciated as professionals. She concludes, "For all its lofty intentions, 'No Child Left Behind' will lead us nowhere unless we broaden our vision of what education can be."

Writing in *The Baltimore Sun*, Gary Ratner, executive director of

Citizens for Effective Schools, Inc., a national nonprofit organization, commented, "When the No Child Left Behind Act of 2001 became law a year ago with the important goal of raising all children to academic proficiency in challenging subjects, the public may have believed that finally there was a complete roadmap for dramatically improving public schooling. But recent experience reveals the opposite."[6] Ratner first points to the huge gap between the law's goal and current student achievement. In effect, he says that the Act mandates that states receiving federal Title I funds test students annually and publish results, provide for transfers to better schools and offer tutoring, train teachers to meet state requirements, certify all teachers as "highly qualified" by the end of the 2005–2006 school year, and ensure that all students are academically proficient by 2014.

One thing the feds do not do is advise states on how to change their educational systems to profoundly improve learning for public school students, especially those groups of low income and racial minorities who have consistently underperformed their educational peers. Ratner quotes Judith Rizzo, former deputy chancellor for New York City's schools as saying, "If you don't know how to get it [federal funds] to the classroom level, [the law] is a waste of money." Not knowing how to comply to the law's purpose to raise virtually all students to academic proficiency, Ratner says, "The states have begun to nullify the act by deeming its goal of academic proficiency to be met by whatever low level of learning they provide with business as usual." Pointing out that states need a "blueprint" for action, Ratner provides four ingredients that such a blueprint ought to contain:

1. Intensive training for experienced teachers in subject matter, individualized mentoring in teaching skills, and regular, scheduled preparation time with colleagues.

2. For new teachers, supplanting the ten- to twelve-week practice teaching programs with at least a thirty-week, academically integrated and closely supervised field placement.

3. For administrators, intensive programs in how to lead their teachers, parents, and communities to raise their expectations and students' learning and incentives to recruit and retain academically skilled teachers and administrators, especially for poor urban and rural areas.

4. Offer adult literacy education, parenting skills, and other programs to all needy families so they can motivate and assist their children to learn.

Finally, Ratner says, "Only the federal government has the authority to lead states to adopt this road map and the capacity to fund its implementation. The government's publication of such a road map is essential to prevent leaving millions of children behind."

One should notice that underlying Ratner's remarks is the view that every educator be respected as a leader—in the classroom, in the school, in the central office, and in the community. This is a worthy goal for states and districts to pursue, and it the vision being singled out in this book. For this to happen, commitments must be made on every level—from the statehouse and to the schoolhouse. Here we are developing, in the most general way, a model of ethical leadership for educators. A review of the literature on leadership reveals the basic tenets of such a model. Within this literature we find that ethical leadership is open and creative, participatory, and that it is laden with meaning and value. It is leadership that begins with a sincere interest and care for those who make up the educational community, including students and their parents. Ethical leadership is also growth-oriented and consistent with Greenleaf's idea of "servant leadership."

To illustrate the differences between an ethical leader and one that is self-centered and motivated by power, the leadership style of two former principals can be highlighted. The first principal was new to his school, and many were skeptical of him. He had replaced the school's first principal, one who was charismatic and allowed teachers plenty of room in decision making and classroom management. This new principal usually walked the halls before and after school with a cup of coffee in his hand and talked with teachers quite naturally in the lounge area or in their rooms. Some felt he was nosey; others thought he had a genuine interest in them. One teacher, who didn't particularly like this principal, recounts his first encounter with him in his office. He observed how careful the principal was to record a phone call that had interrupted their conversation. He noticed that the principal had every teacher's file in a special carriage just behind his desk. He opened this teacher's file and said to him, "You know you should have been receiving longevity checks for the past two years. Why didn't you apply for them? The state owes you back money and the school system owes you an explanation for not filing your claim. Do you want me to handle this for you?" The teacher knew then that this was a principal who left no detail uncovered and seemed to care for a faculty that had obviously distanced themselves from him. Although this principal stayed in this school for only two years, he became an example to the teachers of a servant and ethical leader. He communicated with them about educational and personal issues and made decisions that made their teaching more productive and classroom discipline more effective.

The other principal is one who ruled rather than led his school. In "his" elementary school he only hired female teachers and kept them under his thumb with threats and promises. During his twelve-year tenure as principal of this school, the few male teachers that he was compelled to employ left after a few years. The command and control style of leadership was obvious. Many of the supplies he purchased for teachers were government surplus and unusable. The money raised by students and parents went, for the most part, unspent, as he would brag about the growing bank accounts he held in the school's name. The better supplies he purchased were held in reserve for those teachers who would take on extra duties and respond positively to his demands. Because he had been at this school for well over a decade, he had hired many of the young teachers on the staff and demanded their loyalty.

One incident that happened on a cold and snowy day poignantly demonstrates the dictatorial and demeaning way this principal exerted control over his staff. The superintendent sent out an emergency call to all the schools to report a fast-moving snowstorm coming in from the southwest. He told the principals to ready the buses and get the students loaded and on their way home as quickly as possible. He also said that when the students had left the school, all teachers and staff were to go home. After the students left, however, this principal told the teachers to return to their rooms where they were to work for the remainder of the day. As four-plus inches of snow began accumulating on the ground, many of the teachers became worried. At the same time, their spouses were calling to see if their mates had made it home safely or left for home. Some called the superintendent, who called the principal to find out what was going on at the school. With much anger in his voice, the principal chastised the teachers for calling their spouses and only then allowed them to leave the school. Luckily, no teacher or staff member was injured in his or her drive home. This principal used a dangerous snowstorm to demonstrate his power and authority with little regard for the welfare of his staff. However, when word of how this principal had treated his staff and had ignored the order given by the superintendent reached the board of education, he was soon moved to another school where he retired a year later.

Top-down leadership, especially by one who thinks of himself or herself as "anointed," usually ignores the moral nature of leading. Christopher Hodgkinson has poignantly observed that the principle of leadership always revolves around people and that is why leadership is a "moral art."

People do the work. People communicate imaginative ideas. People develop programs and teach children. He says, "The central problem of administration, then, becomes the motivation of this action, and, more precisely, since administration is always of a collective, it is to reconcile the self-interest of the individual organization member or client with the collective interest of the organization."[7] Educational leadership is principally moral in the sense that it creates value and purpose by setting goals and developing a philosophy for the organization as a whole and because it must bring the self-interest of teachers, principles, and central office specialists in congruence with these goals and philosophy.

Hodgkinson's thesis is entirely consistent with our first principle, namely, that people create meaning and value and the meaning and value created by our actions reveals who we are, deep down. He notes that a great leader is a person who understands individual motives and hidden agendas. The leader's most urgent problem becomes that of reconciling the motives of individuals with the goals of the organization. Phillip C. Schlechty agrees,[8] as he turns his attention to the superintendent as the primary leader of the local school system. Consistent with the prescription that leaders ought to care for their fellow employees and their clients, he also observes that the superintendent is the locus of moral authority within the school system. He says that the values and beliefs of the superintendent will probably be the guiding values and beliefs of the collective school organization. The morality of care being exercised by ethical leaders is a matter of preserving valued connections to others throughout the organization, of preserving the conditions for nourishing care for human purpose and dignity without which the educational environment becomes bleak, lonely, and self-centered, however successful it might be in achieving the politicized educational goals that have been set.

Also, noting the importance of dialogue and communication within the school community and without, to the community at large (see principle #6), Schlechty says the school superintendent should provide a forum from which to lead education in the entire school community. He comments, "… superintendents must exercise strong leadership in developing and articulating throughout the school system a shared vision that is at once compelling and inspiring." He candidly notes that teachers will "respond to the challenge to invent [a] school in which both teachers and students have increased opportunities for success—schools in which every teacher is a leader, every leader is a teacher, and every student is a success."[9] And they will respond to such a vision when they have the moral authority of the superintendent's office behind them.

Schlechty's dominant theme is that the role of the educational leader is a moral one, and the values espoused by this leader—be it a superintendent to his or her staff or a teacher to a group of parents—are always of moral importance. Accordingly, the way educational leaders conceptualize the purpose of their work shapes the way school systems are envisioned and structured. From the individual visions of educators—making a concerted effort to tie their values and beliefs to the values and beliefs of the entire school system—roles, rules, and relationships emerge, meanings evolve, and values are shared. Schlechty does not view schools as institutions to be managed and a set of educational experiences to be organized, but as a living process with evolving activities, technologies, strategies, and values all entirely focused on the learning processes of students.

Principle #2: Recognize the dignity and worth of those with whom you work and serve by placing every educator, student, and staff member on an equal human level.

Associated actions:

1. Support a school and district culture that integrates both community and staff values.
2. Develop and promote a positive culture within the school and school district that fosters such ethical qualities as tolerance, respect, integrity, and the acceptance of individual differences.
3. Include in meetings the contributions of those who have different ideas and points of view.
4. Actively support the social, emotional, spiritual, and physical well-being of staff, students, and parents.
5. Make sure that every staff member is included in sharing the financial rewards of the school and/or school district.

In their newly developed *Manifesto for Adults*,[10] E. Paul Torrance and Garnet Millar, at the Torrance Center for Creative Studies at the University of Georgia, emphasize the dignity and worth of individuals by way of challenging their creative abilities and encouraging them to "be ready to make the creative leap beyond on the way of becoming a *beyonder*." The *Manifesto for Adults* encourages us to not be afraid to make the creative leap beyond our present circumstances. For Torrance and Millar, "being a *beyonder* means doing your very best, going beyond where you have been before, and going beyond where others have gone." It is composed of the following statements which says that *beyonders.*

1. Are tolerant of mistakes by themselves and others,
2. Take delight in deep thinking,
3. Are able to feel comfortable as a minority of one,
4. Love the work that they do and do it well,
5. Have a sense of mission and have the courage to be creative, and
6. Do not waste needless energy trying to be well rounded.

Educational leaders can learn from this manifesto. As it focuses attention on the individual, it makes the assumption that each person, each educator regardless of position in the school system, and each student has a certain human dignity and value that ought to be honored in all planning and in all decision making. No one is to be left out of the equation. The reason for sharing this manifesto is to point out that creativity is not the province of certain people—all of us have a certain amount of creative energy and vitality that should be utilized and respected. We should remember that just because we are in a position of leadership, doesn't mean our creative insights and programs are not open to revision by the creativity and suggestions of those whom we serve and with whom we work. Listening is important. Implementing the best of their ideas and giving them credit for their dedication and hard work is also vital for creating an exciting and interconnecting web of professional relationships.

The quality school and school system embrace positive personal and cultural change. If the system and school are to remain ethical, cultural change will be embedded with ethical principles where change continues to occur but where all effort is taken to see that people do not get hurt. Experience teaches us that all behavior is purposeful. All of us have reasons for our actions, and self-denial is useless. Ethical leadership will remain above these personal defense mechanisms, being open and assertive in its reasoning processes. Frustration rises when what we want to happen doesn't happen. Choosing to negotiate and to actualize our goals and intentions in morally consistent ways reduces this frustration. Putting ethics into leadership and decision making helps us "see" the point of view of others, welcomes their ideas as positive contributions to the school system and school, and releases absolute control of every aspect of the system and school's operation to those educational professionals who have been employed to carry forth its instructional mission.

Many years ago, at the beginnings of the middle school movement in the United States, several elementary principals in a school system where charged with coming up with a plan for turning a designated elementary school into a middle school. After a year of study and travel—visiting middle school programs throughout the nation—one of these principals was awarded the task of converting this school into his vision of an ideal middle school. Others in the school district carefully watched this principal and his handpicked staff. They knew that what worked in this school would be put in place throughout the district wherever middle schools were needed. This principal was the epitome of Torrance and Millar's Manifesto for Adults: he was not overbearing, but was tolerant of teacher mistakes and laughed at his own; he called teachers aside, in small groups and one-on-one, to discuss various parts of the school's program or management plan; he delighted in being unique and liked to have creative teachers on his staff; he loved his work and the teachers loved to work with him and seemed to enjoy what they were accomplishing with students; he had a sense of mission and was focused on developing the best middle school in the district and state.

But there was one fatal flaw that eventually caused this principal to be moved to another school. The flaw was this: the ideas and methods he introduced at this school were "his" vision and, for him, his vision could not be questioned. He asked teachers to share their ideas with him when he needed their input and soon made their ideas his—when in the company of his peers, he seldom gave them credit and or recognized them for their input. The school was such a great place to work that most teachers had overlooked this particular flaw and gone about their business of teaching, counseling, and coaching students. It was during the school's first accreditation that the problem began to simmer and tempers started to flare. What came forth from the accreditation process was that the committee reports by teachers were rewritten to make them consistent with his personal vision. When the various committee chairpersons questioned him about this, he simply ignored them and went on to other things.

Six years into building this ideal vision, many teachers had left, and some of the new teachers were questioning how the school was being managed (or led). An evaluation by a newly appointed superintendent brought further criticism, especially in two areas: student discipline and time management. The time management problem occurred within an area of cultural arts rotation. The main areas of the rotation were band, physical education, choral music, hand bells, art, and vocational studies. Due to an increase in enrollment, all the students could not be accommodated in these classes. The principal then bought board games and other kinds of fun things to do and put classroom teachers into the rotation block to teach recreational methods (as it was called). According to the new superintendent, this was a waste of teaching time when students having problems with reading and math could be rotated into tutorial classes. Also, the noise caused by students "having fun" was added to the noise created by class changes during the rotation movement, which was a concern of the superintendent. He talked with the principal and offered to bring a middle school consultant team into the school for an evaluation, at which time suggestions for improving student movement and teaching would be made.

For several years, some of the faculty of this school had been concerned with these two problems. These problems had been noted in the accreditation process the previous year but were dismissed by the principal as incidental. The faculty had discussed some positive changes among themselves, but no one was willing to present those ideas to the principal. They knew from experience that he would translate their concern and suggestions into "a challenge to his authority." When they heard that the superintendent was going to move the principal to another school and then make the changes he thought necessary, two of the teachers decided it was time to act. One went to the superintendent to talk about the faculty's ideas and how to make the school more productive. The other went to the principal and told him the faculty knew about the superintendent's desire for change and then presented him with the group's ideas. He also asked the principal to take the initiative, call the superintendent, and invite the consulting team into the school. He said that a second opinion is always beneficial for positive change to occur. Both of these teachers had hoped to keep the principal in their school. They thought he might agree to the suggested changes without making a scene or causing hard feelings. They acted as professionals and sought the improvement of student learning and discipline in their workplace. Other teachers agreed that there were problems, but no one else had volunteered to talk with the principal or the superintendent.

Neither of these teachers was successful: the superintendent had already made the decision to remove the principal, and he was to report to the superintendent the next day when he would be informed; the second teacher also received a negative response from the principal. The principal reportedly said, "This is my school, and if you don't like the way I run things, then put in for a transfer." The principal was moved at the end of the school year. A new principal reported to the school, and the suggestions that had been made by the faculty were gradually put in place.

There is no question that this principal was leading from his heart and from a vision that he held dear to him, but he was unable to allow ownership of this vision by his faculty and staff. His inability to share ownership of this vision was a disaster to him personally, and it eventually led to hard feelings between himself and his dearest friends on his faculty. One lesson he had failed to learn was how to serve those whom he led. He covered this with his personality and by allowing teachers the freedom to explore new ideas and innovative methods without much interference from him. But, in his mind, they were there to serve him and support him as he used them to enrich his future and his reputation. The failure to recognize the dignity and worth of those whom we serve and with whom we work is undoubtedly one of the greatest failures in educational leadership today. According to Kay McSpadden, this recognition is not an impossible dream—it is a vision that sustains both young and experienced educators alike.

Kevin Cashman, founder and CEO of LeaderSource, an international leadership executive coaching firm in Minneapolis, Minnesota, takes this perspective as the guiding theme of his work. He calls it, "leadership from the inside out." He has observed that leaders in all arenas of business, finance, and education lead by virtue of who they are. Cashman says, "As we learn to master our growth as a person, we will be on the path to mastery of leadership from the inside out."[11] He labels this as one's essential authenticity and comments, "Anyone who is authentically self-expressing and creating value is leading."[12] Pro-action, not reaction, is needed for implementing this vision. Leadership is responsive to others, but not reactive. Ethical leadership is maintained through an internal referent, one the leader is always trying to self-actualize to some ideal, purpose, or vision.

Joseph Jaworski is a lawyer who left the practice of law to become founder, chairman, and CEO of the American Leadership Forum, a nongovernmental agency responsible for developing collaborative leadership to deal with urban and regional problems in the United States. Jaworski also concludes that there is an inner path to leadership, and his book, *Synchronicity*,[13] is the story of his personal journey of understanding the deep issues of leadership. In this book he encourages those who grapple with the profound changes required in public and institutional leadership to examine the inner path of their leadership development. Jaworski focuses his attention on the way leaders understand and manage relationships. He believes that understanding and managing relationships should be one of the leader's best skills. It is closely tied to the leader's ability to understand the workings of his or her organization and determines how the leader makes commitments.

His idea of leadership encompasses the world of communications, dealing with others, and maintaining individual and group associations. The overarching principle is that of servant leadership—"serving with compassion and heart, recognizing that the only true authority for this new era is that which enriches participants, and empowers rather than diminishes them."[14] This is transformational leadership because it changes, modifies, and alters the values and purposes of the organization. It continually infuses the organization with strong commitments and broad visionary ideas. For Jaworski transformational leadership is creative rather than reactive. He says, "It would embrace the notion that we don't have to be bound by our current circumstances, but that we can literally choose the kind of community, the kind of world, that we want to live in."[15]

In our story above, the principal of the middle school had created the kind of school he wanted—it fit his vision perfectly. His major failure was to incorporate his staff's collective visions into his own in order to create a much wider and inclusive vision of what a middle school could become. He also failed to communicate this vision to the community—who were mostly excluded from the school except on parent nights—and with the superintendent's staff. Having excluded the major stakeholders from participating in the conceptualization and direction of this new middle school, the principal found few who would support him when the chips were down.

Starting a year before this school opened, the faculty had been appointed, the principal chosen, and the population lines drawn, the following activities could have occurred to increase support for the principal and his vision:

In faculty and community meetings, the vision of the school could have been shared in every detail. Input could have been sought from parents, teachers, and central office personnel. Possible weakness in faculty and facility utilization could have been explored. The ideas of others could have been discussed and, where possible, incorporated into the overall vision of the school.

When problem areas began to occur, faculty, community, and central office representatives could have been called in to discuss them. If these were problems mentioned in past planning sessions, the solution alternatives selected during those calm hours of reflection could have been brought into place. This process could encompass an ongoing brainstorming group and be subdivided into other problems areas in which additional faculty, central office, and/or paid consultants could have been brought in to share their ideas.

Bimonthly feedback sessions could have been held with faculty (and other stakeholders) to maintain a continuous assessment of the school's progress.

Executive training could have been arranged for the principal and assistant principal of the school, including problem-solving and conflict-resolution skills, brainstorming, and ways to be more inclusive in leadership style and school management.

What was needed then and remains a present need of schools is transformational leadership. Kevin Cashman agrees with Jaworski's image of transformational leadership and notes that it opens possibilities rather than protects what has been accomplished. Rather than always dealing with problems and coping with limitations, transformational leadership takes a more positive approach: one characterized by innovation, open dialogue, and continuous conversation with institutional stakeholders. Cashman explains that transformational leadership is guided by authenticity, purpose, openness, trust, compassion, courage, inclusion, creating value and contributing, balance and centeredness, fluidity and adaptability, having a peaceful presence, and allowing one's inner being to support the activity of the organization. This type of leadership is put into juxtaposition to "leading from the outside," which is guided by one's projected image; issues of safety and security, fear and control, self-interest; avoidance of issues and people; excluding others from planning and decision making; winning at all costs; being distracted by small issues and personalities; resistance to change; having a dominating, uneasy presence; and doing that which is supported by more doing.

The middle school principal in our story above was on the verge of transformational leadership but just couldn't let go of his projected image. Because a superintendent whom he deeply respected selected him and his ideas for the middle school, he sincerely believed that he had been vaulted above other principals and teachers. Because he couldn't let go of this fading persona, he considered his transfer to another school an act of sabotage and soon retired from public education. Even twenty years after this event occurred, he still talked about his vision and how "his" school was pulled out from under him. The bottom line for Cashman is the choice between looking good—protecting one's persona—or making a difference. He concludes, "Lasting solutions involve dealing with our internal situation in order to transform the external circumstance."[16] And he warns us that leading from character is not easy. He says, "Executive coaching programs often reinforce refining persona, rather than unfolding character— executives are coached how to act instead of how to be."[17]

Principle #3: Become a positive force for improving the human value within your school system.

Associated actions:

1. Share your vision for the school and/or school district with all staff members and the community.
2. Invite feedback from the staff and the community about your ideas through dialogue and critical analyses that redefine, redirect, or prioritize school and/or school district goals and strategies.
3. Make staff training a personal and professional priority.
4. Anticipate emerging problems in the school and/or school district, and solicit alternative perspectives and problem solutions.
5. Collaborate with members of the staff and community when interpreting and resolving organizational and school problems.

One of the most courageous school superintendents I ever met took a large and wealthy school system, that was being managed as it had been since World War II, and, in eight years, set the stage for its growth and renewal. This superintendent was both forward looking and understanding of the circumstances within which he worked. The schools desperately needed to update their technology. The year was 1982, and there were no computers in the system, not even in the central office. Principals in the district had huge sums of dollars in their bank accounts and invested in certificates of deposit but were never encouraged to use this money to upgrade their schools. They had been told to keep it in the bank and let it grow in case there was a disaster. The former superintendent recognized and rewarded them for their fiscal discipline and financial prudence. The new superintendent's first move was to encourage the retirement of many of the principals and central office personnel, especially those who were unwilling to change and update their schools or departments. Those principals that refused to retire were moved to different schools. Many retired, and new principals were hired to replace them. In a period of four years, in the system's twenty-one schools, many principal changes were made, and the money held in their bank accounts was soon spent to create computer centers, upgrade libraries into media centers, and purchase needed classroom supplies. At the central office level, departmental chairpersons were transferred, and gradually a new supervisory staff replaced them. Departments rewrote their mission statements and aligned their goals accordingly.

This was a time of trial and error, and this superintendent was willing to make any change necessary to grow the school system. In his second four-year term, he began a building program to replace every school facility that had been built prior to 1955. Even after this superintendent had moved on to another school district, this building program continued until the year 2000, as did the growth in technology, cultural and fine arts, and improvements of athletic facilities in all of the middle and high schools. His vision had lasting value because the community and school employees had a share in its development and were entrusted with carrying it forward. This superintendent was easy to dislike for his disregard for tradition and his unwillingness to cow down to the "good-old-boy" network that had always operated the school district. It was inevitable that he would move on, but the school system and community leaders understood his value to their educational community and felt fortunate to have had his leadership for eight years.

Early in his second four-year term, he selected what he called his "future committee" from among teachers and principals in the school system. Most on this committee were young, and their brainstorming sessions brought forth many new ideas that were later prioritized and implemented within the district. Members of the future committee soon were leading other committees, each of which focused on one goal of the school district. Excitement and a free-flow of ideas soon resonated throughout the school district. Many said that those eight years were the most exciting days of their careers. They felt important and needed. Their ideas were respected, and the superintendent and his staff were willing to listen and try new strategies and methods. When he left the system he later said, "I'm a mover and shaker, but not much of a maintainer. I like to build and in doing this awaken people to their individual and collective possibilities. I like to challenge them to improve their strengths, and I do my best to provide the resources and the opportunities for them to succeed. I've tried to do that here."

John Gardner has said, "If one is leading, teaching, dealing with young people or engaged in any other activity that involves influencing, directing, guiding, helping, or nurturing, the whole tone of the relationship is conditioned by one's faith in human possibilities. That is the generative element, the source of the current that gives life to the relationship."[18] This also is the world of possibilities emphasized by Jaworski.[19] This was the world of this former school superintendent who was willing to serve as he led, listen as he directed, and praise as he implemented the ideas that were brought before him. An educational leader can be a positive force for improving the value of the entire school organization—from the qualifications and training of employees to the productivity of students and clear and timely communications with the community. This kind of leadership takes courage and shares a broad vision of what education can be.

Jaworski's emphasis on creating a world of possibilities, now and in the future, calls for a fundamental shift of mind, one that is a requirement for creative leadership. His thoughts are a reminder of the superintendent described above and of E. Paul Torrance, the founder of the Torrance Center for Creative Studies at the University of Georgia. First, Jaworski says there is a need for a fundamental shift in the way leaders think about the world. The clockwork-machine-like metaphor views the universe as a closed and fixed system and supports a command/control mentality. It is both destructive and limits the growth of human value within the organization. This metaphor needs replacement by a view that conceives the universe as open, dynamic, and interconnected. This by itself will open leadership to the potential for change. Second, Jaworski says that relationship is the organizing principle of the universe and that current leaders need to accept others as necessary to their own productivity. He understands that organizations can be legitimately looked upon as a network of human interactions. This entails a newfound commitment to listen to others and understand their essential humanness. It is from this commitment—this willingness to acknowledge the personhood of others and listen to what they say—that a certain flow of meaning begins, and we begin to experience the authenticity of dialogue. Jaworski says, "People are attracted to authentic presence and to the unfolding of a future that is full of possibilities."[20]

For Jaworski, these are the pieces of the puzzle he calls "authentic leadership." When they come together willingly, the leader becomes a positive force for improving the human value within the organization. He calls this "synchronicity," where people freely share their ideas and give of their abilities, where doors open and a sense of flow develops. Jaworski says, "You are not acting individually any longer, but out of the unfolding generative order. This is the unbroken wholeness of the implicate order out of which seemingly discrete events take place."[21]

For educators this means aligning practices with an overall mission and goals. This occurs when we close the gap between what we believe and what we do, between our personal and organizational values and our day-to-day activities. Aligning practices will involve change. If our goal is to become an ethical leader, then it means moving from where we are now to internalizing and applying ethical decision making in our daily work habits—it means creating an ethical climate of personal, organizational, and relational growth. Becoming an ethical leader in this sense means that we create opportunities for staff dialogue and invite positive ideas and criticism into our lives. These changes will not occur over night. They will occur incrementally as we improve our own personal skills, attitudes, and behaviors. As we move in the direction of becoming an ethical leader, we can reduce frustration and enhance environmental quality —in others and ourselves—with patience, foresight, and understanding, all of which strengthen the capabilities and dignity of school employees.

The real potential for transforming the educational workplace lies in the willingness of leaders to change. This transformation will take place along seven key dimensions[22]:

1. Organizational structure,
2. Leadership,
3. People and culture,
4. Unity,
5. Knowledge,
6. Alliances, and
7. Governance

Organizational structure change is where hierarchical, command-and-control behaviors give over to centerless networking in which the structure of decision making remains flexible and easily modified.

Leadership change involves everyone being a leader and creating an environment for teacher/student success that is instilled with a capacity for change and growth. Ethical leaders recognize that leadership is no longer the province of the anointed few. The process of promoting select individuals into positions of authority is a relic of a command-and-control culture that paralyzes educational systems and schools dedicated to teacher and student success. When everyone is a leader, an environment has been created for collective gain and success, and the mark of an ethical leader will be to create other leaders within the organization who are empowered to act. This model of cascading leadership is not a luxury; it is an imperative in a world where school systems and schools no longer have the time for day-to-day, top-down decision making and where knowledge throughout the organization must be leveraged and shared.

The people and culture aspect of change is one in which authority is delegated, employees are recognized and valued as knowledge workers, and collaboration is expected and rewarded. Increasingly, teachers and other educational specialists understand that they own their own employ-ability. They are willing to share their knowledge and unique skills throughout an educational system with the understanding that they too will be provided with developmental opportunities. Once their personal development passport has been stamped, however, they may move on to other employment. Recognizing this, school systems need to anticipate and plan for their long-term needs, rather than focusing exclusively on filling slots that have been allocated to them.

The unity dimension of change is one that includes a vision of the educational system and the school that is embedded in employees and students with its impact projected externally. Schools should recognize that extracting 70 or 80 percent of their potential is not good enough; they need to be efficient at generating value at every point in the organization, and principals and staffs need to be ready quickly to innovate and make good decisions about teaching and learning.

The change regarding knowledge is one in which information, expe-rience, and skill are translated (and shared) into student success. Educa-tional offices that are overdepartmentalized and schools that are externally divided by grade levels and subjects have a tendency to hoard their best thinking and avoid sharing or using the best practices for engendering student success. Why restrict meetings to so-called "essential" personnel when open, flexible dialogue on all levels and across traditional chains of command are more productive and meaningful?

Alliances must change, with all educators and educational informa-tion sources committed to cooperative arrangements that enable teach-ers, principals, and system leaders to act faster and smarter with limited resources. Alliances give teachers and curriculum specialists an advan-tage, enhance student achievement, and grow successful schools. They give all educators an excellent way to secure immediate access to those many different capabilities needed for teaching/learning improvement.

Governance involves three different areas that are important issues for ethical leaders. These areas include: governance of the entire school system by the board of education and superintendent, governance of intrasystem alliances, and governance of individual schools. The traditional top-down, internally focused governance structure is today yielding to a more distributed, decentralized model that incorporates both internal and external evaluation. Boards of education are performing more in advisory roles, challenging the effectiveness of school superintendents and principals to improve both the environment of learning and student success. External evaluations are still being used as the superintendent's office continues to evaluate principals and assist with the evaluation of teachers, but internal controls in departments and in schools is encouraged. This allows for greater freedom, a wider distribution of authority, and an emphasis on professional responsibility for each employee.

There is no easy formula, no six-point lesson plan that can bring a leader to this point. It comes from deep within and begins with confidence and a positive attitude about those whom the leader serves. Warren Bennis also recognizes the importance of leading by serving others when he points out that the basic ingredient of leadership is integrity, which includes self-knowledge and a certain maturity in building and maintaining human relationships. Leadership integrity is revealed by one's dedication to be observant, capable of working with and learning from others, never servile, and always truthful. Integrity, he points out, is the basis of trust, the one quality the leader must earn. Bennis says, "It is given by coworkers and followers, and without it, the leader can't function."[23]

Principle #4: Lead from character and with confidence and self-respect, which are the necessary first steps for personal and organizational improvement.

Associated actions:

1. Formulate and articulate a vision for the school and/or school district that prioritizes values, purposes, and actions.
2. Collaborate with staff and community and any other stakeholders to transform this vision.
3. Become aware of the emerging needs of schools, staff, students, parents, and the community.
4. Establish an educational culture which builds cooperation, encourages professional risk-taking, and empowers staff members to actively lead at their levels of work and expertise.

5. Promote a philosophy of lifelong learning for yourself and among staff, students, and the community.

Growing value among school employees and in students can be costly and, if the right methods and strategies are inappropriate for meeting the various needs of the school community, can result in a lost of productivity. Bennis says, "The problem is this: How do we develop a sufficient climate of understanding so that the various publics on whom every present-day institution depends for its support, both financial and moral, as well as the people who take its classes or work in its plants and offices, care about the institution and identify with its destiny?"[24]

According to Bennis, "Empowerment is the collective effect of leadership."[25] Not only must the leader create clear-cut and measurable goals, the leader must make every effort to locate other innovators within the school organization, utilize their expertise, and bring them into the dialogue about school improvement. Bennis says the leader creates a climate in which conventional wisdom can be questioned and challenged and one in which mistakes are embraced rather than shunned in favor of low-risk goals. Transferring what Bennis says about business and financial organizations to the school community, we can say that healthy, spirited educators are the primary source of educational success. The superintendent mentioned in the last section was successful because he created a climate for change and invited all employees and the community to critique what had been happening in the school district and offer ideas for improvement. He then empowered his central office staff, principals, and teachers to take up the challenges offered by these suggested changes. He told them in public meetings and in one-on-one sessions not be afraid of failure, but to learn from the mistakes and move on. The growth in that school district has been phenomenal. The superintendents who followed him have been able to continue the programs he began and ignite the school system to even greater areas of achievement. A foundation, once laid, enriches the productivity of the organization for many years to follow.

Too many superintendents and far too many principals are Teflon leaders. They lead by their authority and not their knowledge and understanding of educational principles or the teaching/learning process. They lead from the outside in and are more concerned about their image than about growing the human value within the school community. They know what they want and give little consideration to the input from the educational expertise that must implement their strategies. These leaders don't mind ordering certain actions to be carried out or even selecting teaching strategies outside their area of proficiency and requiring all teachers to use them. They usually turn a deaf ear to those who share a different point of view than theirs and, when things go wrong—when goals are not met and projects lie uncompleted—are quick to lay the blame outside of their office. Avoiding controversy inside and outside the school system, the reasons for their failures are laid on their subordinates. About these kinds of leaders Bennis comments, "The striving of organizations for harmony is less a conscious program than a consequence of the structure of large organizations. Cohesiveness in such organizations results from a commonly held set of values, beliefs, norms, and attitudes, often summed up as culture. In other words, an organization can be a judgmental place in which those who do not share the common set, the common point of view, are by definition deviant, marginal outsiders. Unanimity leads rather quickly to stagnation."[26] To move anything (organization) or any person takes a certain amount of friction. Friction will come to leaders and to the school system or school. The leader leads most effectively who is flexible and welcomes different opinions and who confronts problems and on most occasions seeks win-win solutions. When the leader invites friction in the form of dialogue and debate, a certain creative tension pushes the organization forward to accomplish its goals.

The goals of the system and those of the individuals who make up the system often work in a subtle harmony. Effective leaders lead from character and with confidence and self-respect, which are necessary for personal and organizational improvement. They also respect and care for those educators with whom they work. When respect and integrity resonate throughout the school organization, there is a certain spirit and dedication to the goals of the entire system that hangs in a delicate balance. The school leader who is most effective understands and respects the ideas brought to the table by teachers, principals, and curriculum specialists. These individuals too must be willing to discuss and modify what they understand as necessary and work with, not against, the school and school system for the productivity of educational excellence. This is a fragile tension, but one that enables productivity rather than stifles it. Russ S. Moxley[27] says this is a process of leadership that is inspiriting, rather than dispiriting, and it is a process that includes all members of the organization in the activity of leadership. He calls this process, "leadership and spirit." Leadership and spirit are a two-lane highway: one lane focuses on the inner character or the inner being of the leader and the other on the activities of the leader. For Moxley, "... in the activity of leadership the who is more important than the what or the how."[28] For him, leadership know-how is a process of developing the inner life of the executive or manager. He says, "Unwittingly and unintentionally, we project what goes on in our depths onto all of our outer experiences, including our practices of leadership. What we project is not always benign; sometimes it is toxic—to ourselves, to others, and to our organizations."[29]

Interestingly, writing in the *Harvard Business Review,* Vanessa Urch Druskat, assistant professor of organizational behavior at the Weatherhead School of Management at Case Western University in Cleveland and Steven B. Wolff, assistant professor of management at the School of Management at Marist College in Poughkeepsie, New York, comment, "Study after study has shown that teams are more creative and productive when they can achieve high levels of participation, cooperation, and collaboration among members. But interactive behaviors like these aren't easy to legislate. Our work shows that three basic conditions need to be present before such behaviors can occur: mutual trust among members, a sense of group identity (a feeling among members that they belong to a unique and worthwhile group), and a sense of group efficacy (the belief that the team can perform well and that group members are more effective working together than apart)."[30]

A role of ethical leadership is to continually push for and help create this climate. Mutual trust and group solidarity are maintained throughout the system by leaders who are self-confident enough to allow the ideas and expertise of principals, program directors, and teachers help guide the mission and purposes of the system. Group solidarity does not mean, especially among educators, that agreement will occur on all means and strategies to reach identified goals. It does mean, however, that all employees feel empowered and encouraged to do whatever it takes to help the schools toward the goal of increased student achievement. As Michael Schrage has discovered, this may mean challenging accepted wisdom, if need be, and making independent decisions based on their own assessments, taking risks, and continuously being on the alert for those moments when someone needs to step up and keep things moving forward. He says, it is "… about encouraging creative people to relate to one another in creative ways."[31]

But not all leaders are ethical leaders. Some can be tyrants, and others are too wishy-washy to be figured out. One day they're for this and the next day—when the idea is not successful—they're against it. For those who serve under such leaders, it's a no-win situation at best, but usually a win-lose situation with the leader always on the winning side. I was familiar with such a superintendent. His first action as superintendent was to tell his central office staff that he owned them from 8:00 a.m. until 5:30 p.m. each day, five days a week, and that they would do as he said. Few respected this superintendent; many feared him. His staff was seldom consulted and rarely included in the decision-making processes. When things didn't go his way, he would, as some say, "pitch a hissy." He made many of his important decisions by consulting a small group of his closest friends, usually far away from the office. The negative influence he had on the decision-making and problem-solving processes carried over to his department heads, many of whom also became top-down, command/control administrators. He was an excellent manager and a superb organizer but an ineffective leader whose autocratic legacy still resonates in that school system many years after his retirement.

Principle #5: Make creative change the norm by
letting go of the old and leading on the edge of possibility.

Associated actions:

1. Promote cross-departmental, cross-grade level, and interschool dialogue and sharing to encourage reflection about teaching and learning practices.
2. Evaluate staff and educational/administrative programs to determine the degree of implementation achieved and where and when changes need to occur.
3. Encourage brainstorming and collaboration among supervisors, principals, and teachers in order to facilitate more effective teaching and learning processes.
4. Use school board policies, purposes, and goals to set high expectations for staff and students.
5. Involve supervisors and teachers in the development of self-evaluation procedures, formal evaluation procedures, and means of self-reflection.

Ethical leadership respects the human value of the school community. Placing the evaluation of teachers, supervisors, and students as a *primary* function of the school system will not increase the productivity of either group, especially if its sole purpose is to ensure that employees are following top-down prescribed methods and programs. This is not to say that evaluation is not needed, for it is a valuable component of school improvement. There are many proven educational methods and strategies for improving student learning over the long run that have been sacrificed for the expedient increase in student achievement scores. Much of my last decade in education was spent in meetings discussing how to raise student standardized test scores. Most of these discussions were led by the superintendent with the support of the testing and accountability department who gave out statistical averages by schools, grade levels, and particular student populations. The focus was on getting scores up "now" and the answer seemed to be more and more practice testing. Little was said about teaching methods, creativity, and developmentally appropriate or long-range strategies. Still less was said about the intense reading program we had started or the gains we had been making in our newly designed mathematics program for middle school students. In the curriculum department, we knew from our research that the scores would rise as these programs impacted the processes of teaching and learning, but it would take time.

Consider the following example of our work during this time. During the 1996–1997 school year, my staff and I wrote the following message in our gifted program handbook:

> Last year, we began a new emphasis for our department. Our goal was to reach more students with high potential and enrich their basic education program. Also, an emphasis on "whole school enrichment" allowed us to provide more effective ways of serving children through our expert team of gifted educators and regular classroom teachers. Through teaming and networking we will be able to build quality programs in our schools to address a variety of special needs of a broad base of able learners.
>
> This new approach creates change—change in the way we plan, change in the way we work together, change in the way we deliver services, and change in the way we train teachers. Our goal is to increase the quality of education of not only those who are classified as "gifted" by our state and local norms, but to also increase the academic productivity of a much larger percentage of those children who are failing to actualize their gifts and who are possibly unaware of their inner potentialities. We accomplish this goal in the following ways:
>
> 1. by providing learning environments adapted to the needs of able learners which concentrate on such areas as creative and critical thinking, mathematical adeptness, the mastery of content-related materials, and the ability to communicate in writing and speaking
> 2. by providing opportunities for students to enhance, develop, and utilize their originality, initiatives, and self-motivation
> 3. by assisting students with the development of their affective and valuing skills
> 4. by providing educational activities which incorporate multimedia and multidisciplinary approaches to learning

    5. by helping students take responsibility for setting personal goals, providing an environment in which students can develop productive peer relationships, and assisting them with extending their freedom of choice and becoming more responsible for their behavior

Our program philosophy simply said:

> The persons whom we employ to manage and teach in our gifted and enrichment programs will be looked upon as human resource systems to whom, for whom, and through whom our programs provide growth, development, opportunity, and rewards. Our first commitment is to our students for whom we strive to provide an enabling educational environment to facilitate in each of them a lifetime of personal and vocational growth.

A part of our program was networking with other school systems, colleges, and the state department. To this end, in 1992, I assisted Lenoir-Rhyne College in Hickory, North Carolina, with the development and promotion of a two-day conference which focused on the educational needs of minority, underachieving, and culturally different able learners in the primary grades. Scholars from around the United States participated in this conference, and the response was well received with educators coming from fourteen states and several foreign countries. One of the products of this conference was an unpublished monograph, which I entitled "Students of Promise." Its primary concentration was developing ways to maximize the learning and vocation potential of this targeted group of students. The conclusions reached in this monograph about programs for young able learners were the following:

1. Programs will primarily concentrate on children and not on curriculum or assessment.

2. More time will be provided for children to think, probe, create, solve problems, and express ideas.

3. We should not hurry children through the curriculum through drill and practice, but allow the curriculum to enrich the child and the child to respond through further explorations.

4. The classroom environment and the leadership of teachers is vital if these goals are to be met. They must keep children motivated and wanting to learn.

5. Engaging them in thinking skill development and creative processes will perpetuate mental and affective growth in children.

6. Finally, by allowing children to grow and help mold the curriculum, learning will become more personalized and, hence, internal.

E. Paul Torrance[32] has recognized that we are probably losing over 70 percent of our able learners by ignoring the above conclusions. During this time, very little attention was given to individual students, learning styles, or teaching styles. We had correlated thinking skills with the state testing program and were training teachers how to integrate creative and critical thinking into their lessons and how to recognize when the state goals called for certain kinds of cognitive operations. Still, the theme was to give students more tests and they will learn how to take tests well. Teachers got the message, and many innovative and affective teaching methods were gradually replaced by the drill and practice required by curriculum administrators. Precious hours and days were lost for instruction as testing became the dominant pastime of educators. Our scores did rise and then level off. Teachers and students tire of such testing, and during the past five years, scores have changed very little save the normal pattern of highs and lows one usually finds in such procedures.

There are numerous educational strategies designed to increase student learning, and today, new brain-based curricular activities are being developed that are pedagogically sound. During the last decade, the deeply enriching and human levels of teaching and learning were brushed aside as educators fell into a testing trap: false positives were generated by narrowing what was taught and how it was taught and by the overuse of testing to produce more efficient testing results. To maintain these levels, schools have to keep on doing these same old things. There are three losers here: the first are our students who are being cheated out of a broad-based and enriching educational experience; the second is our culture which will soon have a great many good test takers applying for jobs, but who will know little else; and the third are our young teachers who are losing their creative and risk-taking edge when it comes to assessing student needs and creating strategies to meet these needs.

Zohar and Marshall[33] talk about a new society (a quantum society) characterized by individuals and groups conditioned to think outside the boundaries, to think in terms of possibilities, and to think the impossible. Sadly, this metaphor has yet to grip the forces of educational change and we are caught in a time when doing the same old thing is yielding the same old results. The quantum society demands quantum leadership, the kind that Millar and Torrance were picturing in their concept of the *beyonder.* Although ideal in nature, the *beyonder* represents a feasible goal for education and is demanded by the problems that beset our post-9/11/01 times. Zohar and Marshall say that if we wish to change our methods of leadership, we must begin by changing the way we think.

Educational leadership is about caring for individuals and about the way we view each other, especially our students. Warren Bennis points out, "Nothing much grows in a stalemate ... but managers and bureaucrats are less gardeners than mechanics—they are fonder of tinkering with machinery than of making things grow."[34] Bennis also says that effective leadership must break away from concrete thinking—thinking only in terms of statistical averages, the bottom line—which is strangling our vision of the future. For Bennis, a leader innovates and is organized. A leader focuses on people, asks questions, and has his/her eyes on both the bottom line and the horizon while challenging the status quo. If, while "reaching for the top" we lose sight of what the top represents, our *reaching* will never change the mission of the schools to teach and educate all students, and we will probably never develop a sufficient climate of understanding so that all who are involved in the reaching, who care about educating youngsters and identify with their destiny, are also thought of as leaders in their schools, offices, and within the community.

Principle #6: Commit yourself to open communication and dialogue by including others in planning, initiating, and decision-making processes.

Associated actions:

1   Encourage and make available opportunities for high levels of participation in school and district decision making and problem solving.

2. Create a collaborative and proactive school and school district culture which anticipates needs, initiates responses, monitors progress toward goals, and allows leaders from the classroom to the central office to lead.

3. Collaborate with staff to transform personal, school, and school district goals into performance objectives.

4. Regularly seek input from the staff and community and openly share information within the school, school district, and community.

5. Practice ethical leadership at whatever level you are working, which includes an ethic of responsibility and relationships and an ethic of rights and rules.

A major purpose of leadership is growing other leaders.[35] This is a powerful idea, one that is entirely consistent with the moral and pedagogical purposes of education. A logical outcome of this purpose is the empowerment of professional leadership from the superintendent's office to the classroom teacher: every educational professional empowered to lead at his or her level of expertise and responsibility, be it a classroom teacher or a program manager. Utilizing the creative and cumulative knowledge of educators at the classroom, school, and district levels is the best way of increasing the human value and productivity of the school system. These individuals are at education's "ground zero;" they are the grassroots of education who are able to articulate and elaborate the vision and mission of the school district to the community they serve.

Implied by this idea is participatory leadership. Educators call this "site-based management." Instituted with prescribed restraints, it has met with varying degrees of success. Allotting a few designated areas for control by principals and teachers in the schools is only a beginning. Participatory leadership entails that staff, working at all levels in the educational district, will be called to serve on major and minor committees, not just in their school, but throughout the system as well. It means that the superintendent and board of education will solicit and take seriously the views of teachers whom they serve and that there will be a leadership mix caused by varying levels of knowledge and expertise with teachers, principals, supervisors, and superintendents sometimes leading and sometimes following. This does not mean that the board of education or the superintendent give up their governance of the school system or their vision. It does mean that the knowledge and skill of those employed to implement this vision are invited to the decision-making table.

Participatory leadership is *servant leadership*. Robert K. Greenleaf says that this concept "emerged after a deep involvement with colleges and universities during the period of campus turmoil in the late 1960s and early 1970s."[36] He further comments, "It was a searing experience to watch distinguished institutions show their fragility and crumble, to search for an understanding of what happened to them, and to try to help heal their wounds." Important to his concept of "servant leadership" is the idea of "followship." His vision and hope was "that leaders will bend their efforts to serve with skill, understanding, and spirit, and that followers will be responsive only to able servants who would lead them—but that they will respond. Discriminate and determined servants as followers are as important as servant leaders, and everyone, from time to time, may be in both roles."[37]

In 1977, while evaluating issues of power and authority, Greenleaf said, "People are beginning to learn, however haltingly, to relate to one another in less coercive and more creatively supporting ways. A new moral principle is emerging which holds that the only authority deserving one's allegiance is that which is freely and knowingly granted by the led to the leader in response to, and in proportion to, the clearly evident servant stature of the leader."[38] Here, the idea of ethical leadership begins to emerge. For Greenleaf, it all comes down to *followship* where followers "will freely respond only to individuals who are chosen as leader because they are proven and trusted as servants."[39] Greenleaf recognizes the unpopularity of this idea, especially among leaders. This is especially true in school districts where principals and teachers, program directors and supervisors are told to do what is expected of them and to avoid meddling in areas where they have no business. This type of leadership is actually a situation of leadership withdrawal and avoids tapping the knowledge and wisdom—the human value—within the school district itself. Don M. Frick and Larry C. Spears have commented, "The times are finally catching up with many of Greenleaf's ideas. Management and organizational thinkers ... emphasize the importance of an ethical base for organizations, the power of trust and stewardship, and the personal depths that authentic leaders must honor as they empower and serve others.... No two resulting organizational charts look the same because each organization adapts ideas according to the experiences and insights of its own people."[40]

The ethical questions are "Do those served grow as persons?" "Do they become servant-leaders within the school district and schools?" A direct part of the human dilemma is measuring the effectiveness of servant leadership. Greenleaf notes that we cannot know for sure and comments that the hypothesis of servant leadership is left under a cloud of doubt. His answer is that we must continue to study and learn, and, from time to time, reexamine the hypothesis itself.[41] He says, "The natural servant, the person who is servant first, is more likely to persevere and refine a particular hypothesis on what serves another's highest priority needs than is a person who is leader first and who later serves out of promptings of conscience or in conformity with normative expectations."[42]

Greenleaf has expressed a credo that summed up his life's work[43]:

> I believe that caring for persons, the more able and the less able serving each other, is what makes a good society. Most caring was once person to person. Now much of it is mediated through institutions—often large, powerful, impersonal; not always competent; sometimes corrupt. If a better society is to be built, one more just and more caring and providing opportunity for people to grow, the most effective and economical way, while supportive of the social order, is to raise the performance as servant of as many institutions as possible by new voluntary regenerative forces initiated within them by committed individuals, servants.

Such servants may never predominate or even be numerous; but their influence may form a leaven that makes possible a reasonably civilized society.

If, for Greenleaf, *followship* is the first ethical principal of leadership, his second ethical principle is *foresight*.[54] He says, "Foresight is the 'lead' that the leader has."[45] Without foresight, the leader can only react to events. Greenleaf views the loss of foresight—the ability to take the right action when there was time and freedom to think and act—an ethical failure because the result is usually serious compromises. The tests of leadership are realistic and exacting. Dreams and large visions stir our blood, whereas little plans and coercive power leave us empty. Nothing much really important can be done with power. Coercive power, although convenient, only works in emergencies. He says, "Beyond that, coercive power must be valued in inverse relation to its use ... the real disabilities of the holder of power become more apparent" as civilization and its institutions evolve.[46]

In addition to followship and foresight, Greenleaf adds *listening* to his list of ethical leadership characteristics.[47] He tells leaders to listen in both directions—to those on the growing edge and to the more conservative pragmatists, and then to all in between these two extremes. This is how we learn, and this is how the leader serves, develops foresight, and grows the organization. This is the way a leader shows his or her genuine respect and care for the persons in the organization. When a person doesn't get an opportunity to put his or her opinion down at the decision-making table, he or she is devalued and discounted as important to the organization. We are moral only as we care for persons, and we will have a moral society only as we create institutions that also care for persons. Greenleaf concludes, "Caring for persons, the more able and the less able serving each other, is the rock upon which a good society is built.... If a better society is to be built, one that is more just and more loving, one that provides greater creative opportunity for its people, then the most open course is to raise both the capacity to serve and the very performance as servant of existing major institutions by new regenerative forces operating within them."[48]

I ran into a situation back in 1977 that puts some of what Greenleaf says in perspective. I was new to the public schools and just starting in the department of exceptional children in our school district. I was assigned to a middle school position where I taught learning disabled and educationally handicapped students. I noticed that the educational psychologist assigned to my school took very little time with students. I had read that a psychological evaluation would take about two hours, but he was spending barely fifteen minutes with each student. I said to him that labeling children as learning disabled is a serious responsibility and commented that it seems you should take a little more time with each child. His comment back to me was quite disconcerting. He said, "You want to have a class don't you? In order to get the state and federal funding we need to pay your salary, we have to label a certain amount of students in this school as learning handicapped." With that he left.

A few months later, a state auditor showed up in my class. He was on his regular rounds through the state and made our school district his next surprise visit. He was with our exceptional children's director and asked to see the private files of my students. The director left and the auditor stayed with me the rest of the day. At the end of the day he ask me if I ever reviewed the files of my students. I told him that I did and that their educational plans were created around the recommendations found in each of their files. He then produced the psychological profiles of each child and asked me what these were. By his voice and the look on his face, I knew that he was not a happy camper. I told him that I was new to the public schools and was unfamiliar with psychological reports and procedures. I had been taking classes at a nearby college, and with the background I had from those classes I had questioned the school psychologist about the time he was spending with our children and the completeness of his evaluations. I also reported how the psychologist had responded to me. With that the auditor left my school.

The next morning I found my principal waiting for me at the door of the school. He escorted me to my room where waiting for me was the exceptional children's director, his assistant, the school psychologist, the superintendent, and the assistant superintendent of our school district. They allowed the exceptional children's director to speak to me first. He wanted to know what I had said to the state auditor. I told him what I had said, detailing what the psychologist had said to me weeks earlier. With that, the psychologist jumped to his feet and shouted, "Listen, we don't air our dirty linen in public." He was angry, and the central office was upset because my conversation with the state auditor caused a 100 percent audit of every exceptional child's file in the school district. The result was a fine and a loss of several hundred thousand dollars of state and federal funding. Following this incident, new psychologists were hired, and the two former ones were reassigned to schools in guidance positions. Also, from that time, all exceptional children's files were moved to a central location with only copies of their educational recommendations left for teachers in the schools.

This was my first taste of the command and control leadership in our school district. My principal said that this incident would cause me a load of professional harm, here and in other school districts if I chose to move. He further said that I would not be trusted and would be watched and evaluated much more than other teachers. If this actually happened, I was unaware of it, but for as long as I stayed in this school district, I never lived down the label of not be a "team player." One year later, after I had assisted the state with developing its second governor's school, the district was sued in civil court for not providing programs for its gifted students. I was then called upon by this same group of individuals to develop a gifted program for the system—one it didn't really want—and moved into the central office for three years.

Leanna Traill, a New Zealand reading consultant, took the title of her 1993 assessment and evaluation of literacy learning—*Highlight My Strengths*—from the Maori saying, "Highlight my strengths and my weaknesses will disappear." She commented, "The fundamental goal of teaching and learning in schools should be that every learner is guaranteed optimal instruction and opportunity to reach his or her educational potential."[49] Our role as educators is to serve our students and, by doing so, to highlight their strengths, and the role of educational leadership is to serve this purpose. Joseph R. Royce says that many of us are too one-sided, too tied up in our own cocoons, too serve this purpose. He calls this "encapsulation," and he labels those who exhibit these characteristics as "encapsulated." He reminds us, "De-capsulation demands that we are able to get inside and outside ourselves, our culture, and our time,"[59] that we are able to lead from the inside out with foresight, followship, and by listening to and understanding the world in which we live. Although this is not always 100 percent possible, just beginning down this road will open us to a new world of human possibilities. It will free us from a command/control mentality and from current prevalent prejudices of race, color, religion, and political party. De-capsulation will free us from the reductionist tendencies of contemporary education that are limiting leadership to the superintendent or principal's office and teaching and learning to practicing and scoring high on a narrow range of standardized tests.

If I have belabored this point, it's because we have lost the image of what this nation can become and the possibilities that lie before a well-educated public. I understand that certain evaluations are necessary, but also labor to point out that the grading and classification of students has replaced, for the most part, creating creative and enriching educational opportunities for them. Royce reaches the following conclusion, "And while it is true that such an open approach to life is very risky for the individual man in the short view, it is clearly more creative and productive, and therefore, more viable for all men in the long run."[51]

Ethical/Servant Leadership

It has been my experience that educators tend to brush off any attempt to discuss ethics, saying that all values are relative, individualistic, and personal. They many times conclude that what is moral for one person may not be moral for another person. In the last quarter of the twentieth century there was a break with scientific and rational cognitive processing that is known today as "postmodernism." Postmodernism is a movement in almost every branch of science, art, architecture, religion, and philosophy, which accentuates the freedom of choice and self-determination as its highest values. Arguing that the scientific method and logical analysis are only one way of approaching truth, postmodernists claim that truth is relative to the truth seeker; that there is no universal truth and no universal values. Ethics, therefore, has been trivialized to "do your own thing," and no ethical horizon outside the self and its happiness is sought.

One major problem with postmodernism is that our identity and values are not merely formed by self-examination but are tied to our work, our families, and the significant relationships built over a lifetime. The postmodern hypothesis narrows ethics to an individualism that flattens moral behavior and ignores our social responsibilities and the richness of life brought through human interaction, love and care for others, and the recognition of each person's personal dignity. This breach with rationalism has reduced ethics to what I like to call "locational values," namely, that morality is ultimately arbitrary and relative to location. Also, the content of ethics and morals is lost in the vacuum where choice—any choice—is the highest value.

A story may illustrate this point more clearly. In October 2002, while picking up my grandson at his school, I overheard two men discussing the sniper who had recently killed and wounded many individuals in the Washington, D.C., and Richmond, Virginia, areas. One of the gentlemen standing near me was a college professor who said that his students posed an interesting question about the sniper, a question which he labeled a "moral dilemma." His students had asked him, "If one had to choose between the sniper never killing again and not getting caught, or killing one more person and getting caught, which would you choose?" The college professor said he had thought about the dilemma for several days and couldn't come up with an answer.

This is the typically false dilemma posed in college classrooms and by those who believe that moral values and ethics are arbitrary—being relative, they have no firm or rational content that can be applied universally. I beg to differ with that point of view. My reasons will become clearer when the question is asked: What if the person the sniper chooses as his last victim is you, your child, your spouse, or someone else close to you? Does that help you answer the question? Let me explain; first, creating an either/or and clean-cut ethical conclusion, when both parts of the disjunction have partial merit, gives one a false impression that ethical principles never work in the real world, that they are relative and each situation must be thoroughly probed for a satisfactory application. The choice in this case is between no more killing and not getting caught, and one more killing and getting caught and punished.

If we rephrase the situation like this: "You may kill one more person if and only if you get caught and are punished," it really doesn't make much sense. It sounds as it we're saying that killing is okay as long as you are punished for your misdeed. But killing is not an ordinary misdeed; it is nonreversible and therefore the most serious negative act that can be carried out on another person. It is blatantly immoral. But wait a minute, we want to catch the killer don't we? If killing one more person is the only way to catch the killer(s), then condoning the killing is the moral sacrifice we must make. But is this our only choice? On the surface it seems to have some merit, but so does the other disjunctive—no more killing and not getting caught.

Before we go further, we must point out that condoning murder begs the question of morality. The purpose of morality and ethics is to promote human dignity and human well-being. Morality is about caring and responsibility, rights and obligations. When we recognize the content and purpose of morality, then we are forced to say—that is, if we are to be consistent with this purpose—that killing is immoral and it would be better for all people and for the "supposed" next victim if the killings stopped now.

Being caught and getting punished are important, but these actions have little to do with the point of view of morality. Punishment is a complement to morality, but not its primary intention or function. When someone breaks a moral principle such as taking a life of another person intentionally, then this person forfeits his or her protection of that same moral principle. The moral principle is "killing is wrong." Punishment for killing, like punishment for breaking other moral principles, follows consistently as a forfeiture of rights to protection by that same rule. This has generally been the reasoning behind developing laws in this country and labeling some actions as crimes, even developing a hierarchy of crimes such as felonies and misdemeanors.

So, how would I answer the student's query about the sniper? There is not a simple answer to this question. It would be immoral and unethical to condone another killing, even if it meant catching the killer(s). But would someone like to volunteer to be the next victim? No killing is a better moral solution. I prize the dignity of the supposed next victim much more—and the victim's family and friends—than I do catching the sniper(s), if and only if, they never kill again. I put the "if and only if" into this last statement to point out just how "iffy" this whole dilemma is. No one can guarantee that they won't kill again—this is the reality of the situation. This is why the student has posed a false dilemma.

This is unfortunate. Although many values are cultural and person specific, there is a core of human values that seek the ideal of desirable well-being. Abraham Edel[52] seeks this valuational base in ideals of human equality, human dignity, and human freedom. We can also locate this base in ideas of justice and responsibility and of caring and building relationships. Lynn Beck and Joseph Murphy[53] have also suggested a framework to govern educators' talk about ethics. First, they believe that each educator should be motivated to think deeply and critically about their personal and professional beliefs and commitments. Second, they believe that we should increase our ability to understand the moral reasoning of others and continue to engage in dialogue on these important topics. Finally, they believe that some sort of foundation needs to be provided for including ethics in educational leadership development programs. I would add to this the belief that if such ethical ideals as human equality, dignity, freedom, responsibility, and integrity are to be articulated in programs for educators, then they must be firmly grounded in human need and rational procedures. Also, this valuational base, if so grounded, should provide a mooring to which a morality may be fastened.

According to Abraham Edel, "The valuational base may be seen rather to contain value conclusions or guiding principles embodying the fullest available knowledge about men's aspirations and conditions."[54] Edel adds that this valuational base will contain both universal and local principles: the universal principles representing fundamental human needs and the local principles representing approved goals or goods and evils, rules of duty and obligation, and virtues and vices.

From the point of view of ethical leadership, the local principles represent state and federal laws and regulations, school board policies, and other rules and procedures pertaining to the legal and professional parameters of the school district. At various levels—the courts, state and federal lawmakers, local school boards, professional organizations, and the like—these policies can be challenged and amended. They are not absolute and were not intended to be absolute. They were developed to meet the changing needs of students and education, and when these needs change again—and they will—these policies will once more be amended. The educator has a professional and legal obligation to carry out these regulations and, if need be, an equal right to challenge them through proper channels. Professional ethics obliges the educator to follow these rules until they are appropriately changed. These values, many of which are contained in codes of professional ethics, are time, place, and situation relative.

On the other hand, universal ethical principles are based on human need and establish a wide variety of beliefs dealing with the general welfare of humans, their societies, and the environment in which they live. Although ethical principles are applied uniformly, to all people alike ("universal" is the term used by ethicists), they are not absolute and can be changed as we learn more about society, culture, and ourselves. These principles may take the form of general goods, virtues, character constellations, obligations and tasks, and strivings and aspirations. We many times demonstrate their importance by embodying them in law and religious doctrine. Fundamentally, ethical principles have been of two types: those focusing on justice and rights detailing a wider and more general view of ethical obligation. These will also include our legal and social obligations. Ethical principles will also include those principles which focus on caring for other individuals and which embrace building and maintaining positive human relationships. This is a more personal ethical point of view and includes our basic responsibility to support and grow human value—including students—within the educational community.[55]

Essentially, this second view of ethics and ethical leadership takes is based on a major principle of Immanuel Kant: *not to treat others as a means, but as an "end" only.*[56] It is universal, not in the sense that it cannot be questioned, but in the sense that it has general application as an ethical principle based on human need and human growth; after all, no one wants to be used by another for his or her selfish gain. As Richard Rorty reminds us, "The self is a centerless web of beliefs and desires which are continually changing through a process of reweaving. This reweaving process takes place through perception, inference, and metaphor."[57] We live and work interactively with others in our educational world and translate the ethical touchstones of our lives and work to those with whom we work and to a greater community of parents, politicians, the religious establishment, and to citizens at large.

It is important that educational leaders, at all levels, have a vision of their work and its impact on students and the community. It would be sad to live our lives through someone else's vision. This uncovers the importance, if not the necessity, of ethical leadership, which places the welfare and happiness of others as one of the leader's primary obligation. Ethical leadership is unselfish and finds satisfaction in the productivity and success of others. As Michael Scriven comments, "in usual circumstances of society, each citizen's chances of a satisfactory life for himself are increased by a process of conditioning all citizens not to treat their own satisfactions as the most important goal."[58] William K. Frankena agrees, "at least it may be that, as our insight into men, society, and the universe increases, we shall more and more come to see that the finally rational way of life for the individual is or at least may be precisely the socially considerate one."[59]

Fundamentally, this is what being ethical means. The ethical leader is charged with treating all colleagues and employees considerately, demonstrating their dignity and worth as individuals and to the school system as well.[60] Modifications and exceptions to traditional norms in the treatment of others must be based on morally relevant premises. Ethical leaders are under pressure to "get the job done," whether it is to increase student learning as measured on achievement tests, build new and better facilities for teaching and learning, or improve the qualifications and training of the teaching staff. They can and should be demanding, but this in no way is a license to treat staff and colleagues in an ethically demeaning manner. As I once said to a superintendent, "You had the authority to hire me, and you have the authority to fire me, but you do not have the moral right to assault my dignity or belittle my worth, either as a professional educator or as a person."

Activities That Promote Ethical Leadership

1. Some have said, "leadership is about people." Examining the major premises of this chapter, how do principles #1 through #4 illustrate this

belief? Discuss your answers in groups of three or four, and give reasons for your conclusions.

2. Robert Greenleaf says that three fundamental principles support his concept of "servant leadership": followship—the idea that leaders serve first in order to lead, foresight—the ability to think long-term and be able to take appropriate action when there is time and freedom to think and act, and listening—at both ends of the organization—the growing edge and the conservative middle—in order to know how to make appropriate decisions.

    a. Assess your workplace and give examples of when and where these three principles were used to maximize benefit—the motivation and productivity of employees.

    b. Greenleaf's three principles are called "ethical principles" in this chapter. What reasons can you give for calling or not calling these "ethical principles"? Discuss your answers within your group, find a common ground, and report back to the whole group.

3. Leanna Trail uses the principle "highlight my strengths and my weaknesses will disappear." In your opinion why is this principle definitive of ethical leadership? Explain your reasoning.

4. The term "universal" was used throughout this chapter to describe moral principles. What is the difference between a universal principle and an absolute principle?

5. Your author says, "Ethical leadership is unselfish and finds satisfaction in the productivity and success of others." As an educator, give reasons why this ought to be thought of as an universal principle. Follow with examples of times when you have witnessed this principle being applied. Finally, talk with your colleagues. Find out how leaders have made them feel because of their individual initiatives and successes. Was their treatment positive or negative? In either way, did it increase or decrease their desire to work harder and be more committed to their professional tasks?

3

Leadership Characteristics: A Focus on Character

Creating Value: The Knowledge Worker

Effective Schools' research[1] has correctly linked student achievement with character development and improvement in the school's learning climate. Safety issues and applying codes of conduct have been shown to be factors in this primary mission of education. Experienced educators fully acknowledge that no student can learn the acceptable norms, habits, and values of a society unless his or her behavior is under control where attention can be given to the various programs and strategies of learning. This being said, even as schools focus on student learning measurements, character education cannot be ignored as a part of the student's learning equation. Parents and educators understand that character education is a means to the development of an educated citizen who recognizes and lives by ethical codes of conduct. Robert Bellah and his associates agree that it is terribly difficult to be a good and productive person in "the absence of a good society."[2]

As a vital component of ethical education, character education requires that teachers, principals, and other school administrators exhibit positive habits of ethical leadership. Modeling ethical behaviors by educators is essential to the mission of education. There can be no compromising on this point; the school system must establish an uncommon ethical linkage among its employees—from the classroom to the office of the superintendent—and within the community that it serves. As the moral environment of the school system improves, the promise is that the discipline and productivity of its staffs and students will increase. Robert Bellah further comments, "Moral ecology is only another way of speaking of

75

healthy institutions, yet the culture of individualism makes the very idea of institutions inaccessible to many of us. We Americans tend to think that all we need are energetic individuals and a few impersonal rules to guarantee fairness; anything more is not only superfluous, but also dangerous.... It is hard for us to think of institutions as affording the necessary context within which we become individuals; of institutions as not just restraining but enabling us; of institutions not as an arena of hostility within which our character is tested but an indispensable source from which character is formed."[3]

Ethical leadership supports the maintenance of enabling educational environments and is a major way of supporting the goal of developing educated and ethical citizens for the future. In all areas of life, building a compassionate and moral society entails compassionate and moral leadership. As we learn, we grow; as we learn to be moral in our relationships and just in our dealings with others, we grow as ethical leaders. As we build our educational strategies and procedures on a calculus of potential, rather than of probability, ethical leadership will take hold in education as it focuses on the value and growth of educators and students within its domain. Only morally sensitive people struggle with the gap between who they are and who they know they ought to be; ethical leaders will always be sensitive to this gap and struggle to improve their moral worth within their community of learners. We can use ethical leadership as a tool for dialogue, for narrative, for persuasion, and for facilitating the moral growth of students, parents, and educational staffs, as well as understanding that the purpose of education is—at its roots—a moral purpose.

One thing ethical leaders have learned is that they will never be autonomous individuals. From ancient times, human beings have sustained and expanded their societies because of a growing internal moral sense that recognized that good and bad actions are judged as they obviously affect the welfare of the tribe.[4] It is my conviction that each leader who chooses to be generous rather than selfish, to be truthful rather than deceptive, represents a vote for a life of generosity and truth rather than selfishness and deception. Leadership is about people; it is about building relationships and, in so doing, increasing the total value and productivity of the educational unit. As some have said, most people are not afraid of dying; they are afraid of not having lived. What frightens many teachers and educational leaders is the dread of insignificance, the idea that they lived, led, and taught and none of it mattered.

Education is at the hub of the learning society, and this is one reason for the attention it is getting from both state and federal levels. Consider the following example: At General Electric Company the value of learning and the human value of its employees is daily recognized. GE is using one form of ethical leadership to assist with their development. Sunita Holzer, vice president for human resources at GE is promoting in-house networking as one technique in this process.[5] Back in the 1970s, when women's networks were beginning to proliferate, many businesses considered in-house networks—organized by employees of the same company—as a threat to management. Holzer says, "In-house networks are important tools for people who want to get together for support and development." She further comments, "Organizations have begun to realize that in-house networks also help the employer recruit more diverse talent, develop careers, and provide mentoring." At GE networks are grassroots initiated and organized by employees. Management also encourages them. Leadership at GE has benefited from these in-house networks because they are authentic learning centers for the corporation. Cecilia Lofters, vice president and senior intellectual property counsel at GE, says that membership in one of these networks, the African American forum, has given her "an opportunity to meet other African Americans, to have informal mentors, and to get to know the company better." Jim Torres comments that his participation in the leadership of the GE Hispanic Forum has given him visibility in the company that otherwise might not have occurred.

Today, education has become the focus of attention in our "learning society." Here, as in the world of business and manufacturing, knowledge is value. Schools can learn from business and industry. The learning society seeks leaders who are adventurous, risk takers, diverse, and participative. These are leaders who are change oriented, who seek innovation, are self-developing, flexible, imaginative, and tolerant. In learning organizations employees are no longer thought of as being loyal, prudent, status quo oriented, tradition bound, rule oriented, and followers of orders. Rather, employees are thought of as persons who bring knowledge and value to the organization and who ought to be treated fairly and with respect. As Bellah reflected, "We believe that the modern ideal of a democracy governed by intelligent public opinion and participation not only is worth redeeming in our own society but requires, as far as possible, extension to the human community as a whole."[6]

Integrity seems to be a key concept for today's ethical leader. That which characterized business and school leadership after World War II was professionalism, control, rationality, teamwork, and efficiency. As the 1980s began, business and industry began searching for a new type of leadership. The ideas of "followship" and "servant leadership" began to appear in leadership literature as examples of *leadership integrity*. But, in education, these concepts were rarely mentioned. Educational management began to understand the importance of verifiable data, objective analysis, and solid strategies to improve the bottom line—standardized test scores. A standardized curriculum and the standardized assessment of both employee and student emerged in the 1980s and soon became one of the chief operational values of the schooling process. During the last decade, much effort went into perfecting these assessments. They were thought of as essential to the school's mission of educating every student.

Little room was left for ethical leadership or vision. Teachers and administrators participated in writing mission statements, but these were little more than goals and objectives that aligned teaching practices to predetermined tests and curricula. Management by these limited objectives still dominates education today. The methods by which teachers are assessed, the ways by which schools are measured, and the ways in which teachers must deliver knowledge and information are characterized by structure, order, and reliability, which are often substituted for substance, content, and vision. During these years, business leaders were interjecting ethics into their mission statements and tempering their visions of "what might be" with the recognition that the human value within their organizations was probably their greatest, single investment—and part of this investment was a recognition of individual worth to the company and worth as human beings.

Interestingly, the same assembly line model developed at Ford Motor Company earlier in the twentieth century was finally being adapted to the schooling process. Perhaps unknown to educational administrators, who welcomed and fine-tuned the command/control model of leadership, the world had changed, and they were one paradigm behind, just beginning to apply the old when others had discovered that in the end, the command, measure, control model is ineffective in an era of globalization distinguished by the knowledge worker. Unlike schools, a growing number of companies began designing ethics programs that addressed human problems in industry and business and provided a model of ethical decision making to address these problems at grass roots levels. Companies with strong ethics programs soon discovered that their efforts reduced potential costly fines, decreased vulnerability, improved production, and provided access to capital that influenced their bottom line. These in turn had positive results on the improvement of employee commitment and customer loyalty.

For example, in 1997, Walker Information surveyed employee views on business ethics. Forty-two percent of the employees surveyed said that a company's ethical integrity directly influenced their decision to work at the company. In addition, a 1994 survey entitled "Corporate Character, Highlights of a National Survey Measuring the Impact of Corporate Social Responsibility," reported that the most important factors for employees in deciding where to work were employee treatment and business practices. These were placed ahead of quality, service, and price.[7]

What I discovered upon entering the public schools as a teacher and then administrator in the mid-1970s was that an orderly, smoothly functioning school was of primary importance to both principals and superintendents. As the 1980s drew to a close, a cloak of accountability had encircled public education, and rising test scores soon became synonymous with a successful school, teacher, or school system. Business calls this looking after the bottom line. In their commitment to coordination, cooperation, and control, professional educational administrators lost sight of their educational mission. They had come to believe that the manipulation of data—teaching to the tests, arranging for more and more pretests to improve test-taking skills, and focusing on "test-bites" as a substitute for knowledge—would improve teaching and learning, at least the perception of teaching and learning.

This was the focus of education in the 1990s and remains so today. Developing a literate citizenry that is creative, motivated, and flexible, or providing superior services—allowing for flexible and adaptable schedules, allowing for creative, frontline decision making, and teaching students of different abilities, languages, and cultures—have become marginal issues. What counts today are high test scores, and this is commonly equated with the quality of students in the classroom and the expertise of the teaching core. Little was said about what this overt overemphasis on testing was doing to children. Few educators gave attention to the socio-psychological fact that human essence lies in developing our unique talents and that the innate moral sense of children is what allows them to be socialized. In our ignorance of ourselves, we have surreptitiously substituted fact for value and content learning for human development.[8]

This one-dimensional view of reality did not survive in the manufacturing world as globalization took hold of American markets in the late twentieth century, and it will not survive in education. It just misses too much that is important about learning and growing up. Up to the latter part of the twentieth century, with no real worldwide competition, success had bred complacency. Instead of promoting individuals of vision and leadership into top executive positions, American companies selected mostly men who were good at organization and control. A similar pattern is found in education. William Whyte's[9] prophesy of a nation of organization men had come to pass. The organization man was a manager, not an owner. He was a company man, not a visionary leader or risk taker.

In 1976, Michael Maccoby became the first of many social commentators to declare the demise of the organization man. He wrote that the traditional description of the organization man was too narrow and time-bound. He said that, with the advent of modern technology, the corporation needed more than one type of person, and those who reached the top in the 1970s were more active and adventurous than the stereotypes of the 1950s.[10] Maccoby sensed a change in the air, but the organization man and his brand of professional management were far from extinct. In 1989, he pointed out that thirty-three years after the publication of *The Organization Man*, reports of the death of the organization man were premature. Just as large companies (AT&T, Du Pont, Ford, GM) still dominated the American landscape, it was the mostly anonymous people in the middle ranks that remained the willing cogs that made the engines run. Surveys have found that 76 percent of middle managers expected to end their careers with their current employers, 80 percent declared their deep commitment to their companies, and 65 percent said they would choose the same career again. They firmly believed that the long hours and many moves they and their families had to make in the name of loyalty and dedication would be rewarded. The economic downturn during 2001 through 2002 has proved them wrong, as many have been temporarily or permanently laid off. Although business cycles are not that uncommon, today's knowledge workers are giving considerable thought to issues of devotion, loyalty, and faithfulness to their employers since their commitments are not always reciprocal.

Schools, like businesses, need leaders, not just professional managers. This is a challenge, for management can be taught and leadership development has always been a problem. And it makes little sense to use the language of business and management in the school organization. Lewis H. Lapham, in a *Harper's* special edition, "New Hope for American Education," said, "The new generation of [education] prophets borrow the vocabulary of the marketing director and the systems engineer. Treating education as a consumer product, they speak of brand value, and pricing strategies, distribute infomercials on videocassette, design their arks of safety and deliverance in the manner of user-friendly theme parks, and deploy out-sources, sponsor intellectual property ventures, inflate the grades."[11] Within education, this has led to confusion, especially about purpose and mission. For teachers who think of themselves as being "called" to teach, and who have been trained in methods and procedures at a teacher college or university, this is strange language, especially when they are compelled to use it to sell their school to the community and compete for students as "market" selection in education becomes more and more important.

The school, as workplace, is coming to look more and more like the Walmarts and Targets of education, competing with one another and losing the soul of their missions in their struggle for recognition. As difficult as it is to understand and manage change in the workplace, it is far more difficult to inspire commitment, create a sustainable vision, and encourage self-management and autonomous work teams. Now the problems of business are the problems of schools. We know how to train managers; we are far less certain about how to train leaders, especially leaders who can manage. A part of our understanding of leadership is examining the nature of what and who is to be led—and where. And doing this means looking at knowledge-based organizations that are peopled by knowledge workers.

Knowledge Workers Characteristics

According to Jack Beatty, in his *The World According to Peter Drucker*, knowledge workers hold the following characteristics[12]:

1. Knowledge workers identify with their work, not with the organization where the work is performed. They identify with the profession or with their craft. They are usually specialists who realize that they know more about their own area of expertise than does perhaps anyone else in the organization. Thus, their loyalty tends to be to themselves and to their profession, not to the organization.

2. What matters to knowledge workers is that they have an opportunity to grow in knowledge and in their profession. They seek work assignments that are professionally challenging; assignments where they can work with state-of-the-art technology or with specialists in their own fields.

3. Knowledge workers have the skills that the information society needs, and those skills give them mobility; they are no longer tied to one

job or to one employer. They know that their knowledge and experience gives them the freedom to move.

4. Knowledge workers are highly committed workers, but they tend not to be loyal in the manner of the organization man of 1956 described by William Whyte. Getting another job is never an issue; finding an opportunity where they can really learn or make a difference is the issue.

5. Finally, in an information economy, workers cannot be managed by the principles of professional management, which is to say the organization-man model. It is not possible to supervise knowledge workers or grade them in traditional ways. They do not work on assembly lines and they cannot be managed as if they did. Since their work involves the formulation, interpretation, and manipulation of information, the command-measure-control model of management will not succeed with them.

Paraphrasing Margaret J. Wheatley,[13] a school system that focuses on its core competencies identifies itself as a portfolio of skills rather than as a portfolio of schools, accounting the number of teachers and students who work and learn there. When the skills of the education knowledge worker are brought to bear on problems and significant issues, the school or school system is able to respond quickly to new opportunities because it is not locked into the rigid boundaries of preestablished roles, departmental territories, and artificially created and preconceived end products. As Wheatley says, "Leadership is always dependent on the context, but the context is established by the relationships we value.... Relatedness is the organizing principle of the universe.... Innovation is fastened by information gathered from new connections, from insights gained by journeys into other disciplines or places; from active, collegial networks and fluid, open boundaries.... Innovation arises from ongoing circles of exchange."[14] This is an *ideal* world, but it is the ideal world of the education knowledge worker.

One of the major errors of American business and education alike is a faith in our ability to measure and rationalize everything. In the 1980s and 1990s, we learned that what gets measured gets taught.[15] Pressure was felt to concentrate on the bottom line of test score averages because that is how schools were now being identified. Also learned was that if certain behaviors could not be measured, they were not worth pursuing. Therefore, ethical principles and character traits were looked upon with suspicion. These were the days in which teachers were forced to write so-called objective goals—those that were statistically measurable—further narrowing the curriculum that was being taught and the methods selected to teach it. Forgotten was the love of teaching that brought teachers into the profession, and forgotten still were the young students who were eager to learn to read and compute, actively engage in scientific experiments, and form networks with their peers that would teach them skills far beyond what was learned in the classroom. The one positive aspect of the account-ability movement is the consistency it is bringing to the school and class-room. Teachers find themselves working together, discussing best practices, and seeking—within the entire community of educators—the most effective ways to enhance student learning. A new sense of community is being developed where once teachers felt isolated and alone in their classrooms.

What is being neglected in this over-managed and tightly controlled educational world is that teachers and their students, principals and cen-tral office specialists are education's knowledge workers. They are creative and innovative because of the information they gather from new connec-tions, from insights gained by intellectual risk taking, from ongoing con-versations with their peers, and through learning networks with fluid, open boundaries. As Wheatley has reminded us, "Innovation arises from ongoing circles of exchange, where information is not just accumulated or shared, but created."[16] Knowledge is not the same as facts that are mem-orized for a test and instilled in us by drill and practice. Knowledge comes from accumulated fact, from dialogue, and from the trial and error of human experience. Knowledge implies understanding, and understand-ing means that what we are learning continues to connect with new infor-mation, people, and situations. Elementary teachers have learned and secondary and middle school teachers are learning that abstract informa-tion needs a connection to the realities of the world in order to become meaningful and fully understood. Wheatley says, "Knowledge is gener-ated anew from connections that weren't there before. When this infor-mation self-organizes, innovations occur, the progeny of information-rich, ambiguous environments."[17]

Lewis H. Lapham has concluded, "We assume that American stu-dents do not go to school to acquire wisdom, or to engage in what the ancient Greeks admitted as, 'the glittering play of windswept thought.' They go to school to improve their lot, to learn the trick of getting ahead in the world, to acquire the keys to the commercial kingdoms stocked with material blessings that constitute our society's highest and most heavenly rewards."[18] Lapham strikes a cord of truth with this observation, but we don't have to be satisfied with this particular state of affairs. Even Lapham allows a measure of idealism to parse the cynicism with which he views today's educational scene. He comments, "If democracy can be understood as a field of temporary coalitions among people of different interests, skills, and generations, then everybody has a need of everybody else. To the extent that a democratic government gives its citizens a chance to choose their own dreams, it gives itself the chance not only of discovering its multiple glories and triumphs, but also of surviving its multiple fallacies and crimes."[19] A problem educational leadership must face in the foreseeable future is the value placed on teachers and students as knowledge workers. How much time is being put into their development and are these individuals allowed to contribute to the growth of the school system and school itself.

Alvin and Heidi Toffler, writing in *Civilization*,[20] observed that humans have moved from an urban-industrial civilization, which lasted approximately 300 years, to a postmodern world that began about 1960. This postmodern world is characterized by global communication; building diverse human, political, and economic connections; and the homogenization of values. This is a world in which innovation has become the norm. In this new order, education and learning are the major keys to success, of being "hooked up" in a new society where knowledge and the flow of knowledge is value. Along these same lines, Peter Drucker encourages us to think outside the traditional causal chains with their coercive demonstrations of inevitability, predictability, and thought-stopping victories. In the place of this cause-and-effect world of modernism, Drucker says we need a discipline that explains events and phenomena in terms of their direction and future state rather than in terms of cause—a calculus of potential rather than one of probability.[21]

Let me put this in perspective by telling a story of how the potential of students in one school district was being written off as "hopeless" and how a planned cover-up did not get off the ground. During the last years of the 1980s, a new golf course community was built on the edge of two school districts. The school district to the east was composed of average-to below-average income families, farmers, a healthy dose of minorities, and trailer parks. It was a large school district, encompassing two small towns and bordering a city school district to its south. The bus ride to the middle school serving this district covered an indirect course of some 25 miles each way. The school district to the west was quite small geographically and was composed of middle- and upper-middle income families who shared more common values with the golf course community. It was basically an urban district which bordered the largest city in the county. Notably, the bus ride to the middle school serving this district would only be three to four miles each way.

The more rural of the two districts had a thirty-year history of low achievement and school dropouts. The more urban of the two was, at that time, the highest performing school district within the school system. On a scale of 1 to 5, with 5 being the highest academically, the average student in the urban district was about a 3.5. The superintendent and school board reasoned that putting the new golf course community into the academically lowest of these districts would raise the average standardized test scores of the two elementary schools, the middle school, and the high school that it included. This was a calculation based on statistical probability. The administration meant well, and they hoped the school profiles in that district would appear better to the public. What was forgotten were the students and educators in that district. No one asked questions such as, "How might we raise the educational potential of the students who already comprise this district?" "What can we do in terms of teacher training to improve the techniques and methods of the educators who work there?" And no one thought to ask the educators who worked and lived in that district for their ideas on how to improve the education of their students.

The parents in the golf course community wrote letters and spoke to the superintendent and many school board members about the upcoming decision. These parents, operating from modern notions of cause-and-effect, persuaded the board to move their children into the high performing school district. They reasoned that these were the class of students they wanted their children to know. After all, they had more in common with them because of economic and learning level. Seemingly, economic levels and social issues ruled the day. The issue was settled politically.

Educational leaders have a responsibility to create environments where knowledge workers can make decisions where they are closest to problems. Because they are professionals and work in a daily teaching-learning environment, their input into problems like the one above is invaluable. Ethical leadership will value and promote the growth of principals and teachers throughout their schools and school system. They will create an environment in which fundamental shifts of mind and different opinions are welcomed—a world recognized by infinite possibilities. They will create a world where there is freedom of choice and understand that choice is an expression of our deepest values and our character. They will create a school system with an expanded sense of identity under conditions involving the loss of boundaries, where there is always an open invitation to contribute one's ideas and energies. Finally, ethical leaders, acknowledging and respecting the knowledge workers on their staffs, will create a world where there is dialogue and where educators with common interests are encouraged to network with others, bring their expertise to bear on problems, and make decisions. The world "dialogue" comes from the Greek, "dia-logos" meaning "a flow of meaning." Dialogue creates meaning, and networking with others preserves one's dignity and individuality.[22]

Kevin Cashman[23] reminds us that ethical/servant leaders in this new environment will lead by ...

following the best interest of those whom they lead,
gaining satisfaction from the growth of others,
caring for those whom they lead,
taking responsibility for their own behavior and for the behaviors of those whom they lead,
being willing to listen, at all times,
giving obedience to a higher mission than serving their own egos, and
managing by ethical and agreed-upon organizational values.

Educational Leadership: The Inescapable Trade-offs

Applied ethics is the branch of ethics that consists of specific controversial moral issues. We are familiar with the issues of applied ethics in such moral dilemmas as abortion, capital punishment, and euthanasia. We perhaps are not as familiar with applications and arguments about ethical leadership. The following general principles[24] are the ones most commonly appealed to in applied ethics and have applications for ethical leadership as well:

1. *Personal benefit*: do the actions of the leader produce beneficial consequences for the individual (leader) in question?
2. *Social benefit*: do the actions of the leader produce beneficial consequences for the organization, for society, for employees (followers)?
3. *Principle of benevolence*: do the actions of the leader help those in need?
4. *Principle of paternalism*: do the actions of the leader assist others in pursuing their best interests when they cannot do so themselves?
5. *Principle of harm*: do the actions of the leader harm others in any way?

6. *Principle of honesty*: do the actions of the leader deceive others?

7. *Principle of lawfulness*: do the actions of the leader violate any laws?

8. *Principle of autonomy*: do the actions of the leader acknowledge a person's freedom over his or her behavior and/or physical body?

9. *Principle of justice*: do the actions of the leader acknowledge a person's right to due process, fair compensation for harm done, and fair distributions of benefits?

10. *Principle of rights*: do the actions of the leader acknowledge a person's rights to life, information, privacy, free expression, and safety?

11. *Principle of caring*: do the actions of the leader demonstrate a willingness to create and sustain caring relationships throughout the school system?

These principles represent the spectrum of traditional normative ethical principles important to living a life of civility and require leadership courage to implement in a broad way throughout a school system. These are called "ethical" principles because they encompass the beliefs that support traditional views of morality. "Morality" is a word that refers to the standards of behavior by which people are judged and to the standards of behavior by which people in general are judged in their relationships with others. Because the differences in "ethics" and "morals" are largely historical and semantical, I tend to use them conjunctively.

Also, when we examine ethical values and legal principles, we again find a close relationship. When one takes a closer look, he or she will discover that ethical/moral obligation and behaviors typically exceed legal duties. For example, although a person is not legally required to give to the poor, he or she might feel a moral obligation to give money to the outreach program of one's church, the Salvation Army, or a local soup kitchen. A person might also feel morally compelled to donate her or his time and talents to Habitat for Humanity, although not coerced to do so by law. The law doesn't say that a person can't hate others or prohibit some in his or her employment from decision-making opportunities. Lying or betraying a friend is not illegal, but most would agree that it is unethical. Yet speeding is illegal, but many people do not appear to have an ethical conflict with exceeding the speed limit.

Law is different than ethics and is intended to regulate social civility, but many laws have their foundation in ethical principles. For example, in America it is legal for a group to organize a private club that excludes certain kinds of people. For years Augusta National Golf Club excluded black members and wouldn't allow black professional golfers to

play in the annual Masters tournament. The color barrier has been bro-
ken at Augusta for about twenty years. Recently, the case of women being
denied membership at Augusta has been in the news. The disallowing of
women, like that of African Americans, raises a moral, not a legal issue.
If the Masters tournament is sanctioned by the PGA and shown all over
the world on television by sponsors who prohibit discrimination in their
own businesses, is it moral for them to sponsor this golf tournament? Do
the professional players have a moral obligation to boycott the tournament because it prohibits female members and female players, especially
in light of their partnership with the women's division of the PGA? Our
entangling social alliances often mask important ethical dilemmas that
we would like to ignore. Ethical leadership is responsible leadership, leadership that is morally consistent.

In schools, all professional employees must evaluate their behaviors in
terms of what is legal—what they must do or cannot do that is prescribed
in law—and what is moral. They have a duel responsibility: one that is legal
and one that is moral. They must reconsider their actions in terms of what
parents and the community will or will not accept, what they are compelled
to do by law, and what they feel that they must ethically do for students.
Superintendents and principals play a vital role in their school district's
legal and ethical performance. They are responsible for seeing that all
employees follow federal, state, and local guidelines and laws and for setting proper examples as moral leaders. With the modern proliferation of
laws and standards at all levels, this is an arduous task and one that must
be carefully monitored and discussed in every leadership meeting.

Being legal and being ethical are two inescapable trade-offs of ethical leadership. Ethical leadership is perhaps the more difficult of the two
because it results from an inner compulsion and not an external one. For
example, in some states and school districts, financial rewards are provided
for principals and their staffs when their students reach certain achievement plateaus. When the achievement profile of the district goes up,
sometimes the superintendent and his or her assistants are rewarded finan-
cially by the board of education. Often left out of this equation are the
many central office curriculum experts who gave their time and resources
to schools needing their help. Although the executive leader is not compelled by law to share his or her rewards with these individuals, it appears
that there is an ethical motivation for such sharing. In ethical leadership
there are inevitable trade-offs. Principles of benevolence, honesty, and justice seem to acknowledge this ethical responsibility. Fortuitously, the
trade-off comes to this: as the executive leader, I must take less of the

reward and share it equally with my staff who carried the resources to "the field of play" and helped deliver a victory for the entire school system.

The school superintendent who dictates teaching-to-the-test and certain prescribed teaching methods that may or may not be workable for all teachers and staffs is also making a trade-off. It comes to exercising executive dominance and power for the diminished creativity and growth of the educators who work in the system. This is called "selfishness," "me-first, you-not-at-all," or "my-way-or-the-highway" mentality. This is one trade-off that will not bear fruit. It limits growth and devalues the human qualities within the educational system. Ethical leaders may at times be self-centered, but they should make every effort to avoid being selfish- or ego-centered, a posture that is demeaning to others, limits their productivity, and devalues their personhood.

The SAS Institute, Inc., an information technology software company located in Cary, North Carolina, provides a model of ethical and servant leadership that others can replicate. SAS is owned individually and provides many resources for its employees, such as daycare on its Cary campus, medical care for employees and families, and a golf course and other recreational opportunities. The focus of SAS is on enterprise intelligence, and they view their employees as their greatest asset. The owner of SAS and its CEO confessed that average normal turnover in employees would cost the company approximately $85 million a year in the course of recruiting, hiring, and training. He said that it was more cost effective to provide the benefits previously mentioned as a way of maintaining company quality and consistency and of keeping company loyalty. Their website says,[25]

> Most organizations find it difficult, if not impossible, to manage enterprise strategy and performance using analytical tools alone. That's why more and more business and IT managers are adopting scorecarding methods to measure and monitor operations throughout the enterprise more effectively and consistently.
>
> Without a suite of solutions that are both intelligent and that work together, knowledge workers won't have the tools they need to be productive—and organizations won't have the agility to stay competitive.
>
> SAS gives you the strategic vision you need to connect traditional business measures with intangibles, such as the health of supplier relationships, the collaborative wisdom that exists throughout your organization, and the profitability of your customers. We call this strategic performance management—a clear, balanced view of how everything fits together today—and where it's headed tomorrow.

The company recommends the following procedures to assure that ethical and servant leadership is operative throughout the organization:

Establish and communicate a shared vision.
Achieve strategic and tactical goals.
Align, track, and measure performance.
Monitor the health of your organization.
Leverage resources intelligently, profitably, and quickly.

Ethical leadership remains a very private struggle for teachers, principals, superintendents, and support professionals within school districts. The challenge is to rise above our petty, self-seeking attitudes and behaviors, to consider the interests of others, and to draw them into the mission of the organization, challenging and allowing them to use their developing knowledge to affect student behavior and learning in positive ways. This will probably be our toughest challenge—to empower all our employees (to leverage resources intelligently, profitably, and quickly) to assess their own strengths and invite them to the table of opinion, criticism, and dialogue; to allow them a voice in the school's mission and an entrance to a decision-making process that will impact teaching and learning in more significant ways. The trade-off comes in giving employees decision-making power and then personally and publicly recognizing their contributions. Although this may seem to diminish the leader's authority and power, it actually grows his or her power and influence and makes correcting the mistakes of others a much easier task. When leaders serve they learn, and when they learn they grow.

The following lists outline the major provisions for building a leadership culture.

Major Concepts[26]

Knowledge worker (Drucker, 1998)
Leaders don't necessarily have to invent ideas, but they have to be able to put them in context and add perspective. (Bennis, 1994)
Centering on principles or core values provides security to not be threatened by change or criticism. (Covey, 1991)
People define leaders by what they do or don't do in small moments. (Bergmann, et al., 1999)
To build achieving organizations, we must replace power with responsibility. (Drucker, 1998)
Commitment is what makes the impossible possible. (Cashman, 1998)
Leadership should focus on an integrated, inside out growth process

which will greatly enhance personal, professional, and organizational excellence. (Cashman, 1998)

Managing by values (Blanchard and O'Connor, 1997)

Leadership Characteristics

Defines mission

Creates flexible environment and organizational structure that can respond quickly to change

Focuses on innovation

Anticipates the future

Directs resources toward opportunities for significant growth

Values people

Identifies and responds to needs

Is accountable

Focuses on team, identifies weak links

Makes and maintains connections

Avoids being reactive

Leadership Strategies

Creates a compelling future by creating a vision, managing change, and setting priorities

Lets teacher and student needs drive the school system by responding to needs, organizing feedback, aligning vision, values, and practices

Creates trustworthiness and value

Involves every mind by trusting and empowering others to make decisions; shares information willingly, supports individual and team efforts, and assists with making decisions that solve problems

Manages work horizontally utilizing cross-functional teams, technical skills, and project managers

Is competent and effective in managing time and resources

Builds personal skills:
   takes initiative
   responsibility
   emotional stability
   caring and compassionate
   credible and accountable

Building Trust Structures

Leaders who empower, serve, and enable the performance of their employees build interdependent and interlinking *trust structures* throughout the school organization. Building trust structures acknowledges the freedom necessary for unencumbered choice—to stay or leave the organization, and, if they stay, to have their value and growth recognized and supported as essential to the value and growth of the organization as a whole. Trust, H. Richard Niebuhr[27] reminds us, is never to be taken for granted, and Robert Bellah and his associates have observed, "In our relation to the world, trust is always in conflict with mistrust. Because of previous experience a degree of mistrust is usually realistic; yet if we are dominated by mistrust we cannot attend or interpret adequately, we cannot act accountably, and we will rupture, not strengthen the solidarity of the community or communities we live in."[28] Mistrust paralyzes action and faith in leadership; it freezes commitment and the leader's faith in employees is lost. In stalemate the school system or school cannot be productive; discord and disharmony, conflict and stress characterize working relationships. When people work without joy there is loss—of productivity, of creativity, and of human and organizational value.

Just recently, I bumped into a retired educator with whom I had worked as a consultant a few years ago. I asked her if she ever returned to the central office where she was employed to visit old friends and inquired about several of them with whom I had been associated. She replied that she had visited with some former colleagues, that they have lunch together periodically, and then said, "Boy, that's a sad place to work these days." My curiosity aroused, I wanted to know what had happened at what was, a decade ago, a vibrant, cutting-edge group of professional educators. She looked at me and simply replied, "Some superintendents elevate and others merely dictate." Top-down, do-as-you're-told administrators simply rob the spirit from knowledge working professionals. Dictators say, "I don't really trust you to make decisions, so just carry out your assignments and don't ask questions."

From situations such as this one, we learn that trust is not an abstract ethical principle and neither is it a character trait to be emphasized one week each year in a character development program. Trust is the essence of human relationships; without it marriages fail and organizations fall apart too. Motivating educators to become ethical leaders in their own right involves building trust structures with them. Trust strengthens our social ties and is the foundation for civility, and the choice to be civil is a cornerstone of one's emerging character development. Ethical leaders in schools depend on the character of other school employees. Philip Selznick[29] finds the foundation of civility and community in the trust structures we build with one another. Bellah and his associates conclude as well, "Our institutions are badly functioning and in need of repair or drastic reform, so that if they are to support a pattern of cultivation, rather than one of exploitation, we must change them by altering their legal status and the way we think about them, for institutional change involves both laws and mores. More than money and power, these need to be at the center of our attention."[30]

Leaders are responsible for developing strong commitments to the mission and purposes of learning and to strong beliefs that structure, support, and communicate the mission and purposes throughout the educational organization. The trusting relationships that sustain productive school systems are built upon these commitments and beliefs. They emanate from our beliefs about persons, such as the following:

1. Individuals can live and work harmoniously through combining personal satisfaction and self-development with significant work and other activities that contribute to the welfare of the family, school, and community.

2. Individuals will develop faith in others if we have faith in them; they can tap their own power to solve difficult problems if we teach them to reason and share their responses.

3. A person's uniqueness will unfold quite naturally as we express respect for her or his abilities as well as possibilities.

4. Each person possesses intrinsic moral and intellectual worth, and we should look upon each individual, as well as ourselves, as natural and good.

5. We do not have to grow at the expense of others. This means that each of us has the ability to reach out creatively beyond our own physical and mental boundaries and maintain ethical consistency and integrity in our lives.

6. Individuals are naturally open and responsive to their environment. Therefore, we must invite them to discuss their ideas, share their values, and model growth-producing ethical behaviors.

7. Finally, individuals are naturally creative and curious, and the more they learn and practice intellectually and ethically, the more abundantly they will produce for themselves and for their families and communities.

Leaders should understand that patience will be required to effectively cultivate these beliefs in themselves and in others. Patience will generate opportunities for understanding, and understanding begs for dialogue, which perpetuates open, flexible communication. Again, we emphasize that the meaning and significance for one's work and involvement in a caring organization is crystallized through making these beliefs apart of the cultural of school systems. Cliff Havener states, "meaning is what affirms to a person that he or she actually exists. Without it, a person lives a purely mechanical existence, going through all the motions of life without feeling alive."[31]

The following trust structures flow from our beliefs about people and create meaning in the workplace. They empower leadership potential in all employees and inspire us to create our own personal vision of what teaching and learning can accomplish. As I look back over a long career and see former students, many of whom are now doctors, lawyers, nurses, teachers, business executives, health providers, and the list goes on, I am convinced that so long as conversations between teachers and students continue; so long as educators at all levels are allowed to lead, and leaders are sometimes willing to follow; so long as we care and respect those with whom and for whom we work; and so long as an ethical foundation for leadership is sustained, there is hope for a more productive and fulfilling tomorrow.

In their book, *Productive School Systems for a Nonrational World,* Jerry Patterson and his coauthors present the following building blocks for erecting trust structures[32]:

Building understanding by
   articulating a set of ethical beliefs and purposes to our colleagues and students
   valuing the importance of dialogue, understanding, and belief
   consistently modeling ethical beliefs and moral behaviors
Building empowerment by
   providing opportunities for skill development
   providing knowledge and examples of ethical decision making
   allowing others to make decisions and helping them evaluate the consequences
Building decision-making power by
   supporting the critical judgment of other educators
   seeking input from others on decisions that affect them
   valuing the decisions of others and praising them even though we may later have to adjust them through dialogue and discussion

Building a sense of belonging by
  valuing the development of fair-minded critical thinking in other
    educators
  treating all others with respect and significance
  allowing other educators to feel ownership of their decisions
Building trust and confidence by
  acting in the best interest of employees and the school system
  believing that others will respond with their best efforts when appro-
    priately praised and recognized
  having and sharing confidence in our employees
Building excellence by
  valuing high standards and expectations—both academic and ethi-
    cal
  valuing an atmosphere that encourages others (and ourselves) to
    stretch and grow
  expressing and living a positive "can-do" attitude
Building recognition and reward by
  offering incentives and encouraging creative and caring behaviors
  recognizing others for their accomplishments
  investing in the academic and moral development of our employees
Building caring by
  valuing the well-being and personal concerns of others
  allowing others to share their ideas in an open and trusting manner
  taking a personal interest in the welfare of our employees
Building integrity by
  valuing honesty in words and deeds
  valuing a consistent, responsible pursuit of goals and intentions
  valuing the unwavering commitment to high personal and ethical
    convictions
Building diversity by
  valuing individual differences in our employees
  valuing and encouraging creativity and different approaches to prob-
    lems
  believing that we are not all alike and that we must remain flexible
    in working with others

In 1987, in the second edition of my *Philosophy for Young Thinkers*[33]
book, I commented, "The vacuum caused by a generation of uncertainty
about teaching values and the move away from a traditional values base
at home is just now having its impact on our schools. Our answer to this

social and education dilemma is the production of a morally centered, pre-college philosophy curriculum for our students. In this curriculum we shall argue for and provide a foundation for teaching such moral values as honesty, integrity, responsibility, honor, courage, and kindness." This need still exists in our schools, and not just for our students, but also for all levels of leadership. This ethical vacuum will be filled when educators, students, and parents develop:

1. Flexible attitudes and abilities that will aid decision making when confronted with difficult social and academic challenges,
2. Better and more creative solutions to urgent personal and societal problems,
3. Intellectual and emotional flexibility, and
4. A universal and unbiased vision of people and their role in our future.

We have learned by working with children that exciting ideas are actively contagious. The concept of ethical and servant leadership is one of those ideas. In schools, it's not enough to just make teaching and learning better; it is also important to make educational leadership better as well. In the many years that I worked as a college and public school teacher and in the ensuing years that I worked as a central office administrator, I discovered that when I was good to myself and respected my own abilities I was able to return this respect and goodness to my staff and colleagues. We certainly gain experience from others, especially others who treat us with respect and dignity. And this point is not trivial. Sowing ideas is one thing; reaping them is another. Over time, if we have faith in our students and in our colleagues, they will develop faith and trust in themselves and others. This is a formula for leadership success, which involves the following behaviors:

1. Listening, discussing, and applying various kinds of information,
2. Understanding that meaning links information with experience through dialogue and application,
3. Committing ourselves to a task, to individuals, and to our beliefs about others,
4. Pledging our faith to these behaviors and being accountable for them,
5. Employing persistence, which enables us to see a project through to completion,
6. Exhibiting fair-mindedness toward others, which is a cornerstone of a morally coherent life, and
7. Taking responsibility, which holds us accountable for our actions.

Here we must take care, for there are limits to the exercise of ethical leadership just as there are limits to the application of any idea. This warning is provided by Elliot Turiel.[34] His research demonstrates that developing character is not only a process of teaching, acquiring habits, and obeying rules and laws. He says that we develop moral, social, and personal judgments over time, and that these judgments entail deep moral understandings and take into account the various and different contexts of people's activities. This comment, he reminds us, was not made to support a moral relativism, but to point out that "in their moral decisions, people take circumstances into account ... people often weigh considerations, as well as try to balance nonmoral with moral considerations.[35]

Based on Turiel's observations, we are unable to characterize societies or cultures (such as educational cultures) in broad and consistent strokes. Change is a constant factor in life and within school systems, change is always operative, peptic, and pecking away at the dominant point of view. Being self-centered—not selfish—may work in an organization's favor, as each of our interests coincidentally tends to check, as well as change, the self-interests of others. Because of these interactions our ethical characters are always under construction; they are never fixed but are continually bumped and prodded by multiple social interactions and sometimes with unexpected effects.[36]

Ethical leadership, like moral development, is largely evolutionary in its development. As adults we can aid this evolutionary process by choosing to make our lives morally coherent. Achieving our personal goals and personal meaning are a part of our concept of the good life, and these goals and meanings point to our essential individualism. A sense of self, developed through our relationships with others, is also needed for a sense of connection. We must recognize that society and culture have been our teachers. Trusting others and engaging in activities that promote the well-being of society can also produce positive change in our lives.

Society is nothing less than a network of communication among people—who share common values—seeking social and moral solidarity, which potentially can have positive consequences for them. Within this context ethical leadership is recognized as an ongoing process, one that is constantly under construction through multiple social interactions. It entails leaders who are involved in the understanding and application of judgments about others, about justice, and about building cooperative relationships that entail organizational and personal responsibilities. Let us be reminded levels of trust in the existing society and organization do not determine ethical leadership, but ethical leaders who believe it necessary to build a level of moral substance in their lives develop trust structures.

The relationship of self and the world is an interactive one in which our beliefs, purposes, and values can be viewed as a set of tools for making our way in the world. It is important to have our own vision; to trust our instincts. Visions are intensely personal. It would be sad to live life through someone else's dreams. This is the difficulty of living and working in a society—any society. But, the requirements of civility and of ethical practice force each of us to check our visions and dreams at the door and to prepare ourselves for certain compromises as we listen to the visions of others who also want their dreams actualized. Trusting others helps build value in our schools and school systems. Our survival, as well as the survival of our schools and school systems, depends not on its absolutes but on its adaptability. Like ideas, our visions are social; they require other people for their development and actualization. Schools, to be successful, must become communities of learners where educators, parents, and students remain connected through a common goal to make learning more effective and teaching more productive. Leaders—especially superintendents and principals—who isolate themselves from this learning community, send other educators a message that their knowledge is not valued and their input unwanted. In such situations, levels of accomplishment and innovation soon wither away.

Activities That Promote Ethical Leadership

1. How would you rate your school or school system's leadership integrity on a scale of 1 to 5, with 5 being the highest and 1 being the lowest? Give three reasons and one example for your rating.

2. In groups of three or four colleagues, discuss each other's ratings. Prepare a new rating sheet, and reach a consensus about how you would rate your school or school system. Share your group rating with that of other groups, and try to reach a new consensus through dialogue and consensus.

3. How has the vocabulary of the marketplace affected your understanding of the purposes of education? Was this the same language used in your college or university school of education? In small groups make a list of the ways education mimics the marketplace and how you would change what is being said and stressed as important to teaching and learning.

4. Looking only at the people in your school or in your central office, make a list of the skills that each person brings to the job. You must assess the strengths of your colleagues. Once this listing has been completed, beside each person's name and skill(s) explain how that person is a "knowledge worker."

5. Within small groups discuss how being ethical sometimes works against one's self-interest. Give a couple of examples of how this has happened to you in the past, and share them within the group. Does the principle of caring sometimes mean that we won't get our way and what we actually want from a situation? Explain.

6. Examine the lists for building a leadership culture: major concepts, leadership characteristics, and leadership strategies. Rate yourself by putting a plus sign (+) by those areas that define your leadership behavior and a minus sign (-) by those that need improvement. In groups of three or four, or in departmental or grade level meetings, share your ratings with your colleagues, and tell them in which areas you are planning to give more of your energies.

7. Trust structures are important for building an ethical leadership culture. Select three out of the seven of these beliefs and explain to your group how practicing these behaviors would make working conditions much more caring and supportive. Share the results of your group's conversation with the entire faculty or central office, and make plans to cultivate these beliefs in your work.

8. Study the formula for leadership success and list three concrete behaviors under each that need improvement by you and your colleagues. Share these with the entire group, and create a leadership success chart listing each of these behaviors along with concrete examples. Make copies of the chart and post them where all can see.

4

Leadership Skills: A Focus on Strategies for Success

Developing a Supportive Climate

Leadership is about people; it's also about thinking outside the boundaries and showing "the way" for the school system, a school, or a classroom. Make no mistake about it, school leaders have the responsibility of articulating and selling visions of what their schools can become. Schools should be organized around the purpose of increased student learning. This purpose is the link between organizational structures and values and the actions of educators. Leaders must also articulate their goals and prioritize practices that promise to improve existing conditions. In carrying out these responsibilities, the school leader will be addressing a mixed bag of clients: employees who may be eager for change and some who will resist any suggestion of change; a community that is perhaps tired of promises and is demanding results; teachers, many of whom have no permanent classroom and have for some time been working in overcrowded conditions; and a board of education that is sensitive to all educational stakeholders and whose decision making is perhaps structured more along political than educational lines.

Leaders are charged with inspiring others to follow them. They begin this task by setting examples in their own behavior and continue by making the right choices. Making the right choices is perhaps the most important part of leadership—not what choices to make, but *when* to make them. Timing is a significant part of making positive changes in the way children are taught. Superintendents and principals should understand that this is no simple task and that their success is not an entitlement—it has to be earned. To generate passion and enthusiasm for their vision requires courage and skill. As many stakeholders (teachers, central office personal, politicians, community leaders, and parents, etc.) as possible need to be included in this conversation. The newly hired superintendent or principal should perhaps dedicate his or her first year to building coalitions. The first year should not end without holding many "town meetings" where sharing and dialogue enrich and solidify support for a clearly formulated system or school vision. "Joining together" should perhaps be a theme for schools and school systems. During the first weeks of leadership, the new principal or superintendent should set the tone for his or her work, not over-promising but holding all levels of leadership accountable for their productivity. The new leader should prepare intensely, anticipate potential problems, and deal with them before they get out of hand. The new leader should learn to be satisfied with small victories because their accumulated effect is a mark of success or the lack of it.

Working in a group is one of the most important factors of our lives. A significant key to successful leadership is not only setting the pace and articulated the vision of the school/school system but using the filter of compromise to move the system and/or school in the direction of positive student achievement. In many ways, positive change improves group solidarity and efficiency. Leaders learn from great teams. In schools, especially, there is a great interest in improving group (classrooms, departments, teams, and committees) efficiency. Helping a school, classroom, or school system grow and change in constructive ways is a major responsibility of educational leaders.

A story may help illustrate this point. During the early 1990s, a newly hired curriculum supervisor was given the responsibility of moving writing scores in grades 6 through 8 from the average range, as measured by state scores, to scores that consistently registered in the top quartile in the state. All but one of his teachers had responded to the methods that he had introduced. This particular teacher refused to teach using practice tests or gear her instruction to the type of test expected to be given during a particular year. She liked to teach creative writing and consistently gave her students experiences in all forms of writing, from expository to narrative writing. Her scores never improved. The supervisor was outdone. Not being able to get her to use new methods or the materials he kept sending her, he lost his temper and resorted to threats. He told her that she would be brought before the superintendent and possibly the board of education. Being a tenured teacher with over twenty years of teaching experience, she simply ignored what he said. Finally, they butted heads.

He threatened her, and she threatened a lawsuit. It was an impasse. The supervisor moved on after a few years, and the teacher retired.

Situations like the one described above are common occurrences in school systems. Supervisors are constantly striving to better understand how the classroom functions as a group, how to positively change teaching practices, and how to build or restore a team approach to educating children. Too often, the central office specialist is viewed as the "enemy" of the classroom teacher, demanding change and putting in new programs that no one wanted to begin with. How to improve central office leadership is a major problem in school systems. Working as a team is to the advantage of all educators. Ethical and servant leadership can positively grow a team approach in school systems. When this begins to occur, there is a higher possibility that there will be improvements in the quality of teaching and learning processes. To improve group productivity a superintendent, departmental director, principal, or classroom teacher needs to develop the following seven sets of complex skills[1]:

1. *Establishing the conditions for modifying followers' patterns of behavior and attitude*   Among other things, this means establishing touchstones of trust with each employee, encouraging each of them to view problems from a group or school perspective, increasing their sense of self-control; and promoting positive identification with the school or school system.

2. *Being a resource expert on how to learn and change within a school or central office setting*   This may mean teaching interpersonal and small-group skills, counseling individual employees (or students), and being able to diagnose problems and situations quickly.

3. *Modeling the constructive use of small-group and interpersonal skills*   The leader may be leading from the heart, but this by itself is not enough to systematically present effective skills to be imitated by other educators; a leader must also be interpersonally effective for these modeled skills to have an impact on other educational professionals.

4. *Helping define and diagnose the problems of employees and provide them with constructive feedback and confrontations*   Confusion over their feelings and actions increases employees' anxiety and fear concerning their problems. A necessary skill of a growth leader is making sure that employees have opportunities for self-disclosure and experimentation with new patterns of thinking. The leader needs to understand that genuine emotion (excitement, anxiety, and fear) often accompanies learning and innovation. Reflection and dialogue with peer groups should be emphasized

to assist educators with the responsibilities of applying their newfound knowledge and skill.

5. *Maintaining a problem-solving environment within their schools and central offices*   Developing effective problem-solving procedures is important for bringing new information and practices to schools. A part of this process will be helping teachers, principals, and others clarify their attitudes about present practices, changing them if need be before moving on to other behaviors. Keeping lines of communication open is essential as this process unfolds. Developing understanding of present practices and the projected impact of new ones, highlighting conflict between desired consequences and actual behavior and thinking, and initiating problem-solving discussions are ways in which a principal, superintendent, or curriculum/technology specialist may facilitate the inclusion of new skills and practices within schools.

6. *Maintaining an effective and cohesive working group*   Whether the group is a classroom of students, the teaching core of a school, central office specialists, or the system's cadre of principals, clarity should be maintained about individual responsibilities, and governance should reinforce group cohesion. The leader must manage group conflict and provide supportive control over the educational system.

7. *Carrying out a variety of executive functions at all levels*   The teacher, especially, will have many decision-making responsibilities involving students and parents, as will departmental or grade-level chairpersons. At all levels of leadership there are executive functions indigenous to the position: developing and operating an overall budget, organizing the group, arranging for facilities, providing needed materials and other resources, initiating dialogue about effective practices for learning improvement and efficiency, providing constant surveillance, solving problems, making decisions, and conducting evaluations. By allowing leadership to emerge at all levels of the school system, educators will encounter challenges that provide hands-on leadership experience and be invigorated to uphold their responsibilities and move forward with productive innovations.

Carolyn R. Shaffer and Kristin Anundsen tell the story of a small town in Pennsylvania that became the focus of medical researchers in the early 1960s. The community of Roseto was an ordinary small American town except in one remarkable way: its residents were among the healthiest in the nation. Their death rate due to heart disease was significantly lower than the national average, and they demonstrated greater resistance to peptic ulcers and senility than other Americans. There were few ordinary clues to support these findings: the citizens of Roseto smoked as much, exercised as little, and faced the same stressful situations as other Americans. Roseto was a closely-knit Italian-American community whose health habits were no better than those of people in any other town in America. After extensive testing, researchers were able to link the health of this small town to their strong sense of community and camaraderie. Dr. Stewart Wolf commented, "More than any other town we studied, Roseto's social structure reflected old-world values and traditions." In his report, Dr. Wolf pointed out, "There was a remarkable cohesiveness and sense of unconditional support within the community. Family ties were very strong."[2]

A follow-up study of Roseto underscored this conclusion. As the young people of Roseto began to marry outside the clan, move away from the town's traditions, and sever emotional and physical ties with the community, the healthy edge Roseto held over neighboring towns began to lessen until, by 1975, its mortality rates had climbed as high as the national average. Mark Pilsuk and Susan Hillier Parks reflect, "The obvious subjective benefits that follow feelings of connectedness to other humans are but the tip of the iceberg in evaluating the benefits of caring relationships. There is now a mass of evidence to indicate that such support may be one of the critical factors distinguishing those who remain healthy from those who fall ill."[3]

Developing a supportive climate in schools and school systems (communities) can have positive effects on learning growth and teacher development. Shaffer and Anundsen point out, "Contemporary medical, psychological, and sociological literature overflows with studies that point to the prolonging, even life-saving qualities of interpersonal support."[4] For these two researchers, "community is the key," not only to good physical health and longevity, but for providing support when a person is in need and stepping into other roles once filled by family. Community gives one a sense of identity and a feeling of belonging; it enables one to grow and makes possible one's "full flowering as an individual." They conclude, "Community can fill your life with enriching discoveries and surprises."[5] Educator Alfie Kohn concurs and points out that to cooperate is not to sacrifice your individuality and your achievement orientation. You can still be a team player. Success is more likely to be the result of working with other people. This is also the source of a healthy self-esteem.[6]

Building Relationships

Building relationships is the first step to resolving many of the problems that will eventually appear at the superintendent's, principal, or teacher's door. When problems do arise, the relationships built during that first year, along with an open and caring attitude displaying flexibility and concern, will set the stage for many win-win situations. Parenthetically, Belgian physicist Ilya Prigogine,[7] who was awarded the Nobel Prize for his theory of "dissipative structures," says that the capacity for being "shaken up" is paradoxically the key to growth. In his theory of dissipative structures, he shows that friction is a fundamental property of nature, and that nothing grows without it—not mountains, not pearls, and not people. Therefore, when problems arise in the educational community, leaders should embrace them for the growth value and possibilities they hold and deal with them directly. Their goal should be not only to resolve the issues that are causing problems, but to learn from them as well. Having ducked (or "passed the buck on") many systemic problems, leaders can console themselves that they haven't failed and that they still have an unshakable vision, but this is a delusion. When we drive into a tunnel, using Plato's metaphor of the cave, we lose reception—the light in our visions dims—and we lock ourselves into beliefs and practices that lack the critical evaluation brought to us by confronting issues openly. Truth, understanding, and wisdom increase as we engage in dialogue about situations and problems that are important to the foundations of teaching and learning. Without open conversation inside and outside the educational system, the results of our educational practices will be inclusive and leave us with no verification, no foundation.

Building a supportive and open climate internally and externally is a continuous process and a prerequisite for making school and systemic changes in years to come. Ethical leaders voice respect for the dignity and contributions of others by including them in mapping the overall definition and direction of the school system or school. Dedication to this process is a first step in ethical leadership and, as the school year moves along, makes for a more comprehensive and honest accounting of goals and practices. Yet, the thought of being a leader is horrifying to many people. Experience teaches that we become leaders by our inner strength, by our character. Leading is not about taking and neither is it about dominance. Ethical leadership is about service and social interdependency. Without this inner meaning, leadership becomes merely a celebration of disorder and superficiality.

As leaders, every sacrifice, every step toward action, and every response we make necessitates a leap of faith and is done without knowing the outcome before hand. It is, as Søren Kierkegaard once described, the epitome of anxiety meeting courage.[8] Only when you try your vision in the world can you test it's truth. But staying on course can be difficult. Facing their calling, many leaders ask, "What is right for me?" On the other hand, followers, facing their leaders ask, "Where am I willing to be led?" Authentic leadership, which begins on the inside of a person, is a path between these two questions. It is illuminated by one's moral compass and has the strength of mind to look beyond the many insignificant problems that tug at one's energies. At every level of educational leadership we find leaders who are also followers. If they are leading and serving and following and leading, they ask and answer both of these questions every day. The challenge of discernment is immense: knowing whether we are being called to lead or follow, knowing how and when to respond, and knowing whether our call to follow or lead or both really belongs to us or not. These challenges force us to walk a path between these questions and to ask them continuously and devotedly in the hope that by doing so we will find our course.

The mythologist Joseph Campbell used to say that we're having experiences all the time that hint at our hungers. He insisted that we must learn to listen for them, and in listening, learn to recognize them. He reminds us that the great sacrilege in terms of the soul's integrity is that of "inadvertence, of not being alert, not awake."[9] As this sequence unfolds, the practical side of leadership will emerge. Leaders with excellent management skills will build strategies that make attaining these goals a reality. The school superintendent usually delegates the development of strategies for improving the school climate, teaching practices, and student learning to principals and curriculum/instruction supportive professionals. These individuals, working together, have the responsibility of improving teaching and student learning. They must also work in tandem to improve the climate of learning. Having the entire school community moving in the same direction is imperative.

The following strategies will help educational leaders build more productive schools:

1. Collecting of reliable data on a regular basis—preferably every week at a prescribed time—covering every aspect of the school or school system's operation,

2. Developing performance indicators that zero in on the core mission of schools to improve student learning,

3. Involving all departmental heads, principals, and curriculum specialists in regular meetings (and at the school level, regular meetings with teachers and other nonteaching staff) to create open dialogue and to receive honest feedback, and

4. Encouraging teachers, principals, central office specialists, and nonteacher staff to submit additional performance indicators indigenous to their work not included in those developed by the governing executive or board of education.

These leadership responsibilities can be immense and, if one is unable to delegate, overwhelming. They will include everything from budget building to creating consensus among participating educators and laypersons. Human and material resources must be located. Research has to be conducted, training undertaken, and problematic situations overcome. Meeting with parents, citizens groups, and faculties and moving everyone in the same direction is imperative. Timing is always important, and this is a skill to be mastered by all successful leaders. Remembering their ties to the superintendent as executive leader, information will flow upward in central office meetings to keep her or him informed of progress or problems that are impacting the implementation of certain desired goals. The executive leader of the school system has the responsibility of reporting sequential progress, or the lack there of, to the board of education and to the public at large.

Putting this process into motion will necessarily involve building relationships, connecting with professionals outside the system who can assist with the accomplishment of goals, and assembling coalitions inside the school and in the community. Fulfillment requires a level of sustained attention and governance at any level—especially that of the principal and superintendent. If these two levels of administration are not kept in the loop of networking, information sharing, program development, and resource procurement, the system and school will not easily be governable, and the loss of their support in creating a supportive climate for change will not easily be recoverable. If the top administrators are not fully informed, the system will be threatened by weakness at the superintendent level and, in the middle, at the principal level. Where communication is not open and freely pursued, the school system is left unsupported by its natural strengths.

Working in a cooperative, ethical environment is essential. Although much of our work will be routine, our first duty is to listen. All around us are educational professionals who have a stake in the outcome of our leadership. And we should be reminded that as we listen to the big ideas that could bring notoriety and reward, we should not ignore the little ideas that are right at our own feet. All voices need to be heard, and the give-and-take found in staff meetings needs to be continuously informed by differing perspectives and the creative input of staff. Experience teaches that when we take care of the small things first, the big issues are more easily managed. So, prepare intensely and sweat the small stuff. This may sound complex, but in reality it is a description of a vibrant and dynamic school system on its way to teaching and learning improvement. In these actions, relationships will be created and networks will evolve in every grade level and subject area. Meeting with teachers across grade levels and subject areas and networking with feeder schools—tandemly organized elementary, middle, and high schools—will engender enthusiasm and earn the respect of those directly involved with classroom operations and student learning.

Another suggestion for improving the ethical environment of schools is provided by Frank Navran of the Ethics Resource Center. He explains seven steps that an organization, especially one facing ethical concerns, can take to change its culture to one that promotes and rewards ethical behavior. These steps have been adapted for educational institutions:

1. *State position, philosophy or belief publicly*   The school system or school (through its superintendent or principal) announces that it has formally adopted a specific set of beliefs regarding fundamental values or principles and that it wants employees to use this statement as the basis for decision making. The statement is written as an integral part of the school/school system's philosophy and is to be applied without exception by every decision-making employee.

2. *Create formal organizational systems*   The school system or school creates and implements the formal systems, procedures, and policies which explicitly define expectations regarding employee behaviors that are needed to guide employees in their day-to-day decision making. Examples of these systems include statements of values, codes of conduct, ethics policies, ethics oversight committees, ethics surveys, employee "help lines," and other ethics management mechanisms.

3. *Communicate expectations through informal (leadership) systems*   Leaders at all levels of the school system or school explicitly and implicitly communicate their expectations regarding employee behavior, reinforcing the explicit systemic expectations detailed through the formal systems and structures. This includes the visible use of the ethics systems in their

own decision making and the requirement that subordinate employees do likewise.

4. *Reinforce policy through measurements and rewards* The school system or school reinforces its statement of position, philosophy, or belief by making adherence to the associated guidelines and policies an integral part of how success is measured and rewarded.

5. *Implement communications and education strategies* The school system or school embarks on a strategic communications and education campaign to ensure that employees understand the stated position and the behavioral expectations, as well as have familiarity with the systems and structures that have been put in place to facilitate employee fulfillment of those expectations.

6. *Use response to critical events to underscore commitment* Superintendents and principals use critical events in the school system or school's history to underscore their commitment to ethical leadership. They make their adherence to the position explicit and use the critical event as evidence of how the highest levels of the organization are accountable to the same standards as are imposed throughout the organization.

7. *Avoid perception of hidden agendas* One of the most critical, yet least controllable, shapers of any school or school system's ethical culture is employees' perceptions of the motives behind the board of education's and superintendent's adoption of the stated position, philosophy, or belief; that is, their hidden agendas. Superintendents and principals need to assiduously avoid any decision or action which could reasonably be expected to communicate a self-serving or selfish motives for imposing the previously referenced position, systems, or measurements on the employees of the organization.[10]

In schools and school systems that operate openly and with flexibility, one cannot predict where ideas and innovations will emerge. Engaging the minds and passions of teachers first—who serve on the front lines of education—and then principals and curriculum/technology specialists will ensure that many voices are heard and appropriate actions are taken. Educators who have had special training and possess vital skills will have contributions to make. Others may wish to pursue such training and may need professional and financial support. Leaders who possess the courage to listen and the passion to grow value in their schools will implement ideas that have merit and support the continual education of those who wish to develop their knowledge and skills. These actions will engender employee loyalty, a vital virtue in any organization.

Enthusiasm is contagious. Communication that is open and flexible and neither tainted with selfish intentions or limited by a "this is my territory" mentality can be the lifeblood, the essential spirit, of an educational organization. Where there is open communication, innovation will follow, educators will be focused on their responsibilities, and the community will be supportive. Of course, for those teachers and administrators who believe they must control every program and claim every workable idea as their own, this will be scary. Input from others is neither welcomed nor held in high regard. Many administrators and teachers would rather remain isolated and work as independent operators within the school setting. Their isolation usually stymies school and systemic growth. Many of these—administrators especially—tend to micromanage the life and work of those around them. When this happens, productivity and growth usually advances at the pace of one. Letting go of micromanaging and allowing leadership to emerge means that leaders will lead by following and followers by serving others in the educational community. Leaders are charged to find the right balance between speed and deliberation. This balance is more easily found by serving and listening to those who are led.

Alan Watts has pointed out that some people, especially rigid people, just can't stand wiggles. "They want to get things straight."[11] Change and growth will always encounter "wiggles." Recognizing the innovative and different ideas of others (the "wiggles") will allow other educators to demonstrate their knowledge and leadership capabilities. We can't grow if we remain isolated and if we are unwilling to listen and learn from others. Only by asking difficult questions, listening to others, and facing difficult problems do we grow as leaders. Authentic leaders seek opportunities to lead—they stalk their calling and locate the most sensitive and alive spot, and plug into that pulse.[12] Where there has been an effort to include employees in decision-making and where self-esteem has been lifted and dignity enhanced, there is a promise of significant growth and productivity.

Engendering Respect

Much has been written about respect,[13] but understanding the origins and interpretations of respect can be complicated. There are several ways in which "respect" is used. First, respect is commonly interpreted as deference to status and hierarchy driven by duty, honor, and a desire to avoid punishment, shame, and embarrassment. This may be respect for a school superintendent qua superintendent or respect for the flag. Sometimes we hear the call for more respectful relationships in health care, urban planning, and education. The call also comes for a more civil society. Here, we do not hear the voices of individuals or the work involved in nourishing respectful relationships; here respect has a vague and organizational connotation. When I was a teenager, my mother said that I ought always, without exception, to respect my elders. My dad usually translated "respect" as listening to and obeying him. These too are traditional forms of respect. Mother used to say to me—even when I was in my forties—that I should "obey" my principal or departmental chairperson without question. This was a pattern of behavior that she developed having grown up working in the textile mills of the South—the mill superintendent was, without question, always right. According to Sara Lawrence-Lightfoot, "The traditional view of respect, though rarely expressed in its pure form, tends to be relatively static and impersonal."[14] She observes, "The remnants of this view survive today and shape our expectations, our apprehensions, and our disappointments."[15]

In her treatment of "respect," Lawrence-Lightfoot focuses on the way respect creates symmetry, empathy, and connection in all kinds of relationships—such as teacher and student, doctor and patient, both commonly seen as unequal. She says, "I am interested in watching it develop over time. I see it not only as an expression of circumstance, history, temperament, and culture, rooted in rituals and habits, but also arising from efforts to break with routine and imagine other ways of giving and receiving trust, and in so doing, creating relationships among equals."[16] Lawrence-Lightfoot's second use of "respect," based on trust and creating relationships among equals, is closely tied to the conception of ethical/servant leadership. Ethical leaders build supportive climates for teaching and learning by developing *respectful* relationships. These relationships are able to sustain the vision of the superintendent about the teaching and learning climate and motivate educational professionals to improve their craft. Respect grows value in schools through dynamic networking and interacting. The carryover to teacher-student relationships is obvious. There are no boundaries. As leaders, we should be aware that when we're too attracted to stability and the status quo, we avoid creativity and change. We soon become disrespectful of those with different ideas and innovative solutions to traditional problems. We view them as a challenge to our authority. Leaders need to understand that growth involves risks, pain, and uncertainty (wiggles). The sensitive servant leader will feel all of these emotions. It will not be easy for a leader with a traditional bent to accommodate the different skills and ideas among his/her professional staff. Traditional leaders need to understand the concept of "knowledge worker" and that the world has gone through a paradigm shift since they were trained in educational administration.

Open Societies

School systems become dynamic open societies and vibrant growing educational communities when its members:

1. Participate freely in common practices,
2. Depend on one another and feel free to call on others for assistance,
3. Make decisions together,
4. Identify their work and the work of the school as something larger than the sum of their individual relationships and visions, and
5. Commit themselves for the long-term to their own, one another's, and the school system's well-being.[17]

Given these behaviors, ethical leaders are charged with creating a climate of growth and a climate of learning in their schools. This educational environment will be of the nature of an open society where different views are recruited and heard. George Soros points out the importance of respect in open societies. He comments that we create open societies because we realize no one is perfect and many contributors are needed to perfect the whole, but he says something else is needed, "some concern for others, some shared values. These values have to be infused by the recognition of our fallibility, but they cannot be derived from it by logic."[18] These values also support ethical leadership. Because education is one of the most important institutions for transferring value and meaning, tradition and culture to youngsters, it should remain open, flexible, and, at its core, moral in nature, recognizing the essential dignity and worth of its employees and parents and, especially, its children.

Soros says, "We are incomplete as individuals; we need to belong to society."[19] And he points out that we cannot have a society without recognizing some common interests that take precedence over self-interests. But how can leaders in educational communities best attain their goals, especially when they conflict with the goals and interests of others? He says we need some ground rules for prioritizing our common interests and how best we can attain them. He then develops two general axioms to govern his choice of these rules: *governance* and *subsidiary*. These two axioms are easily applied to educational communities. First, Soros notes, we need some form of universal governance; some way of regulating the activities of governments, businesses, organizations, and individuals. Translated, this means that some governing board—e.g., school board or a citizens advisory committee—should be set up to review the mission, goals, and practices of the school system and, when necessary, adjudicate conflicting interests that threaten the stability of the institution. A second axiom is the principle of subsidiarity, which says that because it is difficult to decide about the common good, decisions should be made at the lowest possible level.[20] In education, this means developing leadership and decision-making skills at every level of the school system's operation and including all professionals and parents on committees where decisions are being made that will affect the entire educational system. Universal governance is a concept that we need to apply both inside the school system and outside to citizen groups as well. It means we are all responsible for the other and that there is no place within the school system for finger pointing or blame.

From these two axioms, Soros precedes to develop three fundamental principles of an open society.[21] These principles are indicative of ethical leadership because of their moral content and their ability to support ethical climates in which teachers are allowed to pursue their profession and students are allowed to learn at proper developmental increments.

The first principle is that of freedom of thought and expression and the freedom of choice. Soros comments, "Since the ultimate truth is beyond our reach, we must allow people to think for themselves and make their own choices."

The second principle is generated from the first; namely, "freedom of thought allows critical thinking and freedom of choice allows the market mechanism to operate." This entails the creation of value, the movement of individuals up and down the corporate ladder due to their developing new skills or failing to do so. This also means the working out of problems at the school level with principals, teachers, and parents who are closest to the troubles that beset the learning child. Dictation of procedure and method by law is a given, but laws only provide broad directions about how educators are to govern their activities. Allowing many voices to be heard permits growth to occur and allows innovation to permeate all levels of the system's operation.

The third principle is the ideal of human rights, which can be derived from our being thinking agents conscious of ourselves and capable of making autonomous choices. It grants to us a certain professional freedom to pursue the goals and objectives of the school system without too much micromanaging. Micromanaging classroom practices from a distant central office only confuses teachers and compounds local and classroom problems. Micromanaging and top-down control are the antithesis of open societies.

The description given above provides us a picture of an ideal school situation where everyone from the classroom teacher to the principal's office and from the school to the central office of the school district is pulling his or her own weight. Upon reading this description, one school administrator responded, "But who does the weeding?" What the administrator meant is that in the real world of schooling, there are some educators who do not cooperate, who neglect classroom duties, who go their own way and neglect the school or systemic mission, or who may just be sorry teachers hunkering down under the auspices of "tenure" until the day they can retire. Experience reminds us of our imperfections and the continual need for dialogue and an occasional prod or reprimand. In all honesty, it must be said that teachers, like others in our society, are not equally capable nor are they comparably motivated or cooperative. School governance demands that principals and superintendents assert their authority—when other measures have failed—to remedy this situation. Experience taught me long ago that most decisions in education can be made by answering one simple question: "What's best for the child?" Ethical leadership never operates in the realm of the black and white. Most of the time we are operating in shades of gray and pray that our commitments and ethical policies will guide us.

An example of micromanagement that does more harm and raises more questions than the good that is assumed to follow is the de facto censorship of books and other materials from school libraries before anyone in the school or the community raises questions or objects to the materials. It goes without saying that library materials have to be age appropriate. This is a judgment call, but professional educators have local, state, and national organizations to help them make decisions about questionable materials. Sometimes it just comes down to a matter of experience and common sense. On the other hand, many great books have been pulled from middle school and high school libraries that were not questioned in a particular community and that were not offensive to teachers or parents in those schools and communities. No one had challenged them, but they were pulled quietly and purposefully, either by a local librarian or by direction from a central office administrator. The reasons can be many for these actions, but in the case of a central office administrator, the reasons are usually more political than because a specific book or magazine was offensive or inappropriate. Local administrators are aware that certain materials are being challenged and censored in school systems across America on a regular basis. In their effort to avoid potential problems in their own school communities, they make a list of these materials and direct school librarians to systematically pull them from their shelves. Thus, they micromanage not only the daily operations of the schools but the beliefs and values of the schools and community as well by discreetly limiting what students are able to read, view, or study. It would promote the values of democracy and the open society if procedures were established and consistently followed that allowed challenges to take place, discussions and debates about the materials to follow, and decisions to be made by a governing board—rather than one person—acting reasonably and with the goals of education and the values of the community in mind.

George Soros heads Soros Fund Management and is the founder of a global network of foundations dedicated to supporting open societies. He is known throughout the world for his financial intelligence and for his political engagement. He interprets history as a reflexive process in which the participants' biased decisions interact with a reality that is greater than their individual actions and beyond their comprehension. He points out that the interaction between people and between groups and organizations can be self-reinforcing or self-correcting. They probably are both: when the interaction is self-reinforcing it can go only so far before it hits limits set by reality, but it can go far enough to bring about substantial changes in the world or the organization. When the goals of the self-reinforcing organization become unsustainable, it will either self-correct or self-destruct.

Consider the following example: in 1990 through 1991, with the knowledge and permission of the superintendent and his goal of improving achievement test scores, I made it a point to call every school district in North Carolina whose math scores on the state achievement test were in the high range. Our scores were acceptable, but many of us thought they should be higher, especially in Algebra I. I had felt for some time that we should be offering an algebra program for our middle school students and hoped that I could find support for this conclusion by calling those twenty-seven school districts. What I discovered that summer was that twenty-six of these districts indeed offered Algebra I in the eighth grade and the other district was planning to offer the course in the upcoming school year. From that time I began to talk about offering Algebra I for high achieving and gifted eighth grade students. I discussed this possibility with my supervisor, the director of curriculum and instruction, and reported my findings to the superintendent of schools. There was no immediate response, and my impatience got the best of me. I then proceeded to design a three-year algebra emphasis for grades six through eight based on several factors:

1. I had taught middle grade gifted students for a number of years— actually, I had designed a course in mathematical logic for eighth grade gifted students to prepare them for ninth grade Algebra I—and knew that a number of students in each of our four middle schools that could handle such a course.

2. My research into brain-growth periodization[22] told me that 95 percent of sixth graders were in a positive brain-growth period and that here is where the major concepts of Algebra I should be introduced.

3. While researching methods in critical thinking, I discovered the *Arlin Test of Formal Reasoning Applied*,[23] which could be used as part of an assessment package to assure teachers that the students selected for the course were cognitively ready.

4. I had been brought into the central office in 1988 to improve programs for the gifted. We had been working on an advanced literature program for several years and had begun training teachers in critical thinking skill—preparing them to infuse their lessons with thinking processes.[24] The state department of instruction had told us that the new state achievement tests had used critical thinking processes as a skill foundation for constructing their assessments.

5. I also felt that the timing was right to recommend this program to our superintendent. I had thought about it for many years. My research was carefully managed and verified my own experiences with gifted/above average middle grades students. The reality was that there was a small window of opportunity here that had not existed before, and I was convinced that my staff and I could manage the expectations and results of this proposed program.

My staff and I finished the development of the assessment instrument and began the task of selling the program to middle school math teachers. Our elementary gifted consultant discovered the Algebridge[25] program that had been developed for sixth graders, and we felt that our three-year algebra emphasis was ready to go—Algebridge in the sixth grade, pre-algebra in the seventh, and Algebra I in the eighth grade. We anticipated offering all average and above students the Algebridge program, then using a combination of the Arlin Test, achievement tests, report card grades, and teacher recommendations for selecting pre-algebra students, and evaluating only those who had taken pre-algebra—at the end of the seventh grade—for placement in the eighth grade Algebra I class.

Our conversations with principals and teachers uncovered one principal and teacher willing to be the first to experiment with this program. Looking back, we had perhaps moved too fast in putting Algebra I into place. Finding balance between speed and deliberation is a matter of experience and intuition—of feel—as well as knowledge and perception. The director of curriculum and instruction was just beginning to meet with high school math teachers to assess our proposal. A creative tension between that group and my department was an opportunity for examining old procedures and making innovative changes. After several of their meetings, which I concluded were intense because neither I or anyone on my staff were invited to attend them, the high school teachers decided against allowing Algebra I to be taught in the eighth grade. They had three major reasons: first, they believed that eighth grade students could not handle the rigors of abstract thinking required for an Algebra I class; second, they believed no eighth grade teacher could possibly teach Algebra I to the satisfaction of high school math departments; and third, they said this program would take their best students away from regional and state math competitions held during the spring of each year for ninth graders.

My principal leadership mistake was being too aggressive and exclusive; the high school math teachers should have been brought into the conversation early on, and by me, not someone unfamiliar with the research that supported my conclusions. Explaining this to our director of curriculum and instruction, I was invited to the next meeting and explained my reasoning. At that meeting I assured them that this was only an experiment, but that twenty-six school districts across the state had been teaching Algebra I successfully in the eighth grade for a number of years. I made two concessions with this group of teachers: first, that the teacher selected for the experimental class would be a high school certified math teacher (we had several high school certified math teachers in each of our middle school math departments). Second, I told them that each student taking the Algebra I class in the eighth grade would take the state mandated end-of-course test for Algebra I, and if the scores were not high enough, we would not pursue the program any further. With these concessions made, they seemed to think we would not pro-

ceed with our plans. I had not over promised what this new math emphasis could produce but knew that by controlling student entrance into the
program and selecting the right teachers, we could deliver a program that
would be advantageous to both students and teachers.

I know now that there are limitations to the boom or bust model provided by Soros, but he says that his purpose has been to develop the concept of open society as "an association of free individuals respecting one
another's rights within a framework of law."[26] He further says that the
open society seeks to be inclusive, that societies and communities can
have this positive content; they don't always have to be against something. In this way, when "higher-ups" become involved in school/class-
room problems, it's not considered to be a threat to the principal of the
school or the classroom teacher. Rather, it is thought of as a natural and
supportive part of an interactive school system that is managing and self-
correcting itself.

Soros' thesis is intriguing, but like any metaphor, there is no perfect
match with our daily realities. His axioms and principles, when studied
thoughtfully, can become guidelines for personal behavior and organization interaction. He concludes, "Of course, open society is not without
its shortcomings, but its deficiency consists in offering too little rather than
too much. More precisely, the concept is too general to provide a recipe
for specific decisions. Rules cannot be established by deductive reasoning. It would contradict the principle of fallibility if all problems had a
solution. Those who claim to know all the answers would create closed
society. By the same token, the fact that we do not know what the common interest is does not justify us in denying its existence. Specifically,
the belief that the pursuit of self-interest (such as the failure to include
the ideas of others in your planning and implementation of new programs, even when your research is sound and your motives honorable) will
take care of the common interest is an alluring but false idea."[27] I had
begun the middle school algebra program without opening conversations
with all stakeholders. My enthusiasm, therefore, caught on with only a
few, mainly those within my own department. Those who had no knowledge about the research we uncovered were neither impressed with our
ideas nor willing to let us change traditional methods and territories without a fight. Looking back, who can blame them? A first step for leaders
to remember is to open lines of communication within and without, to
all stakeholders, in honest dialogue, and with purpose and understanding.

The vision of a school and a school system as open society remains fascinating. It returns us to another, perhaps even nobler idea, that we are enriched by the creativity and ideas of others. This is an environment in which many voices are heard, problems are shared, dialogue is encouraged, and meritorious solution alternatives are given the opportunity to be actualized. And the value-carryover we derive from this idea can be transforming: teachers will build more open and flexible relationships with students where teaching and learning come first; principals will treat all teachers with respect and support their classroom capabilities with training and resources; where there are weaknesses, efforts will be made to correct them; and all personnel will remain accountable to the bottom line of student learning outcomes. Merit, initiative, and getting learning results will bring rewards—not just to the classroom teacher or the school where there is growth, but to the entire chain of educational professionals whose efforts have sustained and supported teaching/learning initiatives. The open society recognizes we can't go it alone, and in educational communities, attention should constantly be given to strengthening the weakest link in the system—or as one principal said, "Removing it when all else fails"—meeting the needs of students, and building performance indicators that hold us responsible for student learning growth. After all, education is not about power and neither is it about authority. Education is about responsibility, to students first, and the community.

Experience with teaching bright and gifted students and research into what other schools were offering at the middle school level brought to my attention that perhaps our math scores could be improved with changing our approach in grades six through eight. With our brightest students underachieving on state assessments (actually making less than one year's growth in reading and mathematics), there was room for improvement. When the Algebra I scores came back from our experimental group, their average score was in the 98th percentile. The lowest in the class scores did not fall below the 90th percentile. By listening to the research, by planning our student selection process carefully, and by using an open-minded principal to help us select the right teacher, our program was a success. Our only goal was to provide for those students, who were cognitively ready, a program to enhance their academic performance and enable them to move forward with their education. The carryover has been outstanding with our high schools using our assessments for placing students (who did not take Algebra I in the middle school) in math classes and using the AlgeBridge program with many of their slower and below average students. Transformation had taken place: our middle and high school math departments were now working much closer, discussing common problems and evaluating and placing students in classes that best suit their needs. A spirit of community was unfolding, supported by trust and respect for one another's capabilities and sustained by a credibility built on verifiable results.

A careful review of group development reveals five phases[28] through which communities and organizations move on their road to maturity: excitement, autonomy, stability, synergy, and transformation.[28] All of these were revealed in the development of our middle school algebra program.

Excitement: Getting High on Possibilities   The world looks new and the possibilities endless for a first-year teacher or an experienced teacher moving into a new school, for a first-time principal, or for a new superintendent. The focus is on positive outcomes, not future problems. You view your students, teachers, principals, or central office staff professionals in all their potential, and the possibilities for actualizing your vision seem inestimable. Here, one can move too fast. Remember to include all stakeholders in the conversation and communicate within and without and with teachers, principals, and superintendent-level personnel.

Autonomy: Jockeying for Power   The power struggle phase begins when leaders wake up to the awareness that other persons are not what they had thought them to be. When the illusion of unity shatters and educational partners become disillusioned, disappointed, and angry, they will probably respond in one of two different ways: they tend to either start fighting for what they want by changing others around them to see their point of view and be the way they're "supposed" to be, or they unconsciously try to hurt others in retaliation for the disappointment they have experienced. Shaffer and Anundsen have observed that the illusion of power and the belief that threat, force, manipulation, or domination, no matter how subtle, can get us what we want, becomes the main obstacle to achieving self-assurance and fullness. We cannot have harmony without personal struggle.[29] Without knowledge and without being informed or being left out of the decision-making loop, people become extremely territorial, as did our high school math teachers. That's a natural reaction. Becoming an effective ethical leader requires that we give our attention to how our decisions affect all others.

Stability: Settling into Roles and Structures   Chaotic autonomy doesn't last forever. Neither does rebellion and jockeying for power. Healthy conflict—facing issues, working through them, and giving up on power struggles as unrewarding and ineffective—will allow educators to grow beyond their selfish interests and enjoy the stability that comes with confident adulthood. Once teachers, principals, educational specialists, and superintendents learn they can express themselves as individuals—even if it means criticizing the group—and be heard and accepted, the rigid positions they hold will be relaxed, and they will begin to accept their own and others' limitations and set about to fulfill the mission of the school system. Growth is not a given and will not occur without friction—the give-and-take of day-to-day educational activities.

Friction doesn't necessarily entail hurting others or isolating ourselves in our classrooms, our offices, or behind opaque walls of authority and power. Positive conflict has the possibility of opening us to our own weaknesses and biases, as well as to the power and constructive influence of collective thinking. Its power comes in helping to restructure our inner thinking and providing the self-confidence, once lacking, to open ourselves in honest and constructive conversation with others. As all of our middle schools adapted the algebra program to meet their needs, many of the same problems once again appeared, but because we had already faced them in one school, establishing procedures and guidelines, they were easily resolved in the normal course of school decision making. At the end of each year we encouraged our middle school and high school math departments to get together and share information about students and work together to place them in the appropriate classes in the ninth grade.

Synergy: Allowing Self and Others to Mutually Unfold   Synergy is paradoxical. Through it we are able to actualize our individuality and keep our connection with the vision of others. In a synergistic relationship, what is good for a single educator is also good for the entire school or school system. Unity becomes possible when we begin to align our goals with those of the school, share ideas, and dedicate ourselves to remaining more open to others and flexible in assessing their collective points of view. When a teacher makes a commitment to return to college to pursue a higher level degree or to study to become an administrator, he or she is adding value to the entire school system. When a young principal begins a multi year trek to pursue a specialist degree and then a doctorate in education administration, this commitment should not threaten other administrators, especially the school superintendent. This principal may stay after attaining these two degrees or may move on to another school system. Either way, the principal has added value to himself or herself and value to the school community as a whole. Synergy implies that when you know that everything is connected to everything else, acting from your being (your essence rather from your ego) signifies acting with both your own good and the good of the organization in mind.

The value added to our school system through the middle school algebra program has been far-reaching. Of course, our high achieving students have benefited because of the head start this program has allowed them to get in their high school mathematics classes. The program made room for additional math courses such as statistics and probability at the twelfth grade level and freed teachers in the ninth and tenth grades to offer smaller classes in Algebra I for students who needed more individual attention. Many other students have benefited from our work with gifted students. At the high school level, placement in all beginning math classes has become efficient from using the evaluations based on the Arlin Tests. Using the AlgeBridge program has helped students with special needs in mathematics, and, in general, more and more middle grades students have been included in pre-algebra classes.

Transformation: Expanding, Segmenting, or Disbanding   In the last phase of its cycle, a community undergoes a death and rebirth of sorts, either expanding the boundaries of its identity, segmenting into a number of smaller communities, or disbanding entirely and freeing its members to develop further in connection with other people and groups. A city school system can give up its charter and be assimilated into a larger city-county school district, or vice versa. In either way, a new identity is formed and new associations are built. A county with two, three, or four school districts may wish to combine two or more of these into one larger district, thus being able to compete for more higher level government funding or reduce the cost of paying high dollar administrators, since fewer will be needed. New schools will be built with the growth in student populations; school district lines will be redrawn; and personnel will be transferred or reassigned. Superintendents will resign, and new ones will he hired. There are retirements, a yearly ritual in which experience gives way to youth and vigorous anticipation. New board members will be elected or appointed, and the mission of the school system will again undergo reevaluation and motivation. Change is the one constant in the whirlwind of educational activities. Regardless of the way the new organization looks, M. Scott Peck reminds us that healthy organizations are not ones with the absence of problems but are those who are actively and effectively addressing or healing its problems.[30]

It has been over ten years since starting the middle grades algebra program. Early on I let go of my supervision of the program as our teachers were carrying it forward without any assistance. Their needs and dilemmas were best understood and resolved among themselves. The program had created an opportunity for growth and new avenues for innovation. Our department still funded the purchase of materials and assisted with assessments, but, for the most part, the program moved along without needing our assistance. I believed then, and I know now, that a vision once grasped can take on a life of its own. That is one of the joys of leadership.

Improving Communication

Opening Lines of Communication

Within the educational institution, communication is not only essential, but also vital to systemic and school morale and stability. My wife, a second grade teacher for over thirty years, has said, "To a large degree, my success with a particular class of students or with one single student depended on how well I was able to communicate with the child's parents and my willingness to listen as they talked with me. Nothing has ever been able to replace classroom-home communication. It is essential to student success." Here we find a foothold for respect and the beginnings of an open society. Consciously or not, teachers who effectively communicate with children and their parents are becoming ethical leaders in their own right.

Building relationships, respect for others, and communication work together to sustain supportive climates for teaching and learning. Supportive climates are life giving. Individuals and leaders who live their lives as if other people matter, as if their coworkers and students are an extension of themselves, create supportive climates for personal and systemic growth. The essence, the lifeblood of educational organizations is communication—their ability to maintain a give-and-take of ideas, open dialogue, and a continual conversation, freely entered, about ideas that matter. Those who help maintain supportive environments ask on a daily basis, "What can I give others that will improve their value, enhance their self-esteem, support their innovative ideas, and improve their lives?" When the lives of those with whom we work are improved, our lives and work will also improve. A significant commitment of ethical leaders is to grow the leadership value of the school system. In part, this can be accomplished by creating the conditions for sustained and continuous personal growth for all employees.

Open communication throughout the school system is an important tool that enables the emergence of a dynamic web of interrelated conversations that proclaim loudly that no one person and no single part of the education system is more important than another. Each teacher and each principal, every curriculum specialist at the central office level and every technical support person, the superintendent and his or her staff, the board of education, and all parents are important to the life and growth of the school system. During the early years of the 1990s, our central office joined with our maintenance crew and bus garage employees for a monthly luncheon, usually on payday. This was a time of informal bonding, talking about our families, vacations, and the like. It was fun, and each of us brought a special food for our "covered dish" meal. This helped all of us build new relationships and personally recognize the contributions of every employee to the success of our school system. We always looked forward to this time together and made a conscious effort to mention employees who were sick or who had family members that were sick. With over 2,000 employees in our school system, we were proclaiming loudly that every worker, every secretary, and every educator was important to the success of the group—that he or she was a person of worth.

Without these informal gatherings, open communication can be eroded or concluded altogether. Schools and central offices without open and continuous conversation will soon be divided into those that think they have power and those that know they don't have it. A third group will probably emerge that wants to have power and will soon disassociate themselves from those who are perceived powerless and out of the decision-making group. In one central office that had closed down direct communication between the superintendent and staff lower in the chain of command, such as department heads and curriculum specialists, a newly appointed department head was overheard saying, "The problem with this new position is that I don't know with whom to talk and who to avoid." This supervisor soon aligned herself with the third group. It is my understanding that that office soon began its trek to consolidate its top-down management style—a philosophy that permeated almost every department in the building. Soon, a message came that weekly staff meetings would cease. The superintendent let it be known that he only wished to communicate with superintendent-level employees and principals; the rest would have to go through the proper channels to resolve their problems.

Top-down and one-way communication is usually an inefficient and ineffective method for communicating information. Care should be taken when speaking to one person, small groups, or to large numbers of educators. Some basic research has been conducted on what happens to information when it is passed through several persons with little or no clarification, dialogue, and feedback. The more the message is passed from person to person, the more distorted and changed it becomes. Three psychological processes characterize the communication between persons who are unable to communicate directly with the original source of a message—superintendents and principals should remember this when giving major addresses to all system or school employees. These three processes are attempts to reduce the message to a simple one that has significance for the receiver in terms of his or her own interests, experience, frame of reference, and tasks. These three processes can be summarized as leveling, sharpening, and assimilation.[31]

Leveling The receiver tends to reduce the amount of information he or she receives by remembering much less of the message than was presented by the sender. The message tends to grow shorter, more concise, and more easily grasped as it's told. In successive versions, fewer words are used, and fewer details are mentioned. For example, a new superintendent's first conversation with central office and school staffs was an hour-long speech given in a gymnasium to several thousand employees. The superintendent's message was excellently delivered with back up from a huge screen using Power Point for visual reinforcement. A few days later, several teachers were asked what they heard when they listened to the address. For the most part, they responded that the new superintendent wants all schools to have 80 percent of their students on grade level in math and reading as determined by the state achievement tests. One said, "This would make us a system of distinction." What else the superintendent said in the hour-long address was not remembered or thought of as too insignificant to mention.

Sharpening The receiver sharpens certain parts of the information so that a few high points are readily remembered while most of the message is forgotten. Sharpening then, is the selective retaining, perceiving, and reporting of a limited number of details from a larger context. It is the reciprocal of leveling: one cannot exist without the other. Certain points become dominant, and all others are grouped about them. Continuing with the previous example, about a month into the school year, a principal and several of his teachers were asked about their interpretation of the address they had heard from their new superintendent. The answer from all of these individuals was the same: "Get your achievement test scores up!" The message had now been narrowed and sharpened. Everyone understood what it meant to them.

Assimilation   The receiver takes much of the message into her or his own frame of reference and personality. Thus, his or her interpretations and memories of what was heard are affected by his or her own thoughts and feelings. This process involves not only changing the unfamiliar to some known context but leaving out material that seems irrelevant and substituting material that gives meaning in the person's own frame of reference. A subsequent conversation with teachers in the school system of the previous example revealed that the testing emphasis had been assimilated into their thinking. While talking with one group about using critical thinking skills in their daily lessons and perhaps focusing on character education issues, the answer was, "Who has the time. We meet and talk about test items, prepare lessons around these areas, give pretest after pretest, and drill and practice."

The message is quite simple: important information begs for open dialogue, discussion, and feedback where many different voices can be heard and the experience of others is allowed to impact the message and clarify, reinforce, or even change some of its significant parts. Informed leadership, growing individually, and helping grow the school system or school is an indispensable ingredient for future success. Leading is not about taking and neither is it about dominance. With a servant attitude our leadership quotient will breed a sense of life's interdependency and reveal our own value and just how much we need the support of others. This type of leadership is able to unify the mission of the school system or school and bring together a disaggregated group of professionals to focus their energy on the work of the system's overall mission. What was once unmanageable now becomes easily managed.

A Servant Heart

David Elkind, in his much heralded *The Hurried Child*,[32] points out that, ideally, the home and school are places where we are educated in human relations, where we learn how to live within society. Along with religious institutions, the home and school are essential for developing character and self-respect. Here they are positively refined (ideally) through an interaction of life experiences and, during our evolving maturity, challenged by conscious self-examination. The test of ethical leadership is to provide environments that support individual ethical growth.

We give birth to ourselves in the relationships we form. By way of our caring and concern for others, we add to morality and justice both kindness and integrity—the foundations of our spiritual being that enable us to appreciate the uniqueness of other persons and their situations. As our connections with others outside the family continues, we are compelled to remember what it means to be human and in being human, to treat each other with dignity and understanding. Morality and justice are living ideas that define our humanity. They are the human cornerstone for building relationships. They are also fundamental for developing a servant heart.

As ethical leaders, the gift of honest dialogue is the richest and most enduring gift we can give to those in our employment. A servant heart is shaped by the thought that no one is insignificant. It not only reveals our own moral worth but recognizes the moral worth of others as well. Educators should not be coerced by their environments—as tough as they can be at times—but, instead, become a positive force that turns inward for self-examination and outward, to others, in honest and direct communication. Our life and work as educators always occurs in community. A positive sense of self is needed for building these bridges to others. Superintendents and principals, teachers and central office specialists should have many dialogue meetings a year. In these meetings, the leader should not merely share information but listen, try to resolve problems, and invite the input of others. Leaders cannot enhance their influence or authority by one-way and command-control communication. They need to build bridges to others and initiate conversation with confidence and self-respect, which are necessary for our self-improvement and for helping make positive changes in our schools and in our classrooms. Along with responsibility for our own development and work, confidence in our abilities, and respect for self and others, a higher standard of civility and decency is available to all of us.

We are challenged to remember that authentic leadership begins on the inside with a servant heart and moves forward to provide knowledge, guidance, and understanding for those who choose to follow us. Authentic leadership is not about control, nor is it about power and popularity. Rather, the effective life is about living in harmony with others and, on the inside, with yourself. A servant heart harnesses the principles and motives of ethics, building relationships rather than tearing them down.

A lifetime of work has taught me that lasting change in people is an inside job. By living from the inside out, others will know us by our commitment and stewardship, by our lack of a control mentality and our willingness to give rather than take. Leading by controlling and by displaying our authority and power actually diminishes others, as well as the vision of our schools. It only serves the one in power. It is ego driven. It can destroy human relationships. Acting from commitment and with a servant's heart is acting from the foundations. Here is where the motives of ethical leadership are given birth and enriched. It takes boldness to act on principle. It has power and magic in it.

Developing a Leadership Personality

The decisions considered by a leader, as well as when and where the leader makes them, depend on the leader's inner commitments, work ethic, and personality. Mark Mehler, a New York-based freelance writer, writing for *Priority*, a Pitney Bowes publication that focuses on business ideas that make every minute count, describes five different leadership personality types idealists, jugglers, optimizers, traditionalists, and fast trackers. These personality types are indicative of diverse leadership styles.[33] The following descriptions of these personality types have been adapted to educational leadership and, although an imperfect fit, we are able to find education leaders who share their essential traits.

Idealists   As a lawyer with the United States Department of Health and Human Services, Warren Brown usually ended his day in late afternoon and had many hours left to relax with his friends or enjoy a hobby. He says that he could not relax after 6 p.m. because he had nothing to occupy his time. The thirty-one-year-old said that he had nothing that he could use all his talents in and nothing he could feel passionate about. Idealists have to feel passion about their jobs. At age 31, Brown left his government job and founded CakeLove, a take-out bakery that currently employs twelve full-time and part-time workers.

Idealists share the following personality traits. They
1. Interpret success as getting past the details to the "real work" they are passionate about;
2. Have long-term relationships with business associates; in education, teachers and others who are idealists often maintain relations with their college professors, retired educators that have added to their work, and educators in different areas of the country who have similar interests;
3. Develop long-term growth plans;
4. Work hard, network with others, and keep the costs of their contin-ual training at a minimum; and
5. Are most concerned with competition (in business); in education

6. They often specialize in one new skill and seek opportunities to train others and gain the recognition and respect that follows. They have a desire to create something of lasting value in their profession and may be the first to introduce an innovative idea or practice into a school.

Jugglers Jugglers are high-interest leaders who are intent on micromanaging every detail. Jugglers need to focus on their strengths, own up to their limitations, and delegate away their weaknesses. Terri Levine, a Philadelphia-based small business coach asks clients who are jugglers to set aside a "self-care day" each week in which they swear off all business and concentrate solely on a list of one hundred things that are important to them outside of work. One other day each week is dedicated to identifying long-term issues that will enable them to function more efficiently. Levine says the key is just to get them away from the daily grind so they can begin to think about ways to grow their companies without working harder and to refocus their energies.

Jugglers share the following personality traits. They

1. Are totally immersed in their business and hesitate to delegate authority,
2. Constantly look for ways to improve their business, which can result in too many changes too quickly and give the appearance of change for the sake of changing;
3. Think through budget implications before making new investments;
4. Are optimistic about growth but, in education, are concerned about mandated changes at the federal and state levels that will impact the operation of their school system; and
5. Are adept at using technology in their dealings with others inside and outside of the educational organization.

Optimizers In business, optimizers are intent on growing a company by maximizing existing customer relationships and moving into new niches. They revel in the personal rewards of ownership, both financial and emotional. Although an optimizer is intent on keeping costs down, they have trouble with time management. They have perfectionist tendencies and stay involved in every aspect of the business—unable to let go until they have things the way they want them. This total immersion in the business and lacking the ability to delegate can get in the way of systemic or school growth. The leader is often disabled by standing too close to operations and not far enough back for an overall (universal) view of things.

The optimizers share the following traits. They

1. Like to work for themselves and are savvy and confident,
2. Believe that success is growing a business or school system (or school) that is productive and efficient and see growth as gaining recognition as an effective and efficient principal whose learning improvement is the admiration of others; or, from a superintendent's perspective, being recognized at state and national levels and by one's peers for the positive changes in student learning success;
3. Are knowledgeable about financial matters and know how to allocate resources for personnel, for teaching resources and training, and for facility development;
4. Tend to keep their home life and their work life in balance and do not neglect either one; and
5. Plan for growth in an orderly, controlled fashion.

Traditionalists   Traditionalists are conservative-minded and value stability, comfort, and a balanced lifestyle. They believe that they can survive without being on a fast-growth track. In business these are usually small business owners and professionals such as doctors and dentists. They enjoy their independence and relying on word-of-mouth marketing to keep their business alive. Some school principals, school superintendents, and teachers tend to be traditionalists. They often view fast trackers and optimizers with suspicion. In education, they are usually local men and women who have had their training and have come back to their home communities to work and rear their children. They view education as a service and themselves as service-providers.

Traditionalists have these additional traits in common. They
1. See success as keeping things the way they are or making small, incremental changes; they seek comfort and stability;
2. Maintain a good balance between work and family life;
3. Probably started their careers as teachers in the same school system they're now in as an administrator or curriculum/technical specialist;
4. Love to keep day-to-day activities clear and simple; tend to avoid entangling alliances with other service providers, consultants, and the like or joining with other school systems in some creative adventure; and
5. Watch the bottom line and keep their expenses in line with their budget.

Fast Trackers   Fast trackers sweat out every detail of business operations. Darryl Pikoss begins his day by checking on the customer-service department, the warehouse, and the data-entry function, making sure all orders have been processed and overseeing a half dozen other critically daily operations. Then he gets to his work. He comments, "There is no other way I can run a business than to sweat every detail. Above all, the company's success is based on my drive."

Pikoss is a perfect example of a fast tracker says Mark Mehler. He is focused on turning his $2 million company into a $200 million industry giant. He puts in 12- to 13-hour days; has far-reaching growth ambitions; has a strong focus on satisfying old customers and accumulating new ones; is willing to invest his own capital; has faith in technology, especially the Internet; and has a desire not to stifle the initiative of his employees. Pikoss comments, "I need them to grow along with the business. Plus, I have no choice but to delegate authority. I can't be in four locations at once."

Fast trackers share other common traits. They

1. Concentrate on indicators that show the business is growing or, in education, on the number of schools, size of student population, and growth in test scores;

2. Are more likely to invest in the business, even if it means borrowing money or, in education, they will help schools and specialists seek grants to implement innovative practices and are more likely to reallocate funds to support practices that have shown promise of influencing student learning,

3. View the computer as an important tool and time saver; and

4. Think of the school as "their school," and the system as "their system"—the idea of ownership is definitely a factor in their commitment to growing the school organization.

Leaders ought to continuously assess their leadership personalities. Maturity and growth may lead to positive changes or, if negative experiences pile up and one is more interested in maintaining his or her leadership persona than serving the purposes of education, the leader may become stymied at a level or style that is self-denying and defeating. Maintaining positive, trusting relationships over time is a difficult task, but a lack of trust breeds a you-against-me attitude that spawns isolation and tension. When we start believing that whatever we receive from others has a price tag on it, we find ourselves in a defensive position. This puts us on guard and effectively closes the door to open communication.

In 1978, I was brought into the central office of a school system to develop its programs for gifted children and youth. This was to be no easy task. The state law in North Carolina made it clear that all school systems would have gifted programs up and running by the beginning of the school year in 1978. I had just recently completed a doctoral level certification in gifted education and assisted the state with the development of its second Governor's School. My work with the state department and with the Torrance Center at the University of Georgia had given me an edge on how to create and maintain programs for the gifted and creative student. Later on, my summer teaching at the University of Connecticut's summer program for teachers of the gifted would put me in touch with a host of national specialists who would provide knowledge and on-site evaluations of my work.

Permit me to provide the details of my impressions of the central office beginning in 1978. After working in the Governor's School program, I returned to my school and found that no gifted program had been planned. I expressed my disappointment to my principal and reminded him that the state law required a program to be in place that year. I was ready to develop such a program in my own school but was told that the word had come from the superintendent that there would be no gifted programs within the school district. In October of that year a parent filed a lawsuit against the school district asking that the state force it to develop a gifted program. The child in question had an IQ well above 150 and was fluent in three languages. He was an eighth grader.

In October of 1978, I was called on to develop the overall plans for a systemic gifted program. The plan was submitted to a civil court judge, and I was then directed to implement the program. The lawsuit would be settled when and only when the parents were satisfied with the program's implementation. The plan I had written was built on a three-year time scale. Remember, this was a program mandated by law, but one that the superintendent did not want in "his" school district. Every forward step I made seemed to have a price tag on it. First, I was told to tell principals that they alone had the authority to identify students for the gifted program, despite the fact that guidelines for identifying gifted students had been prescribed by state law. Second, the superintendent had an unwritten rule that no central office supervisor could visit a school without the school principal's permission. On two occasions I went out to high schools and found that a call had been made from the superintendent's office that I was on my way. On the days when I visited these schools, the principals were standing in the main doorway and said to me that I was not welcome in "their" school. When I reported back to the superintendent about what I had encountered at those two high schools, he simply said, "Well, it's their school, professor," and just looked the other way. It seemed that having these two principals liable themselves gave him a clear conscience that he had complied with the law but that his subordinates were the ones who did not. It was one of the strangest situations of my career.

Discussing my situation with my department head gave me insights on how to operate under a traditional type of leadership. His advice was, first, stay within the law and never do anything that is illegal. He warned that if I violated state and federal laws this could and probably would be used against me sometime in the future. Second, he said find those principals who want to know what the gifted law says and communicate with them one-on-one; avoid large groups settings where there are watchdogs that will pull rank and disallow my continuing. Finally, he said, push ahead with your plan. The courts have ordered its implementation, and you really don't have any recourse.

My feelings were "What are these people thinking! How long can you continue to get away with illegal behavior? Don't we have an ethical commitment to abide by the law and to provide for the needs of these, our brightest students? Shouldn't we be doing the best we can for our gifted students, helping to grow their value as individuals and future leaders?" I was frustrated and confused and perhaps more angry than I wished to admit at the time. They pulled me out of my classroom and told me to develop, innovate, and implement. I was doing everything they said, but roadblocks kept appearing around every corner. My job with that office lasted the prescribed three years, then I returned to the sanity of my school and classroom. During those three years, I had arranged free tuition at a local college for any teacher who wished to be trained and certified in gifted education. Over 150 of our teachers began the certification process and were put into positions to teach gifted students. Classes were begun in all elementary and middle schools for gifted students. We also began advanced placement courses in three of our five high schools. When the two principals who refused to let me in their schools retired, advanced placement was begun in those high schools as well.

I returned to my classroom in 1981, only to be pulled out again in 1988 to revamp the system's ten-year-old gifted program, which had grown stale and ineffective. This time things were different. We had a new superintendent that I can only describe as a combination *idealist, optimizer,* and *fast tracker.* His philosophy, I soon discovered, was that you grow a school or school system by growing its employees. For him, people were the chief value of the school system, and their growth and maturity would eventually make possible student-learning success. During this time, my staff and I, with the aid of a considerable number of trained teachers, made changes that optimized student learning in our gifted programs. Without seeking the recognition, our program was recognized by North Carolina State University as one of the state's "best practices" programs, and in 1995, the Torrance Center for Creative Studies at the University of Georgia recognized our creativity and innovative practices for developing programs for young, minority, and disadvantaged bright children; for the successful ways we had developed mathematics and reading programs for our students; and for my work (along with Dr. Philip Vincent) in adapting philosophy, critical thinking, and ethics education to the gifted curriculum. Upon my retirement, I felt that we had grown the value of our programs, had witnessed student success over a period of more than twenty-four years, and that the system was poised to make additional changes that would grow the programs even more.

Making Decisions and Governing

Rather than asking, "what can I get from this job, or person," we can ask, "what does this person or job have to give if I cooperate and dedicate my abilities to improving my performance and that of others?"[34] Leadership is about building bridges, increasing personal value, and enhancing the capabilities of others. During the last few decades, leadership literature has pointed out that participatory forms of governance, more than those based on authority and power, has a double effect of boosting productivity and creating a sense of community in the workplace.[35] Shaffer and Anundsen have commented, "The brave ones have turned their neat, pyramid-shaped organizational charts into circular jumbles with leaders becoming servants and line employees experts."[36] Quite amazingly, during the decade of the 1990s, a central office with which I had been associated adjusted its top-down pyramid-shaped organizational chart annually and sometimes more than once a year. One assistant superintendent had a long list of supervisors, departmental heads, and curriculum/technology consultants listed under her name. She was overheard saying that she wanted everyone to know who was the "boss" and how many people reported to her. Peter M. Senge mentions in this regard, "Especially in the West, leaders are heroes—great men (and occasionally women) who rise to the fore in times of crisis. So long as such myths prevail, they reinforce a focus on short-term events and charismatic heroes rather than on systemic forces and collective learning. Leadership in learning organizations centers on subtler and ultimately more important work. In a learning organization, leaders' roles differ dramatically from that of the charismatic decision maker. Leaders are designers, teachers, and stewards."[37]

On January 2, 2003, Bill Parcells was hired as the new football coach for the Dallas Cowboy football team. His speech to the press was articulate and revealed a person who is committed to fundamental leadership principals. Taking notes in my den as Parcells spoke on ESPN, I was able to jot down nine ideas that he espoused.

1. He has a willingness to work with others and build a successful franchise through a competent support staff. He indicated that he would hire the best people available and provide them the resources to become successful.

2. He reiterated his love of the game. Leaders love what they are doing and transfer this love and dedication to the entire organization.

3. Parcells understands that the organization and its purposes (the game of football) are bigger than one person. A leader understands that the goals and objectives—the very existence of the organization (the school system, the sport, etc.) is greater that his or her persona. This understanding provides for the leader's dedication and moral consistency. It enables the leader to operate within the framework of the group as a team member.

4. A leader has a vision. Parcells, a proven leader and winner, set the bar high—to take the Cowboys to a Superbowl in the near future. Effective leaders set goals and establish ways to evaluate progress toward their completion.

5. He said that leadership is a cooperative effort, a joint venture, not a quest for power and authority.

6. Leadership is not satisfied with the status quo. Parcells said, "There will be changes."

7. Parcells said that he is flexible and willing to learn from others. This is a key ingredient of effective leadership.

8. Leaders understand to whom they are responsible. Parcells said that the Dallas Cowboys employed him and that his performance would be evaluated by the team's general manager and owner.

9. Finally, Parcells said that he was looking for team leadership: in coaches, in players, and in the management of the organization. Leaders seek to grow leaders and are willing to follow and serve those they lead.

Parcells has provided a leadership lesson for us and a clue to power dynamics in working relationships. Needless to say, leadership has always operated according to power dynamics. The questions school leaders need to answer are: can they choose to make their power dynamics conscious and, at the same time, cultivate them to match the school system's agreed upon values and vision? Do they dare take a chance of risking their power for harmony, equality or, perhaps both?

We have learned from social psychologists that "power dynamics" entails fluid relationships within an interactive system.[38] They tell us that interactive systems work best in rapidly changing, information-based organizations, that "with easy access to information through technology, power (which depends on information) diffuses in nonlinear fashion throughout organizations and neighborhoods and across national borders."[39] In other words, power is not something to be divided among people, with some receiving larger pieces than others. We share leadership power by our capabilities, credibility, and willingness to follow and lead when called upon. "It is a dynamic that strengthens everyone as it is shared."[40]

There is a practical lesson here. Ethical/servant leaders should base decision-making activity and governing on trust, commitment, and shared responsibility. Yet, many leaders continue to maintain hierarchical organizations based on fear and control patterns that shape their organizational culture. Even ethical and servant type communities are susceptible to fear and control. Employees may not be aware of undermining power issues until it is too late and the department, school, or system begins to dissolve through attrition. Shaffer and Anundsen comment, "Recognizing this and working as a group to change these dynamics can strengthen and deepen your community bonds."[41] This means that leaders will develop, as part of their group governance, a clearly defined purpose or shared direction and find ways to align new and old members with it.

M. Scott Peck reminds us to be on the alert because any person in an organization can come up with the best solution to a given problem and we should be prepared to follow that person's lead.[42] Sharing leadership is the dynamic key to making decisions and governing a school system. Max DePree, in his community-inspiring book *Leadership Is an Art*, defines a leader as a steward and as a servant of his followers with the assumption that developing the potential of each person in the organization benefits the entire group. This, he understands, stretches the concept of leadership beyond its traditional meaning founded on fear and control tactics. DePree advocates "roving leadership," where individuals are allowed to step forward and take charge as needed in their areas of competence regardless of their place in the organization. He reminds us that roving leadership requires a great deal of trust and understanding and a clear sense of our interdependence.[43]

The main theme of my 1995 book, *Bridges: Building Relationships and Resolving Problems* was that by inviting diverse views to the decision-making table, we can release and use the wisdom and power of our organization's diversity instead of crushing it, isolating it, or smoothing it into a world of gray tolerance. This requires cooperation with others and an attitude that together we can accomplish something truly wonderful.[44] There are advantages of joining together with a shared vision and compatible goals:

A group solving problems together will provide the members with a baseline of common understanding and information that cannot be replicated in a memo or by less personal means. Effective communication and understanding and the eventual acceptance of solutions are tied closely together.

A group setting allows members to jointly create with their diversity and provides an environment that legitimizes a variety of viewpoints.

A working group is capable of creating a greater quantity and variety of ideas than the average individual. There will be conflicts, but a true working community of individuals is not conflict avoiding; it is conflict resolving.

A good experience in a group can be contagious as it generates enthu siasm and commitment. Teamwork is able to build consensus, resolve difficult issues, and move forward to the completion of goals and objectives.

New ideas and innovations come from open and free discussions. Coercion and intimidation only cause resentment and bring nothing new to the table. An inviting environment enables the natural creativity of individuals to emerge and invigorates group productivity.

Finally, open discussions and problem solving allow individuals to identify with solutions and actions to be undertaken. Most people feel positive about a decision if they have had an opportunity to participate and have been made aware of the value of their contribution.

Open discussion, as a matter of policy, should not bruise egos. Egos should be checked at the door so that a free flow of ideas can take place. This will enable both innovation to occur and the ability to incorporate the views of many into the performance standards and indicators of the school system.

Practicing consensus can build community. Workplace teams, teachers, principals, and superintendents can practice consensus to make the shift from autocratic leadership to servant/ethical leadership. Such a move, observes Shaffer and Anundsen, will increase your understanding of the point of view of others and your respect for them as well as your perception of yourselves as a group.[45] They list the following behaviors needed to make consensus work[46]:

1. Trust that a wise decision or solution exists and that the group can find it.
2. Commit oneself to the integrity and value of the group.
3. Provide opportunity for everyone to have input.
4. Have a willingness to listen and to pay attention to each other and the nuances they bring to the table.
5. Acknowledge the feelings of others, the stake they have in the decision, and be willing to resolve conflicts with them.
6. Put forth an honest effort to find out what is best for the group.
7. Be patient. Consensus takes longer than a majority vote, especially when conflicts become evident.
8. Be honest and willing to communicate even an unpopular position.
9. Use an experienced facilitator who can discriminate between false consensus (people giving in to stronger members, resulting in weaker commitment) and true consensus.

Making decisions and governing is an activity in consensus building. This is one of the most important strategies for the success of a school or school system. An ethical leader will understand consensus in an integrated group is not necessarily group unanimity. Following the steps below will greatly assist schools and educational groups maintain both their ethical demeanor and their productivity when working with others:

Always express your point of view clearly and directly.
Jointly define the conflict in a way that it can be solved.
Communicate positions and feelings openly and honestly.
Communicate cooperative intentions and hold to this intention.
Take the other person's perspective.
Avoid being judgmental.
Negotiate in good faith.
Reach an agreement that specifies the joint resolution adopted.

In our society there are two beliefs that prevent leaders from becoming ethical and servant leaders and hamper the positive outcomes of conflict resolution. These are a kind of cultural machismo against intimate self-disclosure based on the view that open sharing is a sign of weakness, exhibitionism, or mental illness; and the belief that misrepresentation is necessary to achieve or maintain power and influence in an organization and in society. Working with department heads and superintendent-level educators is difficult if they make it a matter of policy to withhold vital information from their staffs. Withholding information is another way of saying, "There are some who are privileged and some who are not. Guess which one you are?" Relationship-building in those situations is always difficult and strained. The climate is power-oriented and lacks a foundation built on integrity and trust.

The fact is that self-disclosure demands a willingness to assume responsibility for making any changes in ourselves that we think important. Taking responsibility for ourselves first is perhaps our greatest need and one that will open a door to more effective ethical leadership. Channeling change into growth is paramount for each leader, but it is not automatic. There are three different types of change that will challenge our decision making and governing of a school, classroom, or school system.

First-order change occurs within groups and happens to individuals. First-order change usually doesn't change the entire group or organization, but it does change the person and those closest to that person. A teacher may become a principal and now govern those he or she once worked with in more collegial relationships. A student may graduate from a school, then college, and return to his or her old school as a teacher. In either case, the school doesn't undergo massive change, but the relationships within that school and among those who have changed must be adjusted.

Second-order change alters the very fabric of the school or school system. Marriage, birth, illness, and death are second-order changes. A superintendent or principal becomes ill and a substitute is brought in for a while, or the person dies and must be replaced all together. When this occurs, the school or system can be dramatically changed in unforeseen ways. Second-order change may also occur within a person. After many years of hard work, a young principal finally earns a doctorate in education and gains confidence that was never demonstrated before earning this degree; or having tried many times, the superintendent fails to pass his or her exams and doesn't earn a doctorate in education administration.

This failure could result in a loss in confidence and resentment toward those who have earned that particular degree.

Third-order change involves innovation and is one of the keys to effective leadership, problem solving, and decision making. It allows leaders to look at problems and individuals in new ways and search for the added value they can bring to the school system. Whether first-order change or second-order change, opportunities are provided for innovation or to rebuild one's leadership style on a different set of beliefs and values. This often occurs when roles and relationships are changed or when one is given additional responsibilities. For example, a highly trained exceptional children's specialist with many years of experience returns to school and achieves a principal's certification. She applies for and is assigned to a medium-sized elementary school as its assistant principal. In her new role, the old relationships, both at the central office and in her new school, are changed. She not only speaks with authority, she now has the authority to put her knowledge to work at this school. She must rebuild her leadership role on a different level. Her old colleagues at the central office must now serve her needs and those of the elementary school. In a recent interview, she reported that her responsibilities have actually intensified as she is presently charged with getting results in her assigned school.[47]

The variables related to change, innovation, and leadership are many. They may cause us to act negatively or positively when situations occur that cause conflict in our lives. Leaders especially must remember who they are and where they are when dramatic shifts and changes occur in their lives and in the institutions they govern. Somehow and in some way they must muster their inner forces—their character—to positively and effectively build workable solutions in the face of disappointing and difficult situations. Of course, this may not always happen. There are barriers that may prevent us from making effective changes in our lives and within the groups in which we participate. These barriers may include fear of failure, the belief that change is unnecessary, lack of emotional support, not being desperate enough to respond to changing conditions, being afraid to take risks, or adapting an avoidance persona that insulates us from the perceived dangers that change may bring.

A story may illustrate what avoidance can do to a person and an organization. Many years ago I participated in hiring a consultant who had the responsibility of managing, building, and enriching the gifted programs in four elementary schools. During her second year on the job,

I told the entire staff that I would be visiting their schools on a regular basis—not to check up on anyone—but to run an informal assessment of their work and to evaluate the needs they had presented to me in the previous months. I also told them that I would be visiting on the days when they were scheduled to be working at specified schools. I told each of them that I wanted to support them in person and that I wanted our work to become a team effort. I also said that our programs are not about you and they are not about me; rather, they are about providing enriching educational opportunities for gifted children, helping teachers improve their knowledge and methods, and nurturing school leaders to be sensitive to our purposes.

In the course of these visitations, I failed to meet with one consultant. Other staff members were on the job, and some of them had set up meetings with teachers so that I could hear from them how well the consultant was meeting their needs and what other resources they needed to complete their jobs. Over a period of three months I returned to these schools, but I never could find this one consultant. I talked with the teachers in her schools and the principals about her work. They were consistent in their evaluations: "We never see her. We have the materials we request from your office, but she is never here to provide support and consultations."

My first response to this was to talk with the consultant in my office. She assured me she was at each of these schools when scheduled and that I had just missed her. She indicated that she was probably working with some of the students in another part of the campus. Having completed my rounds with the other consultants, I made it a point to follow her schedule and be at each of her schools every morning and in the afternoon. I did not tell her what I was doing, but I had to see for myself what she was doing before proceeding to talk to my superiors about her. I soon became exasperated trying to locate her; she was not in her office and she was not following her reported schedule.

One day, while in a local drug store, I ran into a friend who happened to live beside this particular consultant. He asked me if she still worked for our school system, and I said she did. He looked puzzled and replied that almost every day, when he came home for lunch, she was in her garden working with her flowers. He said the way that she was dressed told him that she probably had not gone to work that day or was taking part of the day off. The problem was that this was not on her schedule or mine. He also said this was not an everyday occurrence, but it was happening two or three times a week. The next week, I checked the consultant's schedule and when I could not find her at her designated school, drove by her house. There she was, working in her flower garden.

Later that day I talked with the assistant superintendent for human services and asked her advice about approaching this problem. The consultant had been an excellent teacher for us for many years. She had no problems indicated in her personnel file that would give us a clue to what was going on with her now. Together we decided that I would talk with her as a friend, letting her know what I knew and what the teachers and principals had said. I would then give her a chance to explain her seemingly strange behavior. We also found a teaching vacancy in one of our schools where she could be moved immediately if that was the decision. The decision was made easy by her own requests during our meeting. I told her about my investigation and that I had discovered her working in her flower garden during working hours. I told her that the teachers and principals in her assigned schools were equally puzzled about not seeing her on her regular weekly rounds. Her response was immediate: she did not deny her behavior or try to persuade me to let it pass. She simply said that she was overwhelmed by the responsibilities of her job and that she would like to return to the classroom as a teacher. The next morning she was teaching reading to sixth graders in one of our elementary schools.

There is another story about trying to avoid responsibility that may help illustrate the problems connected with change, the fear of failure, and accepting responsibility for one's assigned job. One Friday afternoon, when most central office personal had left for the weekend, a call came in from a parent who was ready to sue an exceptional children's coordinator, the superintendent, a principal, and the board of education. She said that the coordinator had to be aware of her problem, one that had been going on for several weeks. At the beginning of that school year, her son had not been placed appropriately in programs for the gifted and talented. All the gifted children in her son's grade level—except her son—had been placed with a teacher who was certified in gifted education. In this way the teacher could more appropriately develop lesson plans and activities that would enhance the students' academic talents. The teacher could write a group education plan for these students, a method that streamlined paperwork and made her job more efficient. This one boy was left of the equation for a reason that no one could figure out. He was placed with a teacher who was also certified in gifted education. While this was seemingly appropriate, research in gifted education had shown that gifted children needed the opportunity to work with one another and interact with each other academically. That too was the policy of the school system. Therefore, when the parent was handed a group education plan to sign, she refused, saying, "What group is my child in?"

The elementary gifted consultant who worked out of the exceptional children's department was aware of this situation and had neither resolved the problem nor brought it to the attention of the departmental director. The situation had continued to simmer for several weeks until the parent had had enough and called the exceptional children's director with a threat of a lawsuit. Upon talking with the gifted consultant, the director discovered that she had known about the situation for quite awhile but did not want to be caught in the middle between a principal and a parent, so she ignored the situation hoping that it would work itself out. Knowing provisions of state exceptional children's regulations and knowing the board of education's policies on this matter, she had both the knowledge and authority to explain this to the principal and resolve the problem. If, when informed of these matters, the principal still refused to follow regulation and policy, the consultant should have taken this matter to the next level and informed her supervisor. This is microknowledge that the director needed but had to find out from the parties involved. Avoidance of responsibility never works; it merely compounds problems and confuses situations as excuses for either not knowing or not acting are handed out. Although it took several days to resolve this problem, the value of the consultant and the principal was diminished in the process. The questions became: "Who can you trust?" and "Who will step up and take on leadership responsibilities?"

Governing and making decisions as an ethical leader means, among other things, that we will have to adapt to change; that we must reorient our lives to different points of view, different values, and different ways that others work out their problems. We will not always be successful, but when we care for people and try to put them in situations where they can be productive and feel good about their work, our moral leadership will become evident. Success will come if we have patience, give ourselves permission to change, find our own comfort zone, and continue to grow our own value and that of our employees. When we add support from friends, family, and coworkers and are persistent and work on learning to trust, leading will become much easier. Our role is to build relationships and resolve conflicts—to build bridges to others—and find support and connection in a fragmented world.

Activities That Promote Ethical Leadership

1. List three to five ways that leadership has to be earned. Discuss your answers in a small group, and include a consensus list on a chart. Share them with the entire group.

2. In your group, choose one of the seven skills for improving group efficiency. Brainstorm ways you and others can improve the efficiency and productivity of groups under your leadership.

3. Explain and give three examples supporting the statement: "ethical leadership is about service and social interdependency."

4. Why is working in a cooperative, ethical environment essential for all school personnel?

5. Do you agree or disagree with George Soros who says those who claim to know all the answers would create a closed society? Explain and justify your response.

6. Give three or four reasons why building relationships, respect for others, and communication work together to sustain supportive climates for teaching and learning.

7. What do you think is meant by the statement, "We give birth to ourselves in the relationships we form"?

8. In striving to become an ethical/servant leader, what might you do to increase the efficiency and productivity of teachers, principals, students, or supervisors in your care? Make a list and share your responses with the entire group?

5

Leadership Climate: A Focus on Growing Leaders

Empowerment and Responsibility

Educational leaders are continuously drawn in different directions. They have a professional and ethical obligation to use their training and knowledge to educate children—to stay on the growing edge of their profession by faithfully updating their methods and networking with others who, like themselves, are trying to grow their value and increase their effectiveness. They must also cope with the annual changes brought about by politicians and their pronounced need to control educational curricula, the methods of teaching, the evaluation of students, and the assessment of teachers. Many times these two goals run in opposing directions.

Colleges of education, especially in research universities, are still producing knowledge workers on the growing edge of their craft, but this is not always the reality of the young teacher's world. Schools of education stubbornly hold to their faith in the efficacy of statistical formulae as the way to resolve the major issues of teaching and learning. And, as Bruce S. Thornton surmises, "all their works create little more than new virtues of false knowledge raising the fever of discontent."[1] He says, "The desire to create new men through rational technique has usually ended up creating new corpses."[2] This is a dilemma in which education finds itself today.

Consider the follow example from Ridgeland, South Carolina: Under the heading, "S.C. Education Accountability,"[3] the Associated Press provided an account of lost accountability in Ridgeland. The report said, "Failing schools in Jasper County are under review by the state. Two three-person evaluation teams visited Jasper County High School and

145

Ridgeland Middle School to review records and interview staff to identify trouble spots." Edmond Burnes, Jasper High principal, said, "I believe
there will be an indication that we need to continue to work toward and
monitor the rigor of instruction, to see whether the instruction is challenging and to see whether the intensity level is high enough." The newly
appointed principal at Jasper High School also reported that academic
plans were in place, "but weren't being followed." I take that to mean that
they were not being followed in the years previous to his appointment
and that he must now force the issue of following mandated procedures
on the educational workforce in the school. In their 2001 evaluation report,
Jasper High failed in another area; namely, not adequately distributing
responsibility for improving student performance among administrators,
teachers, parents, and students.

Jasper County and Ridgeland are located on Highway 17 halfway
between Charleston and Savannah and adjacent to Hilton Head, one of
the major resorts in South Carolina. The Jasper County website says,

> A combination of public schools, private academies and nearby colleges
> reflects Jasper County's sensitivity and commitment to education at all
> levels, including the refinement of workplace skills available through a
> neighboring technical college. A four-year satellite campus for the Uni-
> versity of South Carolina at the Jasper County line is now under con-
> struction. The estimated labor force within a 30-mile radius of the
> county's geographic center numbers in excess of 200,000 people. Also,
> a fully developed infrastructure network assures water, sewer, electric
> power and telecommunications throughout the county and the region.
> Within 30 miles of the county center, five major hospitals can be
> accessed.
>
> Three major industrial parks host a panoply of industrial activities
> within the County. Building material fabrication, musical instrument
> manufacturing, food processing, bulk export and import products, and
> truck chassis manufacture are but a few of the many industrial employ-
> ers in the County. In the November of 1999, Jasper County reported an
> unemployment rate of 2.8%, which is indicative of the health of the
> County's economy. With the large labor force and each park sufficiently
> supplied with water, sewer, electric power, and superior roads, it is no
> surprise that Jasper County's economic engine is running on all cylin-
> ders.
>
> Ridgeland is in the Jasper County School District, a single district
> that serves the entire county. Students who attend public school enjoy
> low teacher to student ratios, small classes, computer labs in all schools,
> and gifted, early education, and special needs programs. The school dis-
> trict has implemented a "reengineering" effort in all schools to rededi-
> cate themselves to the mission and beliefs of the district. Ridgeland has
> one high school (Jasper County High School), one middle school
> (Ridgeland Middle), two elementary schools (Ridgeland Elementary

and West Hardeeville Elementary), one vocational school (The Academy for Career Excellence). A private school is also available in Ridgeland—ages K through 12.[4]

Not knowing the complete details about the Ridgeland community and the kind of families who live there, and not having inside information about the qualifications of the high school and middle school staff, it's very difficult to make a judgment in this case. What we can construe from this report is that there has been an accountability failure. Another way of saying that is there has been an empowerment failure. For example, the new principal of the high school admitted that the level of classroom instruction may not be appropriate—the rigor of the instruction and the level of the instruction were cited. The principal said that academic plans were in place but were not being followed. Improvements were cited, such as the implementation of eighteen programs, including SAT and exit exam-preparation classes that he thinks addresses many of the concerns of the 2001 evaluation report. Finally, the 2001 evaluation report said that educational responsibilities for improving student performance had not been distributed among administrators, teachers, parents, and students.

Mark Bounds, South Carolina's state department of public instruction's coordinator for the state's external review teams, commented that the state department and the local schools are in a partnership. He said, "It's not: we're going to come down there and tell the school what to do. The external review is the beginning of a process. You can't hit a target you can't see, so what we're trying to do is identify the target and what can we do to help." This statement is puzzling for it has already been noted that low student academic performance is the problem at the high school and that accountability by all major stakeholders—teachers, administrators, parents, and students—is part of the solution. Accordingly, once both the state department and the school system decide on measures to improve teaching and learning in Jasper High School and at Ridgeland Middle School, state law requires schools to correct the problems or face state takeover.

Educators at all levels, who desire the freedom to use their expertise without overt pressure from supervisors, superintendents, or state departments of public instruction must be aware that empowerment is not a license to "do as you want." Rather, empowerment entails a professional and ethical responsibility to use one's capabilities to maximize systemic goals, the learning of students, and personal development. The point made by the principal of Jasper High School about not adequately distributing educational responsibility is a point well taken. William Rasberry, writing for the *Washington Post* Writers Group on December 14, 2002,[5] focuses on parental responsibility in the education of youth and asks, "Can we save the children?" He answers, "Instead of saying it's not our fault, let's do something about it." He paints the following picture, "Thousands of black children are drifting downstream toward a deadly waterfall. And we black adults are standing along the bank reassuring ourselves, 'Well, at least it's not our fault.'" He comments that he has no interest in disputing this assertion but would like to focus on the question, "What can we do to save our children?"

Referring to black children, Rasberry says that there is no doubt they are in trouble. He observes that no one questions the origins of this trouble: slavery, Jim Crow, political powerlessness, and disproportionate poverty and their persistent effects today. He points out that in John Ogbu's forthcoming book, *Black Students in an Affluent Suburb*, Ogbu provides an explanation why the children of wealthy black professionals in Shaker Heights, Ohio, lag behind their white counterparts academically. Rasberry says, "Ogbu, a professor of anthropology at the University of California, is inclined to blame a black culture that has successful black parents failing to pass along to their children the values that produced their own success and spending too little time tracking their children's academic progress."

Again the question of accountability is raised in the face of the quest for empowerment. Rasberry quotes Ogbu as saying, "No matter how you reform schools, it's not going to solve the problem. There are two parts of the problem, society and schools on one hand and the black community on the other hand." Rasberry concurs: "We've been ready enough with our indictment of society and the schools.... All I know is that if we see the problem as entirely outside ourselves, we are likely to see the solution as out of our hands."

Rasberry is correct—empowerment entails responsibility—and not just among the African-American community, but also among those where there has been a tradition of educational low performance: in the South, in Appalachia, among minorities, and in our inner cities. For too long we have accepted the statistics on these groups and regions, as "that's just the way things are." Statistics aren't facts, chiseled in stone. A statistical spread on a bell-shaped curve is not an absolute. Statistical numbers change with changing reality. Statistics describe what has occurred and project what probably will occur if present conditions go unchanged. They are not prescriptive, nor are they fatalistic. We should not assume that our students will always mirror the highs and lows of preconceived statistical patterns. Assuming that some students will always be on the low end seems to give us permission to ignore their needs. Parents, community leaders, teachers, and administrators have a responsibility for the education of their youth, of regenerating and improving their spiritual, economic, and academic competence no matter what their present level of academic success or economic status.

So before we discuss the importance of empowerment, we must understand the human and social fact of responsibility. Typically, we tend not to hold people responsible if they are not free; that is, if they do not have the mental or physical resources to make improvements, or are otherwise hampered by their sociocultural history. Of course, none of us are totally free and, therefore, can't be held totally responsible for all the ills of society or education. We are partially free and partially unfree, says Lawrence M. Hinman, and "there is good reason for believing that progress in life consists, at least in part, in moving from a state of unfreedom to one of freedom."[6] He says, "The point here is that, after we realize that we are causally influenced in a particular way, we are often free to choose to accept or reject that influence. Instead of making us less free, knowledge of deterministic influences may actually liberate us from their domination."[7] We are able to conclude that when educational leaders know what problems are plaguing their efforts to educate students, they are able—if motivated and committed—to find solutions that will improve teaching and learning processes.

Harold S. Kushner encourages us to "live a life that matters"[8] and asks the question, "What kind of person do you want to be?" He comments, "Only morally sensitive people struggle with the gap between who they are and who they know they ought to be."[9] When talking about ethical leadership and management, he quotes Kenneth Blanchard, author of *One Minute Manager*, and Norman Vincent Peale, who together authored *The Power of Ethical Management*, as saying, "There is no right way to do a wrong thing." Their book, he observes, is "a plea for integrity in the business world, both as a tactic and as a matter of principle."[10]

What we learn as we read these authors and observe the world of education unfolding before us is that in our quest to reclaim the empowerment and dignity that has been lost under layer after layer of bureaucratic legislation and top-down control by an autocratic administration may not be the bargain we are actually searching for. Throughout my life, whenever leadership was needed in a situation, someone usually said, "Someone needs to step up to the plate." Most will not "step up" and be counted for or against a program, a mandate, or an untenable situation. They cry, "Don't blame me!" when things go wrong, and complain behind the scenes but don't accept the responsibilities that ethical leadership and empowerment bring. As Kushner says, "each person who chooses to be generous rather than selfish, to be truthful rather than deceptive, represents a vote for a world of generosity and truth rather than selfishness and deception."[11] But more than this, if they also choose to lead rather than follow, to be responsible rather than irresponsible, they represent ethically empowered leadership and are in a position to change their world for the better.

The following example adds to our insights about empowerment and responsibility. Bob Herbert of the *New York Times* reports about education in economically depressed communities and concludes, "Commitment leads to excellence in poor, rural area."[12] He was talking about the Gaston College Preparatory School in rural eastern North Carolina, just across the Virginia border. There are only two grades in this school, the fifth and sixth. A seventh and eighth grade will be added over the next two years. Herbert visited Gaston Prep because he heard it was a remarkable school. He says, "It's in a region that is struggling economically and is not known for its academic excellence. Most of the students at the school are black, and nearly all of them are poor. Most of the other schools available to them are burdened with problems that show no signs of easing." He says that the atmosphere at Gaston is almost idyllic. The children are well behaved and the classroom work is intense. Students report that there is no fighting or bullying at the school and that they have to work hard there.

Gaston Prep is one of fifteen Knowledge Is Power Program (KIPP) schools in the United States. This program began in Houston, Texas, and has grown as one of the most academically sound public school programs in the nation. Herbert continues, "The key to the success of the schools seems to be the requirement that there be a strong commitment in the very beginning by pupils, parents, and a team of extremely dedicated teachers to put forth whatever effort is necessary to enable the children to learn." At Gaston, the school day lasts from 7:30 a.m. to 5 p.m., which provides time for additional classroom work and extracurricular activities. After that there are two hours of homework. Students also attend classes every other Saturday, and there are three weeks of summer school each year.

Does all this work pay off? Consider: KIPP students routinely outperform most of their public school peers. In each of its first seven years, the KIPP Academy in Houston has been named a Texas exemplary school. For five straight years, the KIPP Academy in the Bronx, New York, has outperformed all other public schools in New York City in mathematics and reading. Its student orchestra is considered one of the finest in the nation.

One interesting fact about KIPP schools is that they do not seek out top students. Students are chosen by lottery, and some are students with special needs. In the year before they attended Gaston Prep, only 53 percent of the first class of fifth graders had passed the North Carolina statewide reading examination. After only one year, 93 percent passed, including 82 percent of the students with special needs. Gaston Prep is already the highest performing public school in all of the four counties from which its students are drawn. Herbert has his doubts if the KIPP program can be replicated on a wide scale. He says, "I wonder how much of a commitment could be secured from parents in general, or from teachers in general, or students in general." He quotes Mike Feinberg, a Teach for America alumni, who said, "We are never going to end the day shrugging our shoulders and making excuses. If there's a problem, if something is impeding the success of our kids, that needs to be solved one way or another."[13]

Issues of empowerment and responsibility are made quite clear in these examples: if teachers, principals, and other educational professionals wish to have the freedom and empowerment to do their work without overt supervision, then they must take responsibility for the results of their efforts. Responsibility entails accountability, and these two actions are the flip side of empowerment. Bob Herbert concluded, "Long hours, hard work, discipline; like I said, I don't know how easily that gets replicated. But schools that thrive in the inner city and in poor rural areas deserve, at the very least, some very close attention."

We should understand too that "empowerment" is not the same as "willpower." Willpower is personal; it is the ability to "psych ourselves up" to overpower all forms of resistance to achieving our goals. Peter Senge says, "Willpower is so common among highly successful people that many see its characteristics as synonymous with success: a maniacal focus on goals, willingness to 'pay the price,' ability to defeat any opposition and surmount any obstacle."[14] The problem Senge sees with willpower is that the leader is acting alone, without leverage, leaving the underlying system of structural conflict unaltered. He comments, "Despite significant accomplishments, many 'highly successful people' still feel a deep, usually unspoken, sense of powerlessness in critical areas of their lives—such as in their personal and family relationships, or in their ability to achieve a sense of peace and spiritual fulfillment."[15]

To overcome this problem, Kevin Cashman recommends balancing *personal power* with *synergy power* and *contribution power*. He says, "If leaders attempt to use their personal power to achieve results while ignoring synergy power—a common dominant, driven leadership style— real contribution and a people-centered culture are sacrificed on the altar of immediate achievement."[16] Empowerment is important. As Cashman reminds us, "Leadership will not add enough value if it only comes from the top—it needs to come from the very guts of the business itself to make a meaningful and enduring difference."[17] Thus, not only the school superintendent or the school board are the generators of power and do not bear all the responsibility for the education of youngsters in the school system. Principals, teachers, and parents are also empowered to make a difference. They too are to be held accountable for the quality of the role each of them plays. Students too are empowered to learn and should be held accountable for the effort that they put in. Even more significant are the relationships created within the school system between these stakeholders. "Relationships," says Cashman, "are the bridges that connect authentic self-expression to creating value. Leadership is not self-expression for its own sake; it's self-expression that makes a difference, that enriches the lives of others. Leadership does not exist in a vacuum—it always operates in context, in relationships."[18]

Empowerment as Enabling Performance

Reviewing the literature on leadership, we discover that there are three basic views on empowerment, and although they aim at the same results, they rely on fundamentally different assumptions: Some believe that the leader should actively empower others by giving them the authority to act without overt direction from someone in the command chain above them, that decisions need to be made closest to the problem. The second view is that the executive leader and all leaders in between should create a leadership climate within the organization so that those who can lead actually have the opportunity and means to step forward and lead. A third view says that today's knowledge workers don't need permission to act—make decisions, carry out tasks, or problem solve; that they have the knowledge sufficient to complete tasks, carry through with the goals of the organization, and are adequately motivated to make decisions at their level of performance.

Without arguing the merits of these three points of view, we can conclude that empowerment—whether coming from the top, built into the organizational climate, or coming from self-motivation and expertise—has the same goal: enabling the performance of all who work within the school system, including students and their parents. Saying this, we should understand that we are walking a tightrope between personal power and synergy power. Synergy power is the power that comes from our own capabilities and networking with others who share our goals and those of the school system itself. On the other hand, we can't have synergy power or even contribution power without exercising our personal power. Russ Moxley, at the Center for Creative Leadership, speaking of the partnership model of leadership says that power comes from our own gifts and skills, our competence and our expertise. He comments, "No two individuals carry the same combination of talents and challenges. Our task is to appreciate, lay claim to, and begin to use our original medicine. Power is still present in the relationship, but it comes from within the individuals, not from a position. No person has power over others. The partnership model is based on covenant and not coercion, on commitment and not compliance. It may sound quaint, but in the long run personal power is the only source of real power we have."[19]

Moxley urges each of us to claim our personal power, "the power that is based on belief in our self-worth, knowledge of our competence and expertise, and use of our native talents or gifts. This kind of power comes from within. It is not power over; it is 'power to': the power to influence people and have an impact on events."[20] Moxley says that the use of personal power creates trust and openness, builds relationships, and engenders partnerships with others.

Claiming our personal power within a partnership model of leadership means that we speak and act on the truth that is inside us. There is no more saying yes when we want to say no; no more remaining silent when the group is making a decision we know will take us in a wrong direction; no more agreeing with the boss in the public meeting only to openly criticize him during the coffee break. We no longer accept responsibility for the thoughts and feelings of others, and we don't blame others for our personal shortcomings. It is better that we act as if we are 100 percent responsible than blame others. Blaming others gives away our power because it points to our inability to behave responsibly or change existing situations. When claiming our person power we become more proactive, less reactive.

We choose to be involved in the activities of leadership. We expect to be treated as a partner, and we act as a partner. We search for common ground and look for win-win situations where everyone is involved. We learn to respect others, even when they disagree with us. We also learn that collaboration is more meaningful than competition, and community than hierarchy. Finally, we act responsibly and are accountable even if we don't have authority. No more "change has to start at the top" or "they won't let us do it."[21] We realize that leadership begins with us and are willing to take up the mantle.

Steven Covey outlines six basic conditions of empowerment. His reasoning is based on one simple belief, namely, that "sound conclusions can come only from consistent reasoning based on a correct premise or assumption."[22] The premise that forms the starting point for Covey is that in order "to motivate people to peak performance, we must find the areas where organizational needs and goals overlap individual needs, goals, and capabilities."[23] That is, we must join personal power with synergy power. Together, they enable us to contribute to the greater good of the organization; they gel into contribution power. This premise leads us to his first basic condition for empowerment, the need to set up win-win agreements where, when once established, people could govern or supervise themselves in terms of that agreement. Leaders could then become sources of help and assist employees by establishing helpful organizational systems within which self-directing, self-controlling employees could work toward keeping and fulfilling their end of the agreement. Covey comments, "Essentially the win-win agreement is a psychological contract between manager and subordinate."[24] It represents a clear mutual understanding and commitment regarding expectations in five areas[25]:

First, Covey says, "The concept of win-win suggests that managers and employees clarify expectations and mutually commit themselves to getting desired results."[26] This may be a commitment between superintendent and principal, principal and teacher, teacher and student, or a program director and a central office specialist. Each educator should be committed to getting results, letting those closest to the problem help determine the best means and methods to be used. Target dates and/or timelines need to be established for the accomplishment of objectives, which represent the overlap between the organizational strategy, goals, job design and the personal values, goals, needs, and capabilities of employees.

Second, guidelines should be set by communicating whatever principles, policies, and procedures are considered essential to getting desired results. At whatever level, the leader should set forth as few procedures as possible to allow those closest to the situation the freedom and flexibility to complete the job. This unfreezes people and gives them an opportunity to use their initiative and good judgment. What must also be stressed here is the need for consistency in teaching methodology, terminology, and procedures. For example, especially in grades K through 2, reading methods and terminology should generally be the same. When one grade level or one teacher strays too far from the core of what the others are saying and doing, it only confuses children in the beginning stages of learning to read (or compute). When a principal discovers this happening, respect dictates sitting down and discussing the situation and working out the problem amicably. It should be pointed out that using the same methods and the same terminology is not the same as teaching "every child the same way and at the same pace." This usually slows down the reading ability of gifted readers and doesn't provide the individualized procedures needed by the student who has reading difficulties.

Although it is necessary to set up guidelines and expectations, too much control often has negative results. On the other side, when guidelines and expectations are not firmly established, teachers and principals may think they have unlimited freedom and flexibility to do whatever is necessary to accomplish agreed-upon goals and many times end up reinventing the wheel. The ethical/servant leader, understanding the delicate balance between preserving the dignity of the teacher and the goals of the school, should know that there are some areas of responsibility where the initiative level would simply be "to wait until told, while in other areas, higher levels could be exercised, including 'use your own good judgment and do what you think is appropriate; let us know routinely what you're doing and what the results are.'"[27]

Third, Covey says leaders are responsible for identifying available resources, which may include financial, human, technical, and organizational property. In areas of human and technical resources, continuous training is needed for the educator-as-knowledge-worker to compete and stay abreast of current methods, procedures, and programs. Central office professionals and principals may also need to indicate how these various resources could be used to positively influence the teaching-learning process. Networking and sharing experiences are means of increasing knowledge and allowing dialogue. Trail and error can also be used to determine the best use of new information and technology.

Fourth, the leader has the responsibility for defining accountability. Holding everyone responsible for results, Covey observes, "puts teeth into the win-win agreement. If there is no accountability, people gradually lose their sense of responsibility and start blaming circumstances or other people for poor performance. But when people participate in setting the exact standard of acceptable performance, they feel a deep sense of responsibility to get desired results."[28]

Covey provides three ways in which results can be evaluated: measurement, observation, and discernment. These methods are basic for evaluating the educators' performance. Measurement will use statistical evaluation as well as comparing and contrasting student performance over several years. Principals and superintendents will also want to put their eyes on school operations, classrooms, and program implementations. Judgments will be made using one's experience to discern subtle changes in teacher performance and student reactions.

Teachers and other educators should know, up front, how they will be evaluated—the results for which they are held accountable. Principals and superintendents should hold regular accountability sessions, where the trust level is high. In these meetings educational stakeholders at every level should be afforded the opportunity to participate in determining goals, measurements, and means of accountability. Covey says that his experience is that employees will be much harder on themselves when there is a working partnership between employer and employee. He comments, "Also, when trust is high, discernment is often more accurate than so-called objective measurement. That's because people know in their hearts much more than the measurement system can reveal about their performance."[29]

Finally, the leader's responsibility is to assess and determine consequences—whether desired results were or were not achieved. Positive consequences could include rewards such as additional pay, recognition, advancement, additional training, or other perks. Inadequate growth may mean continued observation, discussion with stakeholders, and additional training. It may also entail personnel changes, changes in methods, and the application of needed resources before performance demonstrates an upward growth.

According to Covey, the purpose of these five features of empowerment, of win-win agreements, is to assist employees to work toward self-management. John C. Maxwell agrees. He says, "A key to empowering others is high belief in people."[30] Leadership analysts Lynne McFarland, Larry Senn, and John Childress have also commented, "the empowerment leadership model shifts away from 'position power' where all people are given leadership roles so they can contribute to their fullest capacity."[31]

Serving Others

The stage has been set and the door has been opened for educational leaders to become more ethical in their dealings with each other. In education today, the stakes are too high for superintendents or principals, no matter how large or small the school system or school, to manage autocratically. The age of the knowledge worker calls for positionless power and decentralized decision making. The role of leadership is to serve those we lead to improve their value, our own value, and the value of the educational organization. We have discovered that leadership is found at every level—beginning with parents, in the classroom, the athletic field, in the principal's office, and at various levels within the central office of school districts. Our theme has been "everyone a leader," but just not a leader, an ethical and servant leader. Before moving to the last chapter and a discussion of leadership evaluation, we need to conclude our discussion of this topic with some practical suggestions for serving others in ethically significant ways.

There is nothing in the literature of leadership or in our discussion of ethical and servant leadership that says that leaders should not be tough, demanding, and unyielding with respect to the highest standards of the educational profession. One does not have to give up high standards to become an ethical and servant leader. On the contrary, ethical leadership means holding oneself and others to the highest standards possible. It also means reaching these standards and maintaining the quality of the teaching-learning processes by serving and lifting others rather than by controlling, ordering, and demeaning their value. The point is quite simple: schools will become more productive when leadership is charged with ethical principals and when ethical leaders ask first, "How can I help you?" rather than "Don't ask questions, just do as you are told." Servant leadership induces community into organizations and, when laced with ethical principals, holds the dignity and importance of fellow-educators, students, and their parents in the highest regard. After all, families and the community are the customers of professional educational organizations. As educational leaders, our role is to increase their value through learning. As their value is increased, the importance of schools and teachers is also acknowledged.

David M. Noer, a senior vice president for training and education at the Center for Creative Leadership with worldwide responsibility for the center's training and educational activities, says, "The increasingly voiced question is, 'After all the layoffs, early retirements, downsizing, and restructuring, what is the glue that holds this organization together?'"[32] He acknowledges ethical/servant leadership as that "glue." Noer makes three points that are pertinent to organizations—especially school systems and schools—where leadership change is an ongoing occurrence:

1. Organizational commitment and productivity are not diminished by loyalty to oneself, the work team, and the profession.

2. Leadership is very different in a liberated workforce that is unencumbered by fear, false expectations of promotions, or the distractions of politics and trying to impress the boss.

3. When people stay in a personal relationship because they choose to be there and know they have the no-fault option of leaving, when armies are made up of volunteers and not conscripts, and when people choose to stay in an organization because of the work and the customers, knowing that they may not be able to stay for an entire career, they tend to be much more productive and committed. This is perhaps the most profound learning, which I call *the paradox of freedom. The paradox of job security* is that when people choose to stay for the right reasons (the work and the customer), as opposed to the wrong reasons (false expectations of job security), their job security tends to increase![33]

Noer's recipe for glue contains the following:

1. Use the clear water of undiluted human spirit.

2. Take special care not to contaminate with preconceived ideas or to pollute with excess control.

3. Fill slowly; notice that the pot only fills from the bottom up. He says, "It's impossible to fill it from the top down!"

4. Stir in equal parts of customer focus and pride in good work.

5. Blend in a liberal portion of diversity, one part self-esteem, and one part tolerance.

6. Fold in accountability.

7. Simmer until smooth and thick; stir with shared leadership and clear goals.

8. Garnish with a topping of core values.

9. Serve by coating all boxes in the organizational chart, paying particular attention to the white spaces. With proper application, the boxes disappear and all that can be seen is productivity, creativity, and customer service.[34]

Schools can learn much from this recipe, but as Noer says, they must do their own cooking. "The new glue cannot be bought off the self."[35] It is the responsibility of leaders to "cook" this glue. This requires motivating people rather than controlling them. John P. Kotter, the Konosuke

Matsushita Professor of Leadership at the Harvard Business School, observes that because change is the function of leadership and being able to generate highly energized behavior is important for coping with the inevitable barriers to change, this means, among other things, that a major role of leadership is planning and setting goals and directions and identifying an appropriate plan for improvement. It also means motivating and getting people moving down that path so they will have the energy to overcome the many obstacles that naturally occur in the business world. He comments, "Management controls people by pushing them in the right direction; leadership motivates them by satisfying basic human needs."[36]

In education, especially, superintendents, principals, central office specialists, and teachers will play both roles. In their role as manager, they will help their staffs or students complete routine, everyday jobs successfully. But leadership is different. Kotter says, "Achieving grand visions always requires an occasional burst of energy. Motivation and inspiration energize people, not by pushing them in the right direction as control mechanisms do, but by satisfying basic human needs for achievement, a sense of belonging, recognition, self-esteem, a feeling of control over one's life, and the ability to live up to one's ideals. Such feelings touch us deeply and elicit a powerful response."[37]

Kotter mentions four ways in which leaders are able to motivate people to achieve their ideals.[38] These are the following:

1. The leader articulates the organization's vision in a manner that stresses the values of the educational staff and the purposes of schooling. He says, "This makes the work important to those individuals."

2. Leaders will regularly involve their staffs in deciding how to achieve the school system's or the school's vision. Educators who are involved in "how to" sessions feel a sense of control over their work and are more eager to fulfill their responsibilities.

3. Leaders will support employee efforts to realize the vision by providing coaching, feedback, and role modeling. Such training will help educators at all levels grow professionally. It will also send a signal that everyone is a leader, that the skills of every teacher, principal, parent, and educational professional are needed to enhance the quality of teaching and student learning.

4. Finally, ethical and servant leaders recognize and reward success. This gives teachers and others a sense of accomplishment as well as making them feel like they are a significant part of the school system.

In order to build effective leadership among school professionals and augment the working together of multiple leadership roles, Kotter points out that "people's actions must be carefully coordinated by mechanisms that differ from those coordinating traditional management roles."[39] He proposes the development of strong networks of informal relationships, continuous dialogue among all levels of employees, and the building of trust structures that "allow for an ongoing process of accommodation and adaptation."[40] He observes that "when conflicts arise among roles, those same relationships help resolve the conflicts. Perhaps most important, this process of dialogue and accommodation can produce visions that are linked and compatible instead of remote and competitive."[41]

Caela Farren, CEO of Farren Associates, in Annandale, Virginia, and Beverly L. Kaye, CEO of Beverly Kaye and Associates and vice president of Career Systems, ask the question, "How can one lead a group while standing within it rather than above it?"[42] They anticipate that leaders can no longer assume "a coincidence of interests" between themselves and other employees or between employees and the goals of the organization. Leaders can best serve their employees by creating a mutuality of interests: "If we accept the premise that people are essentially contractors of their services in the workplace, then the key to enlisting their cooperation is to create collaborative projects that enhance their professional portfolio while advancing the strategic aims of the organizations.... The focus of the art of leadership shifts from directing and instructing to facilitating and enabling."[43] They divide the actions of leaders into five broad categories, which are easily adapted for educational organizations. They comment, "To engage people's career interests as a basis for leadership, it is necessary to be proficient at all five roles"[44]:

1. *Facilitator*   As a facilitator, the educational leader will
   help others identify their career values, work interests, and professional (marketable) skills;
   help others understand the importance of long-range career planning;
   create open and accepting climates in which other educational professionals can discuss their career concerns; and
   help others understand and articulate what they want from their career.
2. *Appraiser*   As an appraiser, the leader will
   provide honest and direct feedback regarding the performance and reputation of those they serve;

establish clear standards and expectations by which their performance will be evaluated;

listen to their peers and employees to learn what is important about their current job and their hopes for improving their job performance;

point out the relationship between one's performance, reputation, and career goals; and

suggest specific actions/behaviors that others can take to improve their performance and reputation.

3. *Forecaster*   As forecaster, the leader will

provide information about the school system, state and local laws and mandates, and the profession in general;

help employees locate and access information, training, and other sources that will enhance their teaching and job performance;

point out emerging trends and new developments that may affect the career of associates and encourage their continual training and keeping abreast of new and improved teaching/learning methods;

Help employees understand the cultural and political realities of their jobs, whether at the school level or in the central office; and

Communicate the organization's strategic direction to their departments, schools, or teams.

4. *Advisor*   As an advisor, the leader will

help each employee identify and develop a variety of potentially desirable career goals,

assist individuals in their selection of realistic career goals,

relate potential career goals to the requirements of their job and the strategic intent of the organization, and

help each employee identify possible sources of support and obstacles to achieving their career goals.

5. *Enabler*   As an enabler, the leader will

help employees develop detailed action plans for achieving their career goals;

help them achieve their career goals by arranging useful contacts with people in other schools, school systems, state organizations, universities, etc.;

discuss their abilities with others who could provide them with future opportunities; and

connect them with the resources they need to implement their career action plans.

According to Farren and Kaye, the third of these leadership skills, the forecaster, is perhaps the most important. They say, "Today, however, it is imperative that we study the broader range of systems that affect our career. Only a panoramic view of the present can encompass all the factors we need to consider to anticipate change and plan effectively for the future. The vital leadership contribution of the forecaster is to help others achieve this expanded awareness. This is accomplished by assiduously practicing two future-oriented skills: *trend watching* and *envisioning*."[45] They identify "trend watching" as paying close attention to new and unforeseen developments in the educator's environment and speculating about how these might affect the education profession as a whole and the career options of employees. They say, "Trend watching is a way of thinking about how the future is shaping itself and what that will mean for the organization and the members of the work team."[46] This requires a commitment to the profession and becoming a lifelong, perpetual learner "scanning the culture and the people around you for signs of the new and previously unrecognized."[47]

Lifelong learning entails the ability to "envision" how new ideas, new products, and new methods will affect the present teaching and learning environment. Leaders and the led will often become aggravated because schools are slow to change. Even though new knowledge and technology periodically change the way educators work, it takes time for a new idea, skill, or technology to permeate educational practice. If leaders are not watching trends and encouraging the continuous education of staffs, skills will lag behind educational standards, morale will drop, and productivity will level out and seem to slow. Farren and Kaye conclude, "Leaders are the bridges that connect people to the future. They include others' visions in their own, building alliances and partnerships based on shared aspirations. Taking the long view will make us more effective leaders today and will carry us through our uncertain times to the future we dare to create.... The role of the leader as forecaster is to articulate a future so full of exciting possibilities that no one will be able to rest until it is achieved."[48]

In these five chapters we have made a case for ethical and servant leadership in education. It has been the aim of this book to help educational leaders lead by pointing the way to more effective ethical practices, by serving first and commanding second. Suggestions have been made for making leadership more helpful and serving more unselfish and caring. The theme of this chapter has been "empowerment." Warren Bennis says, "Empowerment is the collective effect of leadership."[49] Bennis observes that in organizations with effective leaders empowerment is most evident in four areas[50]:

1. Empowerment makes people feel significant, that he or she makes a difference to the success of the organization.

2. Empowerment means that learning and competence matter, that there is no failure, only mistakes that give us feedback and tell us what to do next.

3. Empowerment makes people feel part of a community, a team, a unity.

4. Finally, empowerment makes work exciting, stimulating, challenging, fascinating, and fun where people are pulled rather than pushed toward a goal.

Leadership is a creative life; it is exciting, courageous, and task committed. Leadership is facing change and pressure, adapting and surviving. But leadership is much more: it is acting on a vision, drawing others into it, motivating them, and bringing out their best talents and skills. Creative leadership is a challenging life. So many times we want to make a big splash, a contribution that would draw attention to us, but our biggest lesson is learning to listen to the small voices around us—the children, the teachers, and our own inner voice. Here is where our reality lies as educators, and here is where we are able to contribute the most. Leaders lead best by serving, and when they serve those whom they lead, they increase their value to the school system.

There are times when we give special attention to the men and women who are able to withstand the pressures to conform and maintain their creativity and creative instincts throughout their lives. We call them leaders. All of us have known men and women like this. Understandably, leadership usually brings undue stress and anxiety, but with time, it can become a normal way of life. Stress and anxiety can be reduced by consistently acting from ethical principals and by always making decisions that magnify the dignity and skills of those with whom we work.

The skills of leadership are learned from childhood. They must be a part of the leader's inner nature. They cannot be artificially manufactured or conjured up on a moment's notice when circumstances seem to require it. When coupled with an ethical demeanor, knowledge and insights learned in building relationships with others, and an attitude that service matters, leadership becomes a powerful force in the workplace. Robert Greenleaf has said,

A new moral principle is emerging which holds that the only authority deserving one's allegiance is that which is freely and knowingly granted by the led to the leader in response to, and in proportion to, the clearly evident servant stature of the leader. Those who choose to follow this principle will not casually accept the authority of existing institutions. Rather, they will freely respond only to individuals who are chosen as leaders because they are proven and trusted as servants. To the extent that this principle prevails in the future, the only truly viable institutions will be those that are predominantly servant-led.[51]

Activities that Promote Ethical Leadership

1. In a group of three to five, discuss the meaning of the concept of empowerment and reach a consensus about the relationship of empowerment to responsibility. Be ready to share your conclusions with the entire class.

2. The statement, "There is no right way to do the wrong thing," has practical applications in all areas of human life. Think about your role in your school system, and from your own experiences give two or three examples where doing the "wrong" thing caused additional problems.

3. Empowerment's goal is to enable performance. We empower our students by putting them in "the most enabling environment" possible to maximize their learning and growth. As a leader, your role is to enable the performance of your students or staffs. List three to five trade-offs and three to five benefits that come when you create enabling environments in which they can perform their work.

4. Moxley defines "personal power" as the "power to" rather than as the "power over." This is a crucial distinction. He says that claiming personal power in a partnership model enables performance in five different ways. Review the five ways that he mentions. In small groups select two of these and brainstorm what practical results might occur in your work from their implementation. Share these within the entire class.

5. Stephen Covey speaks about personal power, synergy power, and contributive power. Review this section of the book and in your own words define each of these concepts. Give two or three examples of these behaviors from your own work experiences.

6. Covey says we must find areas where organizational goals and the goals of individuals (including their needs and capabilities) overlap. This, he indicates, is where we can get the maximum efficiency and commit-

ment from our staffs. In a small group of three or four individuals, discuss what leaders must do to make this happen. Make a list of these activities and share with the entire class.

7. The theme of this book has been ethical leadership. It has pointed out that effective ethical leadership is about building relationships and serving those whom you lead. Using David Noer's recipe for organizational glue, make a list of the practical things leaders can do that illustrate each of Noer's seven major ingredients.

8. Farren and Kaye list five roles leaders play. List these five roles, and under each role make two columns. In the first column list—in specific terms—those things you have done that are consistent with that role. In the second column, list those behaviors that need improvement. Complete this activity by making a "How Might I Improve" chart. Put each behavior needing improvement on your chart, and list two or three ways you can improve these leadership skills.

6

Leadership Performance: A Focus on Assessment

The purpose of this concluding chapter is to summarize the basic components of ethical leadership and, in doing this, construct a theoretical model that can be applied to educational organizations no matter what the size. This model will have three components: ethical leadership performance components, ethical leadership performance indicators, and ethical leadership performance assessment. Several beliefs have guided the development of this model:

First, the belief that educational organizations that acquire the public trust and that secure employees and shareholders' (students' and parents') confidence are organizations that put integrity first.

Second, the belief that the most successful educational organization, measured in terms of student growth and employee loyalty, is one committed to human growth.

Third, the belief that employees, students, and their parents have an intrinsic value beyond their contribution to the enterprise of education, which is reflected in their commitment to community service.

Finally, the belief that building relationships is a major function of servant and ethical leadership, that when the motives for practicing ethical/servant leadership are pure, the result is not only increased learning productivity among students and growth among educators, but employee and community trust.

Trust is perhaps the value that undergirds our entire educational effort. For example, on January 4, 2003, Chris Leak—who set the national high school record for career touchdown passes with 185 for the Charlotte, North Carolina Independence High School, and who was recruited as an eighth grader by Wake Forest University—stated that his choice of a college among the fifty-eight that are recruiting him came down to trust and which people he trusted with his future.[1] Leak's advisors have been his father, his brother who plays football for the University of Tennessee, and his high school coach. The key to success in any organization is employees trusting their leaders and leaders reciprocating by trusting their employees. In education, this comes down to students and parents trusting teachers and school administrators and all employees trusting each other as well as the executive and governing leaders of the school system.

The working environment of education and student performance in the classroom cannot be improved without continuously, aggressively improving the processes used to serve teachers and students. This improvement is impossible without eager participation from every leader, from the teacher to the principal, to the superintendent, to the governing board of the school system. Only an environment characterized by a highly developed and communicated appreciation of trust can provide this improvement. Servant leadership, based on solid ethical principles and the desire to help others, pays great dividends. Unquestionably, growth within educational organizations occurs most where its members respect and trust one another. The responsible educational organization is characterized by integrity and commitment to serve its students and community.

All too frequently, educational organizations are overmanaged and underled. A successful educational organization doesn't just need someone to be in charge; it requires leadership to set its direction, to give it a vision, and then to translate this vision into reality. Ethical leadership that is servant-based requires leaders who listen to, respond to, and support teachers and staffs, students and their parents. Ethical leaders remove barriers and obstacles that would prevent employees from growing and students from doing their best in the classroom. Such leaders build relationships throughout the school system and the community and make sure opportunities for personal and professional growth are readily available to all educators. An ethical leader embraces human growth and development, giving care and support while upholding the system's expectations of employee performance. The following leadership model mirrors these leadership components and performance standards.[2]

Ethical Leadership Performance Components

Ethical Components

Premise #1: Ethical leadership creates a high trust environment.

Premise #2: Ethical leadership is congruent with servant leadership.

Premise #3: Ethical leadership is founded on personal integrity.

Premise #4: Ethical leadership builds relationships of respect for individual dignity, worth, and capability.

Premise #5: Ethical leadership creates open and flexible environments which sustain dialogue and communication.

Premise #6: Ethical leadership focuses on growth of both educator and student and is accountable for the goals set by those who govern the organization.

Leadership Components

Premise #1: Educational leadership commits itself to the task of learning and human resource improvement.

Premise #2: Educational leadership defines the mission of the school system, anticipates the future, and directs resources toward opportunities for significant growth of students, teachers, and administrators.

Premise #3: Educational leadership clearly defines the purposes of the school system, seeks a shared direction for accomplishing these purposes, and finds ways to align new and old employees with it.

Premise #4: Educational leadership listens to employees, understands the necessity of linking information with experience, and identifies and responds to employee and student needs.

Premise #5: Educational leadership creates flexible learning environments and organizational structures that can respond quickly to change.

Premise #6: Educational leadership commits itself to a sustained belief in the capability of others and is team focused.

Premise #7: Educational leadership is fair-minded, persistent, and responsible; avoids being reactive; and is accountable for organizational purpose, the improvement of the skills of employees, and the learning of its students.

Environmental Components

Premise #1: Educational leaders learn to lead by following and serving others.

Premise #2: As servant leaders, educational leaders have the ability to listen receptively to what others have to say.

Premise #3: As servant leaders, educational leaders build their capacity to lead on capability and credibility and not solely on power defined by position.

Premise #4: As servant leaders, educational leaders are committed to building community in the workplace.

Premise #5: As servant leaders, educational leaders are committed to the growth of students and educators, believing that people have an intrinsic value beyond their contribution as workers.

Premise #6: When the motives of the educational leaders are pure, the result is not only increased systemic and student growth, but employee trust and dedication.

Ethical Leadership Performance Indicators

The performance indicators by which ethical leadership can be assessed are divided into the following three sections, congruent with the performance components above.

Ethical Responsibilities

1. Educational leaders articulate a set of ethical beliefs and responsibilities to employees, students, and the community.

2. Educational leaders value the importance of dialogue, understanding, and communication and make an effort to communicate clearly, openly, and honestly with employees, students, and the community.

3. Educational leaders model moral standards and ethical behaviors in their work and in their community and family activities.

4. Educational leaders support the critical judgment of other educators and students.

5. Educational leaders value the development of fair-minded critical thinking of other educators and students.

6. Educational leaders make a conscious effort to treat all others with respect and significance.

7. Educational leaders act in the best interest of the school, school system, students, and employees.

8. Educational leaders believe that others will respond with their best effort when appropriately praised and recognized.

9. Educational leaders recognize others for their accomplishments.

10. Educational leaders invest in the academic and moral development of students and other educators.

11. Educational leaders value the well-being and personal concerns of others.

12. Educational leaders value unwavering commitment to high personal and moral standards such as integrity, honesty, fair-mindedness, and responsibility.

13. Educational leaders value individual differences in students and employees.

Leadership Responsibilities

1. Educational leaders create communication venues where information is shared and networking among staff and other educational professionals is encouraged.

2. Educational leaders are mission driven.

3. Educational leaders are student focused and value growth in employees.

4. Educational leaders view problems as opportunities for evaluation and transformation.

5. Educational leaders set priorities that are clearly articulated and communicate the strategic plan at all levels of the school system.

6. Educational leaders are committed to innovations that are best for teachers and students.

7. Educational leaders have a tolerance for ambiguity and a positive attitude toward change.

8. Educational leaders govern by policies and laws and ask questions that keep policies up-to-date.

9. Educational leaders communicate and formalize operating protocol to enhance communication at all levels of the school system and within each school.

10. Educational leaders synthesize various viewpoints and invite stakeholders to share their opinions, problem solve, and make good decisions.

11. Educational leaders focus on results, which include improved student achievement and employee skill development and growth toward leadership.

12. Educational leaders encourage problem solving by those nearest the source of the dilemma.

13. Educational leaders value others and build relationships through-out their schools and school system.

14. Educational leaders keep promises and honor commitments.

Service Responsibilities

1. Educational leaders have the ability to listen receptively to what others have to say.

2. Educational leaders lead by serving/following others.

3. Educational leaders are committed to building community in the school system and in each school.

4. Educational leaders are committed to the growth of employees, understanding that the growth of employees is essential to the growth of schools and the school system.

5. Educational leaders create and encourage ongoing circles of exchange between employees and between employees and outside educational professionals.

6. Educational leaders are active in building systemic and school climates that are open, flexible, and interdependent.

7. Educational leaders value individual capability.

8. Educational leaders encourage the growth of other educators as leaders within their schools and within the school system.

9. Educational leaders understand and provide for the needs of employees as "knowledge workers."

10. Educational leaders recognize employees as a portfolio of skills in the service of students and the school system.

Ethical Leadership
Performance Assessment

Following is a checklist provided as either a self-checking device or an assessment that supervisors and principals can use with other employees. The items on this checklist are consistent with the ethical performance components and indicators listed previously.

Directions: Place a ☑ by those items you feel you do on a regular basis. Place an ☒ by those items where you think you need improvement. Only mark those you think are consistent with your role in the school or school system.

☐ 1. Superintendents work with central office professionals, principals, teachers, and noncertified staffs to create and articulate a shared purpose and educational vision focused on learning.

    ☐ 2. Superintendents articulate ethical beliefs and responsibilities to central office employees, to principals, and to each school faculty.

    ☐ 3. Principals and departmental heads reinforce the importance of ethical behavior with their staffs in the treatment of colleagues, students, and their parents.

    ☐ 4. Leaders take collective responsibility for school practices and outcomes.

    ☐ 5. Meetings are held at every level of the school system to discuss board policy, state and federal laws, and systemic or school problems in which every effort is made to listen to any employee who wishes to speak and make a contribution to the meeting.

    ☐ 6. The critical thinking and judgment of others is both solicited and respected.

    ☐ 7. Throughout the school system, authority is based more on professional knowledge and competence than on position and rules.

    ☐ 8. Educators at every level and students are placed on school and system committees set up to discuss educational problems, discipline issues, the adoption of programs and curriculum, and future planning.

    ☐ 9. Educators model moral behaviors and encourage their staffs and students to model moral behaviors.

    ☐ 10.Parents, students, and other educators are treated with respect in their dealings with teachers, principals, and central office administrators.

    ☐ 11. Appropriate praise and recognition is given to students and educators in response to their achievements and other courageous actions.

    ☐ 12. Time each day is taken to reinforce and enhance students' moral development, not just in the classroom, but in all school activities.

    ☐ 13. Educational leaders exhibit unwavering commitment to high personal and moral standards in their treatment of colleagues and students.

    ☐ 14. Individual differences in students and employees are recognized as a value to schools.

    ☐ 15. Principals encourage and make time for networking among teachers and superintendents encourage networking among the central office staff.

    ☐ 16. Superintendents, departmental heads, and principals encourage the continual education of staffs and make arrangements for workshops, information-sharing meetings, and college classes for their continual improvement.

☐ 17. Superintendents, departmental heads, and principals set priorities that are congruent with the mission and strategic plan of the school system and school.

☐ 18. Educational leaders communicate their passion for learning by challenging ineffective practices.

☐ 19. Educational leaders acknowledge the necessity of change and the importance of creativity and innovation and are flexible enough to adjust schedules and plans to incorporate new programs and methods into their strategic plans which benefit teachers and student learning.

☐ 20. Superintendents and principals govern by policies and laws and make arrangements to keep all staff informed and up-to-date on changes that affect their work.

☐ 21. Superintendents, departmental heads, and principals formalize and communicate protocols and procedures to enhance communication, dialogue, and feedback at all levels of the educational organization.

☐ 22. Educational leaders make decisions after synthesizing various viewpoints from educational stakeholders who have been invited to share their ideas and join in the problem-solving process.

☐ 23. Superintendents, departmental heads, and principals encourage problem solving by those nearest the source of the dilemma.

☐ 24. Educational leaders accept conflict as normal and use it as a creative stimulus for change and growth throughout the school or school system.

☐ 25. Educational leaders are open to multiple approaches and solutions rather than relying on single answers and past practices.

☐ 26. Academic time and support for teachers are given so they can keep students engaged in learning.

☐ 27. Emphasis is placed on students acquiring essential skills and knowledge at high levels.

☐ 28. Students are viewed as knowledge workers and are engaged as active learners and coconstructors of knowledge.

☐ 29. Throughout the school system, thinking skills are emphasized for all students rather than an almost total emphasis on the rote acquisition of basic skills and unapplied information.

☐ 30. Educational leaders focus on results, which include improved student achievement, employee skill development, and growth toward leadership.

☐ 31. Superintendents establish academies for training leaders within the school system.

☐ 32. Superintendents, departmental heads, and principals provide opportunities for others to lead (committees, curriculum evaluation, departments or grade levels, etc.) and are committed to following decisions made by others.

☐ 33. Educational leaders make a concrete effort to build school and school system climates that are open, flexible, and interdependent.

☐ 34. Roles in schools and in the central office of the school system are flexible and interdependent rather than rigid and hierarchical.

☐ 35. Educational leaders value, recognize, and support individual capability.

☐ 36. Teachers have considerable autonomy and discretion to plan curriculum and organize instruction within an overall framework.

☐ 37. Teams are used to plan and implement school and system improvement.

☐ 38. Parents, community leaders, and students are encouraged to participate in decisions about schools.

☐ 39. Superintendents, departmental heads, and principals recognize other educators as knowledge workers who have portfolio of skills in the service of students and the school system.

☐ 40. Human growth in educators and students is recognized as the primary mission of education.

Activities that Promote Ethical Leadership

1. In a group of three to five, discuss each of the three areas outlined in this chapter. With your knowledge and experience, add to each of the items in these areas. Be sure to justify any additions that you make.

2. Review the performance checklist and complete it according to the directions. Note that not all areas of school management are included in this device, only those areas important to ethical and servant leadership have been included. List those areas where you noted that you need improvement and make plans for your improvement. If you are a principal, departmental head, supervisor, or superintendent and are using this device to rate your staff, make a combined list of areas needing improvement and set up training sessions to improve the ethical and leadership skills of your employees.

Appendix A
Manifesto: Ethical Leadership for Educators

This "manifesto" summarizes ideas presented in this book. It captures the major points of ethical leadership for educators and sets them forth as a *policy statement*.

There are eight different areas. Each of these areas is critical to understanding not only "leadership," but ethical leadership. The intent of this manifesto is to combine three different concepts—leadership, servant leadership, and ethical leadership—into an applicable prescription or directive for changing school leadership as it is now practiced. Educators are encouraged to post this manifesto in full view as a daily reminder to instill their leadership practices with the attitude of a servant and with ethical practices.

VALIDITY

Work is carried forward within a framework of legal prescriptions and regulated norms and with a focus on human need.

Responsibility is taken for building strong commitments to the mission and purposes of learning.

Ethical behavior makes possible a culture that cares for the welfare, development, and growth of others; leadership divorced from ethics is reduced to mere technique.

Today's educators must have the behavior of a leader while serving others and the discipline of a manager while being the steward of the school's and school system's vision, mission, and purposes.

CREATIVE CHANGE

Progress depends on the ability to see reality accurately, to think, and to problem solve—faith in human possibility is the norm.

Thinking outside the boundaries is encouraged and rewarded, for there is not one way to lead, and leaders are not routine minded.

Problems are viewed as opportunities and possibilities for positive change, for leaders accept adversity as the purification process.

Time is provided for thinking, probing, creating, solving problems, and expressing ideas in order to identify the internal and external forces of change.

Nothing happens until someone makes it happen.

PRODUCTIVITY

Everyone is accountable; thus, self-assessment is crucial for effective leadership.

Individual achievement is linked to one's inner purpose and the commitment to spend time each day laying the foundation to get there, to lifelong learning.

Educators are a positive force for improving human value; as leaders, they create value through performance, not promises.

Real and lasting productivity and improvements come from the hearts and minds of people.

Leadership development is a process of lifelong self-development and transformation.

FOLLOWSHIP

Leaders follow in order to lead by managing themselves, managing change, and serving others, which regenerates the ability to lead.

Individuals are chosen as leaders because they are proven and trusted servants.

Leaders serve with compassion and recognize that the only true authority is that which enriches and empowers others.

Leaders understand that as they give, they receive.

TEAMWORK

We learn best from great teams; learning gives leaders an effective edge.

Success is based on the commitment to open communication and includes a high level of participation, cooperation, and collaboration.

Teamwork recognizes the dignity and worth of those with whom and for whom we work.

Educational leaders work best that solicit many different points of view that pull rather than push others forward knowing that pushing will be costly in terms of time, vulnerability, and exposure.

FAIR-MINDEDNESS

Fair-mindedness is achieved by an impartial treatment and evaluation of others based on their contributions to the goals and purposes of education.

Caring for others is the first step toward ethical leadership.

Ethical leadership is based on respect for the human value within the school community.

Leaders build unity without requiring uniformity.

INTEGRITY

The effectiveness of a leader is determined by the integrity of his or her private life as ethical leaders take responsibility for their own behavior and for those they lead.

A successful learning environment is consistent with its mission and its core values, and its foundation is built on carefully crafted trust structures that permeate the organization.

Leadership is about building relationships and providing for human growth knowing that followers buy into the leader before they buy into the leader's vision.

Ethical leaders lead from character and with confidence and self-respect.

Leaders create meaning, inspire trust, and care for others.

RESPONSIBILITY

Leaders cannot help followers who will not help themselves.

Leaders are accessible to everyone.

Leaders sense problems before they occur and generate questions from questions.

Leaders who grow leaders believe people can change, see us for what we can become and not for what we have been, approach us in terms of the present and the future rather than the past, want us in the game with them, and bring us alone one step at a time.

We look for leaders who do what they say they're going to do (integrity), know what they are doing (competence), paint a picture of the future (forward thinking), and are excited about what they are doing (inspiration).

Appendix B

Becoming an Ethical Leader: Tools for Self-Evaluation

Educators who are trying to change their behaviors and styles of leadership can use the material in this appendix for self-evaluation.

Begin with the worksheet, which first requires you to define your major responsibilities in general terms. Specific tasks and jobs can be listed separately, but the purpose here is to "get a handle" on roles and responsibilities. This is done best by summarizing the major responsibilities tied to your work as a teacher or school administrator. After completing this first step, you should give serious thought to your leadership style as it now is. On a separate sheet of paper, define your style of leadership and mark with an asterisk areas where you really want and need to change.

Your second step on the worksheet is your goal statement. With reference to the notes you have taken, challenge yourself to become an ethical leader by completing the statement, "My goal is to become:"

The third step is to create a timeline and date(s) for completing each phase or part of your goal. Continuous improvement is the purpose of this process, and periodic evaluations will help.

The fourth step is to imagine results and then act on this vision. Space has been provided for you to write about what you imagine, but you may wish to write or type a much longer response. The important thing is to use this vision to get started.

After the worksheet comes some tips for evaluating the results of your changed leadership style. You should perform this self-evaluation about twice a year. Sample questions have been provided. Each time you answer these questions, compare them with previous answers. You may invent a code for marking strengths and weaknesses. The goal is consistency and continuous improvement. These do not happen automatically but must be planned for and worked at for steady improvement in leadership results.

Name: Date:

Position:

Defined Responsibilities:

Goal Statement: With reference to becoming an ethical leader, my goal is to become

Steps for Accomplishing This Goal: Create a time line with dates

1.

2.

3.

4.

5.

Imagining Results and Acting on the Vision: In the space below, write a future narrative of how your school, classroom, department, or school system might appear because you started becoming an ethical and servant leader. When the narrative has been written, start the change process with step #1 above.

Evaluating the Results of a Change in Leadership Style

Periodically (at least twice a year) complete a self-evaluation focusing on the results of your changed leadership style. This evaluation can be completed informally or formally.

Formally: simply create a questionnaire from the Manifesto's major points. Give this to all staff members to complete. (These questions can be reformulated as a questionnaire for your staff.)

Informally: ask these questions of yourself and apply a self-rating. Find areas for improvement and go to work. The focus should be on the effects of your leadership style.

1. Do you follow to the letter, all legal prescriptions and school board regulations and hold your staff to these same requirements?

2. Do you take responsibility for the carrying out of the mission and purposes of the school system/school?

3. Do you genuinely care for students under your supervision?

4. Have you made an effort to model ethical leadership behaviors for your staff?

5. Are you a creative thinker and problem solver? Give two or three examples.

6. Do you seek out opportunities for positive growth and change in yourself and your staff?

7. Do you hold yourself as well as your staff accountable for the progress or lack of progress in student learning?

8. Are you a lifelong learner?

9. Do you have faith in your staff and in your students?

10. Are there times when you follow the lead of other staff members? Give two or three examples.

11. Do you think you are trustworthy?

12. As a school leader, do you focus your attention on what you can do to serve students, parents, and other educators?

13. Are you in active in building leadership and problem-solving teams in your school/school system?

14. Do you feel comfortable in saying "I don't have all the answers?"

15. Do you actively solicit the opinion of others?

16. Have you built unity in your school system/school without requiring your staff to blindly following your ideas?

17. Do you encourage an open, free-thinking environment?

18. Are you true to your own beliefs and the mission of the school system/school?

19. Are you accessible to everyone?

20. Are you consistent in thought and behavior?

Appendix C
Web Resources

EDUCATIONAL LEADERSHIP WEBSITES

The following website provides hundreds of additional sites related to leadership programs in the United States and abroad, especially to leadership certificate and degree programs at major colleges and universities: http://search .msn.com/results.asp?F%20%20ORM=MSNH&RS=CHECKED&aq=educational+leadership&q=Educational+Leadership&v=1

American Association of School Administrators (AASA)
http://www.aasa.org

AASA, founded in 1865, is the professional organization for over 14,000 educational leaders across America and in many other countries. Its mission is to support and develop effective school system leaders who are dedicated to the highest quality public education for all children. The four major focus areas for AASA are improving the condition of children and youth, preparing schools and school systems for the twenty-first century, connecting schools and communities, and enhancing the quality and effectiveness of school leaders.

American Educational Research Association (AERA)
http://www.aera.net/about/about.html

AERA is concerned with improving the educational process by encouraging scholarly inquiry related to education and by promoting the dissemination and practical application of research results. Its 20,000 members are educators; administrators; directors of research, testing or evaluation in federal, state and local agencies; counselors; evaluators; graduate students; and behavioral scientists. The broad range of disciplines represented by the membership includes education, psychology, statistics, sociology, history, economics, philosophy, anthropology, and political science.

The Association for Supervision and Curriculum Development (ASCD)

1703 North Beauregard Street, Alexandria, VA 22311-1714 USA
Phone: (703) 578-9600 or 1-800-933-ASCD, Fax: (703)-575-5400
http://www.ascd.org/frameedlead.html.

ASCD is an international, nonprofit, nonpartisan association of professional educators whose jobs cross all grade levels and subject areas. Founded in 1943, ASCD's mission is to forge responsible relationships in teaching and learning for the success of all learners. The Association publishes Educational Leadership, intended primarily for leaders in elementary, middle, and secondary education but also for anyone interested in curriculum, instruction, supervision, and leadership in schools. The 96-page, full-color magazine is published monthly September through May except bimonthly December/January. Subscriptions are included in ASCD membership. Stand-alone subscriptions are also available for $36 a year.

Clearinghouse on Educational Management, College of Education, University of Oregon

http://eric.uoregon.edu

This website is another ERIC dedicated to the dissemination of educational management research.

The Education Commission of the States (ECS)

http://www.ecs.org/ecsmain.asp?page=/html/aboutECS/home_aboutEC S.htm?am=6

ECS is an interstate compact created in 1965 to improve public education by facilitating the exchange of information, ideas, and experiences among state policymakers and education leaders. As a nonprofit, nonpartisan organization involving key leaders from all levels of the education system, ECS creates unique opportunities to build partnerships, share information, and promote the development of policy based on available research and strategies.

Educational Leadership

http://educ.queensu.ca/~reesr/leadership.html

Educational Leadership is a website designed to help anyone interested in locating information on leadership in education. This site contains a bibliography on books in educational leadership, websites on educational leadership, articles on educational leadership, and Ruth Rees's M.Ed. course outline on educational leadership. Over time, this website will evolve in response to others' input. Case studies, interactive checklists, etc., will be added over time. Contact Ruth Rees at reesr@educ.queensu.ca if you wish to add information.

Educational Leadership Links
http://www.leadership.sa.edu.au/LinksAE.htm

These links, selected by SACLE Leadership Consultants, provide avenues to additional information about educational leadership.

Education Leadership Toolkit
http://www.nsba.org/sbot/toolkit

Education Leadership Toolkit is a project of the National School Boards Foundation implemented by National School Boards Association's Institute for the Transfer of Technology to Education with a grant from the National Science Foundation. This toolkit is a collection of tips and pointers, articles, case studies, and other resources for education leaders addressing issues around technology and education. Educators may register for the School Board of Tomorrow E-mail Group to join in an ongoing conversation with school board members from around the country. Suggestions and experiences are requested.

ERIC
http://www.indiana.edu/%7Essdc/about.htm

ERIC, which serves teachers, parents, administrators, policymakers, researchers, students, and anyone else interested in information on education, consists of sixteen subject-oriented clearinghouses across the nation. Each clearinghouse specializes in a broad subject area as it relates to education; ERIC/ChESS, for instance, specializes in social studies, social science education, music education, and art education.

The George Lucas Educational Foundation (GLEF)
http://glef.org/foundation.html

GLEF is a nonprofit operating foundation that documents and disseminates models of the most innovative practices in the nation's K through 12 schools. This mission includes the creation of media—films, books, newsletters, and CD-ROMS. The website contains all their multimedia content published since 1997. "Edutopia" is a word used in this website to describe a vision of powerful teaching and learning. Edutopia Online, celebrates the unsung heroes across our nation who are making edutopia a reality by showing what can be done, often with the same number of resources as other schools and sometimes with fewer. The Video Gallery is a robust archive of short documentaries and expert interviews that allows visitors to visualize what these innovations look like—in the classroom and in the words of teachers and students. Detailed articles, research summaries, and links to hundreds of relevant websites, books, organizations, and publications are also available to help schools and communities build on successes in education.

Global SchoolNet
http://www.globalschoolnet.org

Global SchoolNet, a leader in online education since 1984, partners with schools, communities, and businesses to provide collaborative learning activities that prepare students for the workforce and help them to become responsible global citizens. It is free to all educators.

Institute for Educational Leadership, Inc. (IEL)
1001 Connecticut Avenue, NW, Suite 310, Washington, DC 20036
Phone: (202) 822-8405, Fax: (202) 872-4050
E-mail: iel@iel.org.
http://www.iel.org/about.html

IEL's mission is to improve education, and the lives of children and their families through positive and visionary change. Supported by foundations, corporations, and generous individuals, IEL teams often include the most innovative federal, state, and local government agencies and many of the nation's leading nonprofit organizations.

International Center for Leadership in Education
http://www.dagett.com

Dr. Willard R. Daggett is president of the International Center for Leadership in Education. Known worldwide for his efforts to move the education system toward more rigorous and relevant skills and knowledge for all students, he founded the International Center after serving in various management positions at the New York State Education Department, where he spearheaded a series of restructuring initiatives to focus the state's education system on the skills and knowledge students need in today's technological, information-based society.

Journal of Cases in Educational Leadership (JCEL)
http://www.ucea.org/cases/statement.html

JCEL is an electronic publication of the University Council for Educational Administration in cooperation with the University of Utah. JCEL publishes in electronic format peer-reviewed cases appropriate for use in programs that prepare educational leaders. The University Council sponsors this journal in an ongoing effort to improve administrative preparation. The journals editorial staff seeks a wide range of cases that embody relevant and timely presentations of issues germane to the preparation of educational leaders. Cases published in JCEL may be downloaded and duplicated for nonprofit use by any individual or education/public agency. Such reproduction must bear the citation of the article, including authors name, title of case, journal name, issue, and page numbers. Commercial use of this journal in whole or in part is strictly prohibited.

The Lab Network
http://www.nwrel.org/national

The Regional Educational Laboratories are educational research and development organizations supported by contracts with the U.S. Education Depart-

ment, Institute of Education Sciences (IES) (formerly known as the Office of
Educational Research and Improvement [OERI]).

MiddleWeb: Exploring Middle School Reform
http://www.middleweb.com/mw/aaAboutMW.html

MiddleWeb is produced by the Focused Reporting Project with grant support from the Program for Student Achievement of the Edna McConnell Clark Foundation. MiddleWeb provides a wealth of resources for schools, districts, educators, parents, and public school advocates working to raise achievement for all students in the middle grades. In addition to MiddleWeb's large collection of reform-oriented materials, this site includes hundreds of articles and links about curriculum, teaching strategies, teacher professional development, parent involvement, classroom assessment, and much more.

The National Academy for Academic Leadership
http://www.thenationalacademy.org/About/about.html

The National Academy for Academic Leadership educates academic decision makers to be leaders for sustained, integrated institutional change that significantly improves student learning. Its curriculum is based on research and best practices. Its programs are designed both for institutional teams working on campus projects and for individuals—presidents, board members, vice presidents, deans, chairs, and key faculty members—with role-specific responsibilities and concerns. The Academy recognizes the considerable variation among institutions in their readiness for change and their resources for leadership development, and so programs are geared to the unique institutional contexts and specific needs of participants.

School Leadership: A Profile Document
http://www.oise.utoronto.ca/~vsvede

School Leadership: A Profile Document is a website where educators may select the dimension of leadership practice which is of particular interest and click on the appropriate box. Then, for each subdimension, moving from top to bottom, pick the box which most accurately describes present practice or the ideal practice toward which you strive. At the end of each subdimension you can reflect on and write about your own situation. Additional resources are provided at the end of each subdimension for your information. Background: This website was created by Valda Svede and Diane Jeudy-Hugo as one of the assignments for the computer conferencing Master's Level Course 1048: Educational Leadership and School Improvement taught by Dr. Paul Begley at the Ontario Institute for Studies in Education at the University of Toronto. An extensive original bibliography by topic is provided.

University Council for Educational Administration (UCEA)
205 Hill Hall, Columbia MO 65211
Phone: (573) 884-8300
http://www.ucea.org

The UCEA is a consortium of sixty-seven major research universities in the United States and Canada. The dual mission of UCEA is to improve the preparation of educational leaders and promote the development of professional knowledge in school improvement and administration. UCEA headquarters is currently hosted by the University of Missouri–Columbia. The Council fulfills this purpose by promoting, sponsoring, and disseminating research on the essential problems of schooling and leadership practice; improving the preparation and professional development of educational leaders and professors; and positively influencing local, state, and national educational policy. UCEA is also a part of several national networks of educational administration organizations focused on improving the field, including the National Commission for the Advancement in Educational Leadership and the National Policy Board for Educational Administration.

SERVANT LEADERSHIP WEBSITES

A search of the following website will provide additional information, centers, and training opportunities in servant leadership. http://search.msn.com/results.asp?FORM=MSNH&RS=CHECKED&aq=servant+leadership&q=Servant+Leadership&v=1.

The Greenleaf Center for Servant-Leadership

http://greenleaf.org

The Greenleaf Center is an international, not-for-profit institution headquartered in Indianapolis, Indiana. Its goal is to help people understand the principles and practices of servant leadership, to nurture colleagues and institutions by providing a focal point and opportunities to share thoughts and ideas on servant leadership, to produce and publish new resources by others on servant leadership, and to connect servant leaders in a network of learning. The Center's mission is to fundamentally improve the caring and quality of all institutions through a new approach to leadership, structure, and decision making. See also, http://www.leadership-innovations.com/Articles/Servant%20Leadership.html.

Intentional Community

http://www.ic.org

This is an inclusive term for ecovillages, cohousing, residential land trusts, communes, student co-ops, urban housing cooperatives, and other related projects and dreams. The website serves the growing communities movement and provides important information and access to crucial resources for seekers of community, existing and forming communities, and other friends of community. Information is provided on the site about the Robert Greenleaf Center and its relationship to the community's movement.

Leadership Direct

http://www.leadersdirect.com/index.html

Leadership Direct provides articles, executive coaching, counseling, and feedback for leaders. It asks the following questions, "How is the nature of leadership changing to meet the challenges of our knowledge-driven age? What is the role of management? What of hierarchy and formal authority? How can you manage yourself in the face of rapid change and the pressure to do more with less?" The topics explored by Leadership Direct include lead: learn about the real essence of leadership, not the Hollywood image; manage: management is as vital as leadership but portrayed as mechanistic. Modern management is much more human than this sterile conception; self: manage yourself more effectively—assertiveness, self-esteem, time management, career development, self-development, anger control, stress tolerance, coping with personal transitions, making decisions, etc.; self renewal group services—business psychologists for individual and organizational renewal.

Leadership in Newaygo County
http://www.nclinc.org

The group's mission is "to create an informed, committed and diverse network of leaders who will embody the wisdom, awareness, knowledge, understanding, integrity and vision to help Newaygo County be an even better place to live and work." Its responsibility, "Critical to Newaygo County's ability to adapt and prosper well into the twenty-first century, will be the development and acquisition of resources. An integral part of our success will be the capacity of our fellow residents and other community stakeholders. We must build the infrastructure and create a broad resource of leaders who are capable of effectively guiding the greater Newaygo County into the future."

Margaret J. Wheatley
http://www.margaretwheatley.com/writing.html

The website is a library of articles by Margaret J. Wheatley that is updated frequently and may be downloaded free. Users wanting multiple copies for courses, books, or handouts should seek permission. She invites others to join with her in her work with the Berkana Institute, which "supports life-affirming leaders around the globe. Berkana intentionally supports those who are giving birth to the new forms, processes, and leadership that will restore hope to the future. Since 1991, Berkana has gradually expanded its work to reach pioneering leaders and communities in all types of organizations and in dozens of nations. We define a leader as anyone who wants to help, who is willing to step forward to create change in their world."

The Servant-Leader Development Center
http://www.servant-leadercenter.org/index.cfm?id=189

The Servant-Leader Development Center offers public and individually designed workshops and consultations that integrate servant leadership concepts through experiential education designs. Participants come away with the knowledge and skills needed to incorporate servant-leadership concepts into their daily lives and the capacity to develop those skills in others. The results include enhances relationships, more effective teams, and higher performing organizations.

Servant Leadership Retreats

http://www.leadership-retreats.com/index.htm

Register online for servant leadership retreats. Retreat objectives include:

Becoming familiar with the concepts and characteristics of servant leadership and Robert Greenleaf, beginning the process of understanding one's personal stance in regard to servant leadership, building a servant-leadership learning community, beginning the process of understanding one's organization in light of servant leadership, experiencing several of the key components of the servant leader, gaining a sense of renewal and commitment to one's personal and organizational leadership journey, having a clearer vision and action map that incorporates key servant-leadership principles, and using a workbook of resources for one's personal and organizational leadership journey as it continues after the retreat.

ETHICAL LEADERSHIP WEBSITES

A search of the following website will provide additional pages on ethical leadership. http://search.msn.com/results.asp?FORM=SMCRT&RS=CHECKED &aq=ethical+leadership&cfg=SMCINITIAL&nosp=0&origq=Educational+Lea dership&q=Ethical+Leadership&submitbutton.x=32&submitbutton.y=14&thr&v =1.

Academy of Management

http://www.aom.pace.edu

The Aspen Institute

http://www.aspeninst.org/about/index.html.

Association for Moral Education

http://www.amenetwork.org/ .

The Beard Center for Leadership in Ethics

http://www.bus.duq.edu/Beard/staff.html

The Beard Center for Leadership in Ethics, at Duquesne University, Pittsburgh, seeks to become an internationally recognized resource for businesses, not-for-profit organizations, professional associations, and universities interested in promoting applied business ethics training programs or ethics education. To this end, the Center strives to be at the leading edge in providing employee ethics training programs, forums discussing critical business ethics issues, and effective, innovative learning techniques used in business ethics instruction. The mission of the Center is to promote moral integrity and behavior through ethics education and training to those who encounter, or are preparing to encounter, moral challenges in the business world.

Center for Applied and Professional Ethics
http://www.ethics.ubc.ca/resources/business

Center for Civic Education
http://www.civiced.org/index.html

The Center for Civic Education is an organization that promotes civic education in order to preserve and improve constitutional democracy. It is a nonprofit, nonpartisan educational corporation dedicated to fostering the development of informed, responsible participation in civic life by citizens committed to values and principles fundamental to American constitutional democracy. The Center specializes in civic/citizenship education, law-related education, and international educational exchange programs for developing democracies. Programs focus on the U.S. Constitution and Bill of Rights; American political traditions and institutions at the federal, state, and local levels; constitutionalism; civic participation; and the rights and responsibilities of citizens. The Center administers a wide range of curricular, teacher-training, and community-based programs the goals of which are to help students develop an increased understanding of the institutions of American constitutional democracy and the fundamental principles and values upon which they are founded, the skills necessary to participate as effective and responsible citizens, and the willingness to use democratic procedures for making decisions and managing conflict.

The Center for Ethical Leadership/
The LBJ School of Public Affairs
http://www.utexas.edu/lbj/research/leadership

Through the creation of a Center for Ethical Leadership in the LBJ School of Public Affairs, the school intends to self-consciously promote the development of leadership potential among students and other constituents. The Center prepares graduates for leadership positions in the public, private, and nonprofit sectors and for the ethical challenges they will encounter throughout their careers. The Center for Ethical Leadership rests on four premises: the long-term success of an organization, community or society depends on good leadership, not just on technical proficiency and skillful management; good leadership must be grounded in ethical values; ethical leadership involves recognizing and reconciling tensions between personal values and goals, on the one hand, and organizational, community, or societal values and goals on the other; although leadership is a complex form of human behavior, most of what we think of as leadership is learned and, therefore, can be taught. The mission of the Center for Ethical Leadership is to promote ethical leadership in our society through education, research, and service to community. The Center will serve as a teaching, research, and information focal point for students and educators from all disciplines as well as for practitioners and other interested parties. To meet the goals of the Center to advance ethical leadership, programs are offered in the following areas: education: graduate courses in leadership to students from all disciplines in the area of ethical leadership, a leader-in-residence program to bring outstanding leaders to the LBJ School and an international leadership education conference, and a fellowship in public leadership; research: on topics relating to leadership theory and practice in the public sector and nonprofit organizations, to determine the impact of leadership on the ethical quality of public sector work organizations, to compare effectiveness of different leader development strategies, including evaluation of both classroom and experiential learning methods; service to community: seminars for leaders in government, business, and education, and consultation for organizations that are struggling with leadership challenges.

Center for Ethics and Public Responsibility
http://www.smu.edu/ethics_center/home.htm# .

CHARACTER COUNTS!
http://www.charactercounts.org

Character Counts! is a nonprofit, nonpartisan, nonsectarian coalition of schools, communities, and nonprofit organizations working to advance character education by teaching the six pillars of character: trustworthiness, respect, responsibility, fairness, caring, and citizenship. The coalition grew out of the Josephson Institute of Ethics in 1993 at the Institute's Aspen's conference. Members of the coalition, a national, diverse partnership of schools, communities, education and human-service organizations, are committed to using the six pillars of character in their individual and joint programs. The hope is that by using a consistent language with students, the lessons of good character will be reinforced and better understood.

The Content of Our Character Project, A National Conversation on Generational Ethics
http://www.contentofourcharacter.org/index.html

The Content of Our Character Project is an initiative dedicated to the future generations who will occupy, work, and lead the experiment called America in the years ahead. It asks, "What can they learn from us, the living generations? What can, or have, we learned from one another? And what do we really know about our American moral fiber?" In anticipation of its National Conversation on Generational Ethics, a conference hosted by the Content of Our Character Project at Duke University in June 2002 and attended by more than one hundred extraordinary civic leaders from across the country, the Content of Our Character Project posed the following questions: "What core principles, values, and ideals do you associate with your generation? What type of moral leadership can your generation provide America?"

Hartwood Institute for Ethics
http://www.heartwoodethics.org/index.asp

The primary mission of Hartwood Institute is spreading understanding and practice of courage, loyalty, justice, respect, hope, honesty, and love. The Institute provides curriculum development, training, and resources in character education and ethics. This site provides additional links to a large variety of web pages that focus on ethics, character, and civics education.

The Hendrickson Institute for Ethical Leadership
http://www.smumn.edu/academics/ethics

The Hendrickson Institute, at Saint Mary's University of Minnesota, is founded upon the premise that it is both possible and essential to integrate leadership models and ethical principles so that leaders, regardless of their profession or field of work, will be moral leaders. Traditional training programs, seminars, and courses have focused exclusively on leadership skills and techniques. Programs of the Hendrickson Institute expose participants to sound, dynamic and innovative leadership theories and models, all within an ethical context.

The Hoffberger Center for Professional Ethics
http://www.ubalt.edu/hoffberger

The Institute for Ethical Leadership
http://www.creative-learning.ca/IFEL

The Institute for Ethical Leadership is a membership association formed in February 1998. It is sponsored by Creative Learning International to act as a catalyst in promoting positive development in society. Based on the belief that healthy societies are grounded in ethical principles, the Institute seeks to promote leadership action based on these principles. The Institute provides a forum for leaders to come together for learning and fellowship and to plan and carry out positive programs of work in five theme areas: stewardship and the environment, health and wellness, spirituality and personal development, youth and education, and business and sustainability. Members may choose to participate in one or more of these theme areas as an ongoing activity by joining the respective steering committee. Each steering committee takes responsibility for arranging the program of a meeting of the Institute so that the whole membership continues to grow in knowledge about all these areas.

Internet Resources by Topic and Ethics/Social Responsibility/Environmental/Centres
http://www.ucs.mun.ca/~rsexty/cb+s.htm

The Joseph and Edna Josephson Institute of Ethics
http://www.josephsoninstitute.org

The Josephson Institute of Ethics is a public-benefit, nonpartisan, nonprofit membership organization founded by Michael Josephson in honor of his parents to improve the ethical quality of society by advocating principled reasoning and ethical decision making. Since 1987, the Institute has conducted programs and workshops for over 100,000 influential leaders including legislators and mayors, high-ranking public executives, congressional staff, editors and reporters, senior corporate and nonprofit executives, judges and lawyers, and military and police officers. The Character Counts! youth-education initiative is a project of the Institute. The Institute provides materials, seminars, consulting, and training. One special feature is their "Ethics in the Workplace" seminars and training of trainers program.

The Kenan Institute for Ethics

http://kenan.ethics.duke.edu/mission.asp

The Kenan Institute for Ethics is a university wide initiative at Duke University that supports the study and teaching of ethics and promotes moral reflection and commitment in personal, professional, community, and civic life. Its work is guided by the conviction that universities have a responsibility to prepare students for lives of personal integrity and reflective citizenship by nurturing their capacities for critical thinking, compassion, courage, and their concern for justice. Its goals are to create and sustain a strong focus on ethics at Duke University in teaching, training, research, and everyday life, encouraging ethical inquiry across the curriculum and moral reflection about campus practices and policies; to support creative innovation in the teaching of ethics at all levels, from K through university, with particular attention to approaches that not only strengthen critical reflection but also enrich moral imagination and inspire personal integrity and civic engagement; and to develop university-community partnerships and institutional collaborations that address ethical challenges of public concern within and across communities.

Soderquist Center for Leadership and Ethics

http://www.soderquist.org/about_us/index.asp

Soderquist Center exists to equip people in the corporate and nonprofit community with the transforming power of ethical leadership. Founded in 1998, the Center is a nonprofit organization located in Siloam Springs, Arkansas, and affiliated with John Brown University. It exists to equip people in the corporate and nonprofit community with the transforming power of ethical leadership.

The University of North Carolina at Charlotte

http://www.uncc.edu/colleges/arts_and_sciences/philosophy/center.html.

A compendium of websites can be found at Ethics on the Internet: http://www.ethics1.org/ethiclinks.html#Ethical.

Glossary

Absolute   The "absolute" is defined as that which is believed to be unlimited, unconditional, certain, and despotic. For example, certain rules and regulations can be given absolute status. That is to say, they are beyond questioning. In religion, God is considered to be absolute—one who's word is not to be questioned but believed unconditionally. Also, leaders can take on an aura of absolutism. When this occurs they can become autocratic, tyrannical, authoritarian, and repressive. Authoritarianism is the belief that knowledge is validated by the will of a source (king, god, leader, etc.) entitled to unquestioning obedience rather than by independent or competing efforts to discover what is true or false. "Totalitarianism," a word that implies absolutism, is the view that the state or a certain leader is supreme and the interests of that state or leader take precedence over those of individuals in relationship to some end or goal that is considered good.

Authenticity/authentic leadership   Within the literature of leadership, "authenticity" and "authentic" imply that a certain leader is honesty (has integrity) and behaves consistently with the mission and purposes of the organization. "Authenticity" generically means "genuine." Leadership that arises from one's ethical character—the essence of who we are—is thought of as "authentic leadership" the purpose of which is to transform and to open up possibilities and potentialities within the workplace.

Bell-shaped curve   The Bell curve is a theoretical construction of the distribution of values (such as intelligence or IQs) but does not correspond to the real conditions in its outer tails. The uncertainty at extreme values is very large. The bell curve is another name for the normal distribution, which is a common type of graph that more or less has the shape of a bell that is highest in the middle and lowest on the sides. The standard deviation tells you how spread out numbers are from the average calculated by taking the square root of the arithmetic average of the squares of the deviations from the mean in a frequency distribution. Normal distributions are a very important class of statistical distributions. All normal distributions are symmetric and have bell-shaped density curves with a single peak. The normal distribution is a shape of graph into which many observations in psychology fit very well. Student scores, IQs, and various student behaviors are usually plotted statistically on a bell curve to reveal groupings and patterns of behavior.

Beyonder   "Beyonder" is a twenty-first century concept referring to the creative adult. In E. Paul Torrance and Garnet Millar's research on creative adults, "beyonder" is used to refer to those who dream and plan, who are curious about the future and wonder how much it can be influenced by their individual efforts. In the opinion of Torrance and Millar, the beyonder is a rare creative individual who possesses both courage and tenacity. The concept of "beyonder" has a distinctive eastern flavor. Eastern philosophies have some components relative to creativity, in particularly, Buddhism (including Zen Buddhism) and Taoism. It is believed that we cannot create adequately from the control and illusion of the mind. One must go beyond it, beyond its power, and just let the mind be free to express anything it wants. As soon as we try to create, we start controlling. We have to learn to loosen control, to let the mind be. Instead of forcing anything, we let it come, or more appropriately, we give it a chance to come (although this does not work with everyone).

Character   The word "character" as used in character education literature refers to the distinctive ethical and civil qualities of a person such as honesty, civility, responsibility, fair-mindedness, and so on. Used in this way, "character" has a distinguishing moral overtone, which places one as either consistent or inconsistent with the moral traditions of his or her culture and nation. Hence, even patriotism would be thought of as a sign of character. Character educators usually intertwine "character" education with "moral" education, "civic" education, "values" education, "ethics," or "moralogy." They tell us that these areas are roughly equivalent and that character education—in any form—involves providing appropriate moral values and guiding students to realize them in their character. "Emotional intelligence" is sometimes equated with character or character traits.

Creative thinking   Much of the education delivered in public schools takes the form of academic or intellectual education and education in technical skills. However, creative thinking, focuses on exploring ideas, generating possibilities, looking for many right answers rather than just one. A simple definition is that creativity is the ability to imagine or invent something new. It is the ability to generate new ideas by combining, changing, or reapplying existing ideas. Creativity is strongly linked to receptiveness to life and what it has to offer. It means being open to what is true, about ourselves and about others. Creativity flourishes when the truth about things is admitted to oneself. Since creativity depends on accurate information about one's environment, one's lack of concern for others becomes a roadblock to creativity.

Curricular standardization   In an effort to make the transition from elementary school to middle school and from middle school to high school, state departments of education have created a standardized curriculum for all students. This means that at every grade level in every school within a particular state, teachers will be teaching the same content—knowledge and skills—to all students. Testing departments at both state and local levels have created grade-appropriate assessment to evaluate the progress of students in mastering the skills and content of this curriculum. Without curriculum standardization, accurate assessment would be difficult if not impossible.

Effective Schools Model For over thirty years, the Effective Schools Movement has sought to improve the education of our children based on the common characteristics—or correlates—of effective schools. These correlates are based on decades of research as to why some schools are effective and others are not. The principles of the Effective Schools Movement—the ability of all children to learn, the principal as instructional leader, and high expectations for success—are fundamental to the core beliefs stated by Ron Edmonds in the 1980s. Many believe current Effective School Movement consultants have distorted these principles.

Empowerment Technically, "empowerment" means to empower or authorize. When applied to leadership, empowerment entails the leader divesting himself or herself of certain decision-making powers and giving this authority to subordinate leaders within the organization. Leadership education teaches that when leaders empower others to lead, both the leader and the ones who have been newly authorized to make decisions at their level of expertise are responsible for the outcomes of the organization. Therefore, for empowerment to work, leaders must invest in training for all personnel, allow them problem-solving and decision-making time, and evaluate them appropriately.

Encapsulated man A term coined by psychologist Joseph R. Royce in 1964, "encapsulated man" is one who claims to have the whole of truth when having only part of it, looking at life partially and proceeding to make statements concerning the whole of life, or living partially because one's daily activities are based on a world view which is meager next to the larger meaning of existence. Encapsulation is the dilemma of contemporary specialism—that only certain views are correct and that only certain people have the proper background to have these views. It is the narrowing down of vocational tasks brought on by the industrial revolution, a situation in which a person dares not comment "outside his field." According to Royce encapsulation is the fragmentary ethos of the twentieth century.

Ethics/ethical leadership Ethics usually focuses on established or professional codes of conduct, often on their moral content—good or bad, other-centered or self-centered. Also, ethics is an area of academic concern where one studies the language of ethics, the meanings of ethical words (meta-ethics), and the applications of ethical concepts (normative ethics). The word "ethic" is often substituted for "morals." Thus, in philosophy, the ethical point of view or the moral point of view reflect universal and unequivocal norms and codes of conduct. Ethical principles generated from this belief include honesty, fair-mindedness, responsibility, caring for others, integrity, trust, respect, and equality.

Ethical leadership   is leadership that follows ethical principles and applies them on a daily basis in dealing with other people.

Followship   "Followship" is a basic principle or belief of those who promote both servant and ethical leadership. It says that a leader leads best by following or serving those he or she leads. It implies listening to the experts on staff and following their lead. It also means that the leader respects the integrity of those on staff and treats them with a certain dignity.

Growing leaders   A major function of leadership is "growing other leaders." To do this, leaders must invest in lifelong learning for themselves and for those they serve. Growing staff as leaders entails creating a leadership culture within the organization which encourages people to give and teaching them that by giving they gain influence and lifetime relationships that positively affect the productivity of the organization.

Human value   As used in leadership literature, "human value" refers to the collective or individual value that employees bring to the organization. It may be counted in experience, skills, or various abilities such as the ability to work with others, problem solving, and communication. From the ethical point of view, all humans have moral value, but from a business point of view, we add to their moral value the skills, abilities, and experiences they may possess.

Knowledge workers   A term used by Peter Drucker. Knowledge workers are independent and highly mobile and own the means to production. One aspect of the life of modern organizations is that loyalty can no longer be obtained by a paycheck but by the worker being able to put his or her knowledge to work. The knowledge worker is judged by his or her contribution to the missions and purposes of the organization rather than any built-in superiority or inferiority. The modern organization—that employs knowledge workers—cannot be managed from the top down. It must be organized on an egalitarian basis—as a team.

Leadership   Some definitions of "leadership" focus on what the leader does—vision, judgment, creativity, charisma, drive, etc. The content of this book focuses on what the leader is inside—the essence of leadership—through authentic self-expression and creation of value. This can be done through ideas, systems, or through people. From this perspective—making a difference from within—as a person grows internally, he or she grows as a leader. This is leadership by character rather than by position. The essence of leadership becomes not giving things or even providing visions and mission statements, but offering oneself and one's spirit.

Leadership culture   Leadership cultures promote and create the conditions of leading at all levels of the organization. Leadership cultures invest in lifelong learning for all employees and are committed to problem solving and problem finding. Such cultures encourage people to lead by giving, building strong relationships, networking with others, and mentoring potential leaders. Within leadership cultures, new ideas are encouraged and accepted as the organization focuses productivity and success. Leadership cultures are learning cultures.

Leadership from the inside out Leadership from the inside out, a phrase made popular by Kevin Cashman, deals with an awareness of one's inner identity, purpose, and vision and a dedication to an intentional manner of living. From this point of view, all significant growth and development begins with self-leadership and the mastery of oneself.

Leadership integrity Leaders who lead with integrity take responsibility for themselves as well as employees, practice personal mastery, and lead with their character rather than by a projected image or persona of themselves. Leading with integrity means that the leader listens to others, is aware of hidden beliefs, and is willing to learn from others and change in order to prepare for future leadership challenges.

Learning Organizations Learning organizations are populated by their most essential resource, knowledge workers, who are qualified, knowledgeable people committed to learning and growth. Learning organizations have the ability to create their own futures and continually strengthen their ability to shoulder their own burdens

Management and Leadership Management is that leadership element of an organization that has the task of making people capable of joint performance, of enabling the organization and each of its employees to grow and develop as needs and opportunities change. Management's job is to integrate people in a common venture and is built on a structure of effective communication and on individual responsibility. Management is disciplined and structured leadership at the point where the organization meets its customer or where a school encounters its students.

Micro-managing Management comes in two very distinct types. The first type is more akin to leadership in that it focuses on the growth of employees and creates learning environments where teamwork and networking are made possible and decision-making—within the overall parameters of the mission and purpose of the organization—takes place on all levels. Micromanaging, in contrast, is top-down, where decision making is made by managers and department-level heads. Orders are then funneled down to subordinates who merely carry out the plan that has been developed without their input. Micromanaging tends to destroy individual initiative and is the antithesis of a learning culture.

Moral relativism Moral relativism is the view that right or wrong depend on when and where one is and the point of view of the person—any person. This means that there are no interpersonally valid moral norms. In epistemology (theory of knowledge), relativism means that there is no universal, valid truth. Right and wrong, like truth, will vary from generation to generation, person-to-person, and place to place. In the late twentieth century, moral relativism has been linked to postmodernism because the latter recognizes different forms of reasoning other than strictly scientific reasoning or empirical reasoning.

Morality   "Morality" usually refers to the actions and character of persons; in contrast, "ethics" normally refers to standards of right and wrong. Most commonly, ethics and morals are used interchangeably. Living morally means being good in conduct and character according to civilized standards of right and wrong. Morality is the relative right or wrong of one's actions. The word "virtue" is often used in the placed of either moral or morality. Ethics has to do with formal or professional rules of conduct. Both morality and ethics are related to custom and habit (Latin moralis meaning custom; mores, meaning manners; ethos, meaning custom or habit).

Multiculturalism   Multiculturalism is fundamental to the belief that all citizens are equal. Multiculturalism ensures that all citizens can keep their identities and can take pride in their ancestry and have a sense of belonging. Acceptance gives diverse individuals a feeling of security and self-confidence, making them more open to, and accepting of, other cultures. Multiculturalism encourages racial and ethnic harmony and cross-cultural understanding, and discourages ghettoization, hatred, discrimination, and violence. Multiculturalism recognizes the potential of all individuals, encouraging them to integrate into their society and take an active part in its social, cultural, economic, and political affairs. One view of multiculturalism holds that an individual's identity and personal worth are determined by ethnic/racial membership and that all cultures are of equal worth, regardless of their moral views or how they treat people. It holds that ethnic identity should be a central factor in educational and social policy decisions. Some believe that this view would turn this country into a collection of separatist groups competing with each other for power.

One-dimensional man   Herbert Marcuse's One-Dimensional Man was written in 1964 and can be seen as an analysis of highly developed societies. In it, Marcuse criticizes both communist and capitalist countries for their lack of true democratic processes. Neither type of society creates equal circumstances for its citizens. Marcuse discusses the factors which inhibit criticism and analysis of society. He draws on Marx primarily because his analysis focuses on how the economy limits the potential of people.

Open Society   The "open society," as defined by George Soros, assures freedom of thought and speech and gives ample scope for individuals to experiment and use their creativity. In opposition, a closed society claims to be in possession of the ultimate truth (a false claim) and enforces it only by imposing their views on those who differ.

Phonics-based instruction   Some schools and reading textbooks teach the child to recognize whole words and stress the meaning of the text (whole language).

Others first emphasize the study of phonics—that is, the sounds represented by individual letters or combinations of letters—and the development of independent word-recognition skills. Nearly all current programs combine both techniques; they try to teach a child to recognize words and to learn phonics. For more than 60 years, research has shown that early, systematic phonics instruction produces high reading achievement, at least until the third grade. The most common means of phonics-based instruction is the basal reading program, consisting of a reader, workbook, and other associated materials.

Portfolio of skills Knowledge workers in modern society are valued in the workplace not only because they are human beings, but also because of the skills they have developed and are continuing to refine and improve. This portfolio of skills increases their human value for the organization and is why some have called the modern day worker a "knowledge worker." Knowledge workers defined by the portfolio of skills they bring to the workplace require less micro- and top-down managing. Such workers need time to think, create, develop, and problem solve. They also require opportunities for networking with others who compliment their skills.

Postmodernism Postmodernism is a negative and parasitic term that depends on the negation of something else for its self-definition. It is, therefore, something that succeeds, rejects, overthrows, or transcends the "modern." This is a question that has yet to be fully and completely established. Beginning with Descartes, the "modern" was the desire for an all-encompassing mastery of reality by rational and/or scientific means. It was a quest for absolute knowledge. The modern was always marked by exclusion. It excluded or negated that which was deemed to be nonrational and nonscientific; namely, religious belief. Postmodernism cracks modernity's exclusiveness and inhabits the borders and margins of the modern, continually questioning and disrupting it. The modern and the postmodern are two contrasting sensibilities that have coexisted for many decades, perhaps centuries. Modernity never comes to a final end, for as the postmodern interrogates the modern, it remains indebted to it. The term "postmodern" was coined by Federico de Onis to describe a conservative "reflux" within modernism itself. This reflux opens everyone to alternatives and to the unimaginable. It allows for narrative knowledge and for religious discussion. Whereas narrative knowledge approaches scientific discourse as a variant in the family of narrative cultures, scientific knowledge questions and dismisses the validity of narrative statements altogether. The chief characteristic of postmodernism is its move away from exclusive, scientific discourse toward narrative knowledge.

Problem-solving procedures The procedures used in problem solving include defining the problem clearly; stating what is already known about the problematic situation, e.g., building on experience; seeking options—variables, alternatives, values—that solve the problem; trial and error, including evaluating consequences; and choosing a final answer or solution, which involves understanding and synergy. Problem solving works well with small groups and can enhance the productivity of the organization; therefore, a leader needs to create a learning environment conducive to creative thinking, critical thinking, and problem solving. The problem solving ability of groups can be strengthened with the extensive use of inquiry, hypothesis formation, differentiating relevant from irrelevant information, using analogies and metaphors, making predictions, evaluating alternatives, and finding conclusions.

Rationality   Rationality is the view that the mind has the power to know some truths that are logical prior to experience and yet are not necessarily true. Rationalism is not to be construed narrowly as scientific proof, but as critical appraisal of any idea, thought, or position rather than its acceptance on faith or authority. Rationality is marked here by the demand for the revalidation of accepted truths, by the refusal to accept a claim through habit and routine. Rationality uses interrogative (problem solving) methods based on continual reappraisal and revalidation. The indefinite progression of new appraisals, criticisms, and the production of new judgments to meet the new demands is rationality.

Reflective morality   Reflective morality consists not only of forming moral judgments but of setting forth the reasons for them. Rather than accepting a set of universal moral principles and/or virtues prima facie (on their own merits), the reflective moralist will examine and carefully consider the motives, means, and consequences involved in the selection of each possible line of action. Reflection or reasoning will bring to one's attention values and consequences, applications and considerations that would have been overlooked had the person merely followed authority, impulse, and custom (tradition, belief, or habit). Reflective morality will always take place within a frame of reference or within a structure of beliefs and agreements. It will respect the traditions, agreements, and commitments into which one has entered, since the deepest and richest experiences of life arise only within a community of trust and confidence.

Reflexivity   Reflexivity or reflexive thinking is the theory that, in the social sphere, what we think has a way of affecting what we think about. Knowledge of this introduces an element of uncertainty both into our understanding and into the events in which we participate. Although reflexivity is not the only source of uncertainty, either in our thinking or in reality, when it occurs it constitutes an additional source of uncertainty. For the acquisition of knowledge, we must distinguish between thinking and reality, but it does not follow that the facts are always separate and independent of the statements that relate to them. This is especially true about social events which are contingent on what the participants think and do. The thinking participant seeks to understand the situation in which they participate and they participate (are a part of) in the situation that they seek to understand. This interference introduces indeterminacy into both functions that would perhaps be absent is the two functions operated independently of each other.

Servant leadership   Servant leadership was a concept extensively used by Robert K. Greenleaf to describe the modern empowerment movement in business leadership. Greenleaf's Center for Servant-Leadership, an international nonprofit educational organization, has as its mission to improve the caring and quality of all institutions through a new approach to leadership, structure, and decision making. Greenleaf advocates that the servant leader is one who wants to serve others' needs so that those served grow.

Synchronicity The relation that exists when things occur at the same time is what Joseph Jaworski calls "synchronicity" or inner path of leadership—when things come together in almost unbelievable ways, when events that could never have been predicted seem remarkably to guide us along our path. For Jaworski, synchronicity is a journey of self-discovery involving the discovery of how ethical and moral standards mess with issues of leadership and how the real leader sets the stage on which "predictable miracles," seemingly synchronistic in nature, can and do occur.

Synergy "Synergy" is the interaction of two or more agents or forces so that their combined effect is greater than the sum of their individual effects. Applied to leadership, "synergy" means the smooth working of leaders and employees to build, create, solve problems, and increase the human and organizational value of the group beyond the value of any single person in the organization.

Teflon prophet "Teflon prophet" is a term coined by Thomas Sowell in his book, The Vision of the Anointed. The term refers to "self-congratulation as a basis for social policy" and, for Sowell, is equivalent to the vision of the anointed and the effort made to maintain their reputations in the face of repeated predictions that proved to be wrong. The word "Teflon" comes in to play because all blame for their failures "slides off of them" as others take the kick in the teeth for their failures.

Thinking outside the boundaries Thinking outside the boundaries is a form of creative thinking in which problem solving and decision making are released from the structures imposed upon them. Such thinking is also transformational where old problems are now viewed as fresh possibilities and old ways of thinking that gave organizations the same old results are given up. Thinking outside the boundaries is future oriented and is not trapped in the past. It is results oriented and rejects the status quo. For these reasons, thinking outside the boundaries is life giving—giving new life to what was once stale and stuck in the quagmire of one-dimensional thinking.

Top-down leadership Leadership that serves only the top leader or leaders, imposing control and single-minded thinking on the organization, is top-down leadership. Top-down leadership micromanages the work of employees, as the purpose of the organization is to serve those at the top rather than the mission, purposes, and goals of the organization. It often neglects the human value within the organization except in its service to the top.

Torrance Center for Creative Studies The Torrance Center for Creativity and Talent Development is a service, research, and instructional center concerned with the identification and development of creative potential and with gifted and future studies. Its goals are to investigate, implement, and evaluate techniques for enhancing creative thinking and to facilitate national and international systems that support creative development. All programs and activities sponsored by the Torrance Center build on the legacy of Dr. Ellis Paul Torrance, who is a pioneer in research on the identification and development of creative potential.

Transformational leadership   According to Michael Maccoley, transformational leadership is the ability of a leader to bring together different types of people for a common goal and to transform adversarial competition into principled problem solving leading to consensus. Instead of accepting the status quo and the roles we are assigned, the transformational leader focuses first on self-reflection, which becomes a process of personal transformation—the evaluation of our goals and values.

Trust structures   Trust structures are the ethical principles undergirding the development and growth of all human relationships. Without trust, relationships and human organizations cannot grow. Leaders who empower, serve, and enable the performance of their employees build interdependent and interlinking trust structures throughout the school organization. Building trust structures acknowledges the freedom necessary for unencumbered choice—to stay or leave the organization, and, if staying, to have one's value and growth recognized and supported as essential to the value and growth of the organization as a whole.

Universal principle   In ethics and a system of morals, principles can have universal appeal (or authority) without being thought of as absolute. Being absolute means being beyond the reach of reason; beyond question. On the other hand, a universal principle—such as the categorical imperative—although unconditional and morally binding, is not above examination and critique. Moral philosophy takes it upon itself to examine, clarify, support, and criticize ethical principles and practices—even those thought to be universal. Ethical theorists take as their role finding general principles (amid all the confusion about issues such as stem cell research, capital punishment, and the like) that allow one to take a reasoned and consistent stand on different questions. They search for universal or even instrumental principles that point to the morally relevant differences between cases that allow for consistent and reasoned decision and practice. These sought-for moral principles, moreover, must not have unnoticed logical consequences that would be unacceptable when applied to actual or hypothetical situations. This would diminish their universal appeal.

Whole language   Whole language is a reading philosophy about valuing children and trusting every child as a learner. Whole language is a philosophy that allows children to use their innate abilities to make sense of the world around them, to construct their own meaning and knowledge, and to create their own realities. It allows them to think, comprehend, remember, imagine, and create stories in their minds. It also allows them to question, talk, and learn.

Notes

Introduction

1. *Ethical leadership* will be defined as "leadership which is guided by principles of caring, trust, honesty, responsibility, etc., and which treats all people, regardless of level of employment, fairly and equally.

2. Sally Helgesen, "Leading from the Grass Roots," in *The Leader of the Future*, edited by Frances Hesselbein, Marshall Goldsmith, and Richard Beckhard, San Francisco: Jossey-Bass Publishers, 1996, p. 23.

3. Peter Senge, "Leading Learning Organizations," in *The Leader of the Future*, edited by Frances Hesselbein, Marshall Goldsmith, and Richard Beckhard, San Francisco: Jossey-Bass Publishers, 1996, p. 45.

4. William Bridges, "Leading the De-Jobbed Organization," in *The Leader of the Future*, edited by Frances Hesselbein, Marshall Goldsmith, and Richard Beckhard, San Francisco: Jossey-Bass Publishers, 1996, p. 17.

5. *Ibid.*

6. Max DePree, "Servant-Leadership: Three Things Necessary," in *Focus on Leadership*, edited by Larry C. Spears and Michele Lawrence, New York: John Wiley & Sons, Inc., 2002, p. 94.

7. John Burkhardt and Larry C. Spears, "Servant-Leadership and Philanthropic Institutions," in *Focus on Leadership*, edited by Larry C. Spears and Michele Lawrence, New York: John Wiley & Sons, Inc., 2002, p. 239.

8. John W. Work, "Leading a Diverse Workplace," in *The Leader of the Future*, edited by Frances Hesselbein, Marshall Goldsmith, and Richard Beckhard, San Francisco: Jossey-Bass Publishers, 1996, p. 73.

9. Warren Bennis, *On Becoming a Leader*, Reading, Mass.: Perseus Books, 1989, pp. 140–141.

10. Max DePree, *Leadership Is an Art*, New York: Doubleday, 1988.

11. Peter Senge, *The Fifth Discipline*, Boston: Doubleday, 1990.

12. Joseph P. Hester, *Teaching for Thinking*, Durham, N.C.: Carolina Academic Press, 1994.

13. Kevin Cashman, *Leading from the Inside Out*, Provo, Utah: Executive Excellence Publishing, 1998, p. 18.

14. "Growing leaders" is attributed to Bennis, *On Becoming a Leader*, op. cit., pp. 180ff.

15. Rosamund Stone Zander and Benjamin Zander, *The Art of Possibility*, Boston: Harvard Business School Press, 2000, p. 1.

16. Bennis, *On Becoming a Leader*, op. cit., pp. 114ff.

17. *Ibid.*, pp. 120–121.

18. E. Paul Torrance, *Education and the Creative Potential*, Minneapolis: University of Minnesota Press, 1963, p. 17.

19. *Ibid.*
20. H. Darrell Young, *Leadership under Construction: Bridge to the Next Century: A Training Manual Focusing on Unity of Vision, Transformation of the Workplace, and Developing Leadership,* Marietta, Ga., 2000.
21. Zander and Zander, op. cit., p. 26.
22. Fritjof Capra, *Hidden Connections,* New York: Doubleday, 2000, p. 124.
23. Cashman, op. cit., p.126.
24. *Ibid.* p. 35

Chapter 1

1. Zander and Zander, op. cit., p. 96
2. Torrance, op. cit.
3. Philip C. Schlechty, *Schools for the 21st Century: Leadership Imperatives for Educational Reform,* San Francisco: Jossey Bass, 1990, p. 21–22.
4. William Rauhauser, *America's Schools,* Chapel Hill, N.C.: New View Publishers, 1995.
5. Larry Lezotte, "Distortions and Misconceptions of the Effective Schools Movement," http://www.effectiveschools.com/defend.html a response to Donald Thomas and William Bainbridge, "The Contamination of the Effective Schools Movement," *The School Administrator* 58, 3 (March 2001): 55.
6. Schlechty, op. cit., pp. 22–23
7. *Ibid.,* pp. 17–33.
8. Thomas Sowell, *The Vision of the Anointed,* New York: Basic Books, 1995, p. 65.
9. *Ibid.*
10. Schlechty, op. cit., p. 24.
11. Christopher Hoenig, *The Problem Solving Journey,* Cambridge, Mass.: Perseus Publishing, 2000, pp. 3–5
12. *Ibid.*
13. Rudolph W. Giuliani, *Leadership,* New York: Talk Nilramax Books, Hyperion, 2002, p. 93.
14. *Ibid.,* p. 156.
15. Young, op. cit.
16. Giuliani, op. cit.
17. Peter Drucker, *On the Profession of Management,* Boston: A Harvard Business Review Book, 1998.

Chapter 2

1. Andrei G. Aneinikov, editor, *The Future of Creativity,* Bensenville, Ill.: Scholastic Testing Service, Inc., 2000.
2. E. Paul Torrance, editor, *On the Edge and Keeping on the Edge,* Westport, Conn.: Publications in Creativity Research, 2000.
3. Aneinikov, op. cit. pp. 43–47.
4. The Future Problem Solving Program (FPSP) is designed to help students enlarge, enrich, and make more accurate their images of the future. Dr. E. Paul Torrance developed Future Problem Solving in 1974 as an academic activity for gifted students at Cedar Shoals High School in Athens, Georgia. In 1976 through 1977, the activities grew into a year-long program with interscholastic competitions and became international in scope. Today, an estimated 300,000 students in 41 states and several foreign

countries are involved in the futures studies and creative problem-solving activities comprising the FPSP. Teams of students, in grades K through 12, address complex scientific and social problems of concern today and in the future. Each year, five problem topics are chosen for which the students work to find the solution. With assistance from adult coaches, students gather information, develop problem-solving and thinking skills, and improve communication skills. The Incubation Model is a three-stage instructional model that integrates creativity objectives with content or subject objectives. These three stages are heightening anticipation, deepening expectations, and keeping it going. It makes explicit the methods that successful teachers use in helping their students become better thinkers.

5. Kay McSpadden, "School Dreams Won't Be Built without Money," *The Charlotte (N.C.) Observer*, October 5, 2002, 11A.

6. Gary Ratner, "Needed: Education Roadmap," *Special to the Baltimore Sun*, January 16, 2003. http://www.sunspot.net/news/opinion/oped/bal-op.education16jan16.story.

7. Christopher Hodgkinson, *Educational Leadership, the Moral Art*, Albany: State University of N.Y. Press, 1991, p.46.

8. Schlechty, op. cit., p. 128.

9. *Ibid.*, p. 137.

10. E. Paul Torrance and Garnet Millar, *Manifesto for Adults*, Athens, Ga.: The Torrance Center for Creative Studies, 2001.

11. Cashman, op. cit., p. 19.

12. *Ibid.*, p. 20.

13. Joseph Jaworski, *Synchronicity*, San Francisco: Berrett-Koehler Publishers, 1996.

14. *Ibid.*, p. 60.

15. *Ibid.*

16. Cashman, op. cit., p. 49.

17. *Ibid.*, p. 50.

18. John Gardner, "The Anti-Leadership Vaccine," in *Annual Report of the Carnegie Corporation of New York*, New York: The Corporation, XXXX, pp. 3, 12.

19. Jaworski, op. cit., p. 66.

20. *Ibid.*, p. 185.

21. *Ibid.*

22. Gary L. Neilson, Bruce A. Pasternack, and Albert J. Viscio, "The Seven Dimensions of the E. Organization," *Strategy & Business*, 18 (First Quarter 2000), 52–61.

23. Bennis, *On Becoming a Leader*, op. cit., pp. 40,41.

24. Warren Bennis, *Why Leaders Can't Lead*, San Francisco: Jossey-Bass, 1989, p. 13.

25. *Ibid.*, p. 22.

26. *Ibid.*, p. 24.

27. Russ S. Moxley, *Leadership and Spirit*, San Francisco: Jossey-Bass, 2000, pp. 43–70.

28. *Ibid.*, pp. 105ff.

29. *Ibid.*, p. 130.

30. Vanessa Urch Druskat and Steven B. Wolff, "Building the Emotional Intelligence of Groups," *Harvard Business Review* (March 2001): 80–91.

31. Michael Schrage, "Playing Around with Brainstorming," *Harvard Business Review* (March 2001): 149–154.

32. Torrance, op. cit.

33. D. Zohar and Ian Marshall, *The Quantum Society*, New York: William Morrow, 1994.

34. Bennis, *On Becoming a Leader*, op. cit., p. 21.

35. Bennis, *Why Leaders Can't Lead*, op. cit., pp. 22–23.

36. Robert K. Greenleaf, *Servant Leadership*, New York: Paulist Press, 1977, p. 3.

37. *Ibid.*, pp. 3, 4.

38. *Ibid.*, pp. 9, 10.

39. *Ibid.*, p. 10.

40. Don M. Frick and Larry C. Spears, editors, *On Becoming a Servant Leader: The Private Writings of Robert K. Greenleaf,* San Francisco: Jossey-Bass, 1996, pp. 3, 4.

41. Greenleaf, op. cit., pp. 13ff.

42. *Ibid.,* p. 14.

43. Frick and Spears, op. cit., p. 5.

44. Greenleaf, op. cit., p. 14.

45. *Ibid.,* pp. 24, 25.

46. *Ibid.,* p. 337.

47. *Ibid.,* p. 49.

48. *Ibid.,* pp. 52, 53.

49. Leanna Traill, *Highlight My Strengths,* Crystal Lake, Ill.: Rigby, 1993.

50. Joseph R. Royce, *The Encapsulated Man,* Princeton, N.J.: Van Nostrand Company, Inc., 1964, p. 165.

51. *Ibid.,* p. 199.

52. Abraham Edel, *Ethical Judgment,* New York: The Free Press of Glencoe, 1955, pp. 293ff.

53. Lynn G. Beck and Joseph Murphy, *Ethics in Educational Leadership Programs,* Thousand Oaks, Calif.: Corwin Press, Inc., 1994, pp.; 55ff, 77, and 81ff.

54. Edel, op. cit. pp. 293ff.

55. Mary Jeanne Larrabee, editor, *An Ethic of Care: Feminist and Interdisciplinary Perspectives,* New York: Routledge, 1993. See also: Carol Gilligan, *In a Different Voice: Psychological Theory and Women's Development,* Cambridge: Harvard University Press, 1982.

56. John Rawls, *Lectures on the History of Moral Philosophy,* Cambridge: Harvard University Press, 2000.

57. Richard Rorty, *Achieving Our Country,* Cambridge: Harvard University Press, 1998.

58. Michael Scriven, *Primary Philosophy,* New York: McGraw-Hill Book Company, 1966, p. 237.

59. William K. Frankena, "Recent Conceptions of Morality," in *Morality and the Language of Conduct,* edited by Hector-Neri Castaneda and George Nakhnikian, Detroit: Wayne State University Press, 1965, pp. 2–8.

60. Kurt Baier, *The Moral Point of View,* New York: Random House, 1965, pp. 331–335.

Chapter 3

1. Rauhauser, op. cit.

2. Robert Bellah, et al., *The Good Society,* New York: Vintage Books, 1991, p. 4.

3. *Ibid.,* p. 6.

4. Charles Darwin, *The Descent of Man,* New York: D. Appleton, 1909, p. 121.

5. Sunita Holzer, "In-house Networks Help Employees Develop," *The Charlotte (N.C.) Observer,* October 14, 2002, p. 18D.

6. Bellah, et al., op. cit., p. 15.

7. "Business Ethics," www.bsr.org/resourcecenter/topic_output.gep?topicID=192.

8. Frances Moore Lappe, *Rediscovering America's Values,* New York: Ballantine Books, 1989, p. 14.

9. William Whyte, *The Organizational Man,* New York: Anchor Books, 1957.

10. Michael Maccoby, *The Leader: A New Face for American Management,* New York: Ballantine Publishing, 1983.

11. Lewis H. Lapham, "Notebook," *Harper's Magazine* (Fall 2001): 9–11.

12. Jack Beatty, *The World According to Peter Drucker,* New York: Broadway Books, 1998.

13. Margaret J. Wheatley, *Leadership and the New Science,* San Francisco: Berrett-Koehler, 1994, p. 113.

14. *Ibid.*
15. Rauhauser, op. cit.
16. Wheatley, op. cit., p. 113.
17. *Ibid.*
18. Lapham, op. cit.
19. *Ibid.*
20. Alvin Toffler and Heidi Toffler, "Supercivilization and Its Discontents," in *Civilization* 7, 1 (February 2000): 52–53.
21. Drucker, op. cit., pp. 55ff.
22. Jaworski, op. cit., p. 110.
23. Cashman, op. cit., pp. 199ff.
24. "Applied Ethics," *The Internet Encyclopedia of Philosophy,* www.utm.edu/research /iep/a/appliede.htm.
25. SAS Institute, http://www.sas.com/. See also, "What's Right In North Carolina: Thoughts on Leadership, Compassion, Discovery, Hope, Talent, Innovation, and Conversation," *Our State: Down Home in North Carolina* (January 2003): 38–43; and Art Fry, "Creativity, Invention and Innovation: A Corporate Inventor's Perspective," *Communique* XIII (Fall 2002): 1–5.
26. See the following: Peter Drucker, op. cit.; Warren Bennis, op. cit.; Stephen R. Covey, *Principle-Centered Leadership,* New York: Simon and Schuster, 1991; Horst Bergman, Kathleen Hurson, and Darlene Russ-Eft, *Everyone a. Leader,* New York: John Wiley and Sons, Inc., 1999; Kevin Cashman, op. cit.; Ken Blanchard and Michael O'Connor, *Managing by Values,* San Francisco: Berrett-Koehler Publisher, 1997.
27. H. Richard Niebuhr, *The Responsible Self,* New York: Harper and Row, 1978, p. 61.
28. Bellah, et al., op. cit., p. 284.
29. Philip Selznick, *The Moral Commonwealth,* Los Angelus: The University of California Press, 1992, pp. 390–392.
30. Bellah, et al., op. cit., p. 284.
31. Cliff Havener, *Meaning,* Edina, Minn.: Beaver's Pond Press, Inc., 1999, p. 110.
32. Jerry L. Patterson, et al., *Productive School Systems for a Nonrational World,* Alexandria, Va.: ASCD, 1986.
33. Joseph P. Hester and Philip F. Vincent, *Philosophy for Young Thinkers* series, Monroe, N.Y.: Trillium Press, 1983, 1989, p. ix.
34. Elliot Turiel, *The Culture of Morality,* Cambridge, U.K.: Cambridge University Press, 2002, p. 15.
35. *Ibid.*
36. *Ibid.*, pp. 16–18.

Chapter 4

1. David W. Johnson and Frank P. Johnson, *Joining Together: Group Theory and Group Skills,* second edition, Englewood Cliffs, N.J.: Prentice-Hall, Inc., 1982, pp. 443ff. See also, M. A. Leiberman, "Group Methods," in *Helping People Change,* edited by F. Kanfer and A. Goldstein, New York: Pergamon Press, 1980.
2. Carolyn R. Shaffer and Kristin Anundsen, *Creating Community Anywhere,* New York: The Putnam Publishing Group, 1993, pp. 21–22.
3. Mark Pilsuk and Susan Parks Hillier, *The Healing Web: Social Networks and Human Survival,* Boston: University Press of New England, 1986.
4. Shaffer and Anundsen, op. cit., p. 22.
5. *Ibid.*, p. 28.
6. Alfie Kohn, *The Brighter Side of Human Nature: Altruism and Empathy in Everyday Life,* New York: Basic Books, 1990.

7. Gregg Levoy, *Callings*, New York: Three Rivers Press, 1997, pp. 8–9.

8. Søren Kiekegaard, as quoted by Gregg Levoy, *Ibid.*, p. 11.

9. Joseph Campbell, *The Hero with a Thousand Faces*, Princeton, N.J.: Princeton University Press, 1973.

10. Frank Navran, "Seven Steps for Changing the Ethical Culture of an Organization," Ethics Resource Center, 2003, http://www.ethics.org/resources/article_detail.cfm?ID=785.

11. Alan Watts, *On the Taboo against Knowing Who You Are*, New York: Vintage Books, 1972.

12. Annie Dillard, *Pilgrim at Tinker Creek*, New York: Bantam Books, 1974.

13. Sara Lawrence-Lightfoot, *Respect*, Reading, Mass.: Perseus Books, 1999, pp. 8–10.

14. *Ibid.*

15. *Ibid.*

16. *Ibid.*

17. Shaffer and Anundsen, op. cit., p. 10.

18. George Soras, *Open Society*, New York: Public Affairs, 2000, pp. 121–122.

19. *Ibid.*, p. 129.

20. *Ibid.*, 130.

21. *Ibid.*, p. xxiii.

22. Joseph P. Hester and Patricia J. Hester, "Brain Research and the Middle School Curriculum," *National Middle School Journal*, (November 1983): 4–7, 30.

23. Patricia K. Arlin, *Teaching for Thinking: The Arlin Test of Formal Reasoning Applied*, East Aurora, N.Y.: Slosson Educational Publications, 1987.

24. Joseph P. Hester, [to come], op. cit.

25. College Board and Educational Testing Service, Algebrigde Program, New York: McGraw-Hill, 1990; see also, http://www.sra4kids.com/everydaylearning/about/glencoe.html.

26. Soros, op. cit., p. 135.

27. *Ibid.*

28. Shaffer and Anundsen, op. cit., pp. 207–221.

29. Shaffer and Anundsen, op. cit., pp. 22ff.; see also, Susan Campbell, *The Couple's Journey: Intimacy as a Path to Wholeness*, New York: Impact Publishers, 1980.

30. M. Scott Peck, *The Different Drum: Community Making and Peace*, New York: Simon & Schuster, 1987.

31. Johnson and Johnson, op. cit., pp. 214ff.

32. David Elkind, *The Hurried Child: Growing Up too Fast too Soon*, Reading, Mass.: Addison-Wesley, 1981, see chapters 2 and 3.

33. Mark Mehler, "Who Are You?" *Priority* (October/November 2002): 15–22.

34. The Center for Conflict Resolution, *Building United Judgment: A Handbook of Consensus Decision Making*, Madison, Wis.: The Center, [xxxx].

35. *Ibid.*

36. Shaffer and Anundsen, op. cit., p. 271.

37. Peter M. Senge, *The Fifth Discipline*, op. cit.

38. Shaffer and Anundsen, op. cit., p. 272.

39. *Ibid.*

40. *Ibid.*

41. *Ibid.*, p. 273.

42. Peck, op. cit.

43. DePree, *Leadership Is an Art*, op. cit.

44. J. P. Hester, *Bridges: Building Relationships and Resolving Conflicts*, Chapel Hill, NC: New View Publications, 1995, pp. 95–97.

45. Shaffer and Anundsen, op. cit., p. 282.

46. *Ibid.*

47. Hester, *Bridges*, op. cit., pp. 117–118.

Chapter 5

1. Bruce S. Thornton. *Plagues of the Mind: The New Epidemic of False Knowledge,* Wilmington, Del.: ISI Books, 1999, p. 15.

2. *Ibid.,* p. 14

3. The Associated Press, "S.C. Education Accountability," *The Charlotte (N.C.) Observer,* December 13, 2002, 5B.

4. http://www.ridgelandsc.com/education.htm

5. William Rasberry, *Washington Post* Writers Group, *The Charlotte (N.C.) Observer,* December 14, 2002, 13A.

6. Lawrence M. Hinman, *Ethics,* New York: Harcourt Brace College Publishers1998, p. 137.

7. *Ibid.,* p. 138.

8. Harold S. Kushner, *Living a Life That Matters,* New York: Alfred A. Knopf, 2001.

9. *Ibid.,* p. 42.

10. *Ibid.,* pp. 90–91.

11. *Ibid.,* p. 149.

12. Bob Herbert, *New York Times,* quoted in *The Charlotte (N.C.) Observer,* December 18, 2002, 17A.

13. http://www.kipp.org/our_focus/history.html
"The Knowledge Is Power Program (KIPP) began in 1994 when Mike Feinberg and Dave Levin completed their two-year commitment with Teach for America in Houston Independent School District and launched as a fifth grade program at Garcia Elementary School. Their mentor teacher, Harriett Ball, motivated the two young men to remain in education and do everything possible to ensure their students were achieving at the highest possible levels in the classroom. The students' academic success and interest in learning inspired Feinberg and Levin to expand the program beyond one classroom. The following year, KIPP Academy opened in Houston, and Levin founded KIPP Academy in the South Bronx, New York. Today, both are recognized nationally as outstanding schools. The achievements of the first two KIPP schools captured national attention. In 2000, Doris and Donald Fisher, founders of The Gap, Inc., formed a unique partnership with Feinberg and Levin to replicate the success of the two schools. Following their belief that great schools need great leaders, Feinberg, Levin, and the Fishers created a new organization to recruit, select, and train educators who would plan, open, and lead their own KIPP Schools."

14. Senge, *The Fifth Discipline,* op. cit., p. 158 ff.

15. *Ibid.*

16. Cashman, op. cit., p. 109.

17. *Ibid.,* p. 108.

18. *Ibid.*

19. Moxley, op. cit., pp. 96–97.

20. *Ibid.,* p. 154.

21. *Ibid.,* pp. 154–155.

22. Covey, op. cit., p. 190.

23. *Ibid.,* p. 191.

24. *Ibid.,* p. 192.

25. *Ibid.*

26. *Ibid.*

27. *Ibid.,* p. 193

28. *Ibid.*

29. *Ibid.,* p. 194.

30. John C. Maxwell, *The 21 Irrefutable Laws of Leadership,* Nashville, Tenn.: Thomas Nelson Publishers, 1998, p. 130.

31. *Ibid.,* p. 126.

32. David M. Noer, "A Recipe for Glue," *The Leader of the Future,* edited by Frances

Hesselbein, Marshall Goldsmith, and Richard Beckhard, The Drucker Foundation Future Series, San Francisco: Jossey-Bass Publishers, 1996, pp. 141–145.

33. *Ibid.*, p. 144.
34. *Ibid.*, pp. 144–145.
35. *Ibid.*, p. 145.
36. John P. Kotter, "What Leaders Really Do," *Harvard Business Review on Leadership*, Boston: Harvard Business Review Paperback, 1998, pp. 37–60.
37. *Ibid.*, p. 48.
38. *Ibid.*
39. *Ibid.*, p. 49.
40. *Ibid.*
41. *Ibid.*
42. Caela Farren and Beverly L. Kaye, "New Skills for New Leadership Roles," in *The Leader of the Future*, edited by Frances Hesselbein, Marshall Goldsmith, and Richard Beckhard, The Drucker Foundation Future Series, San Francisco: Jossey-Bass Publishers, 1996, pp. 175–188.
43. *Ibid.*, p. 178.
44. *Ibid.*
45. *Ibid.*, p. 181.
46. *Ibid.*
47. *Ibid.*
48. *Ibid.*, 187.
49. Bennis, *Why Leaders Can't Lead*, op. cit., p. 22.
50. *Ibid.*, p. 23
51. Greenleaf, op. cit., p. 10.

Chapter 6

1. Ron Green, Jr. "Sources: Leak Picks Florida," *The Charlotte (N.C.) Observer*, January 5, 2003, F1.
2. The leadership model in chapter six was based on information from chapters one through five and the following sources:

"Servant Leadership: A Model That Can Pay Great Dividends," *Dallas Business Journal*, August 31, 1998, http://dallas.bizjournals.com/dallas/stories/1998/08/31/smallb4.html?t=printable .

Ethics Today Online 1, 4, December 2002. http://www.ethics.org/today/et_current.html.

Education Leadership Tool Kit, A project of the National School Boards Foundation implemented by NSBA's Institute for the Transfer of Technology to Education with a grant from the National Science Foundation, http://www.nsba.org/sbot/toolkit.

Ethics, Leadership & Organizational Integrity: Six Styles and Five Modes of Ethical Leaders, http://www.ethicaledge.com/quest_4.html.

Dave Ulrich, "Credibility x Capability," *The Leader of the Future*, edited by Frances Hesselbein, Marshall Goldsmith, and Richard Beckhard, The Drucker Foundation Future Series, San Francisco: Jossey-Bass Publishers, 1996, pp. 209–219.

James A. Joseph, "Leadership and the Changing Role of Ethics in Public Life," Austin: Center for Ethical Leadership, Lyndon B. Johnson School of Public Affairs, The University of Texas at Austin, Texas, http://www.utexas.edu/lbj/research/leadership/publications/conference1/LeadershipChangingRoleofEthics.html.

"Ethics, Compliance & Responsibility: Nature of the Responsible Business Enterprise," Washington, D.C.: EPIC, http://ethicaledge.com/responsibility.html.

Bibliography

Aneinikov, Andrei G., editor, *The Future of Creativity*, Bensenville, Ill.: Scholastic Testing Service, Inc., 2000.

"Applied Ethics," *The Internet Encyclopedia of Philosophy*, www.utm.edu/research/iep/a/appliede.htm.

Arlin, Patricia K., *Teaching for Thinking: The Arlin Test of Formal Reasoning Applied*, East Aurora, N.Y: Slosson Educational Publications, 1987.

The Associated Press, "S.C. Education Accountability," *The Charlotte (N.C.) Observer*, December 13, 2002, 5B. http://www.ridgelandsc.com/education.htm.

Baier, Kurt, *The Moral Point of View*, New York: Random House, 1965.

Beatty, Jack, *The World According to Peter Drucker*, New York: Broadway Books, 1998.

Beck, Lynn G., and Joseph Murphy, *Ethics in Educational Leadership Programs*, Thousand Oaks, Calif.: Corwin Press, Inc., 1994.

Bellah, Robert, et al., *The Good Society*, New York: Vintage Books, 1991.

Bennis, Warren, *On Becoming a Leader*, Reading, Mass.: Perseus Books, 1989.

_____, *Why Leaders Can't Lead*, San Francisco: Jossey-Bass, 1989.

Bergman, Horst, Kathleen Hurson, and Darlene Russ-Eft, *Everyone a. Leader*, New York: John Wiley and Sons, Inc., 1999.

Blanchard, Ken, and Michael O'Connor, *Managing by Values*, San Francisco: Berrett-Koehler Publisher, 1997.

Bridges, William, "Leading the De-Jobbed Organization," in *The Leader of the Future*, edited by Frances Hesselbein, Marshall Goldsmith, and Richard Beckhard. San Francisco: Jossey-Bass Publishers, 1996.

Burkhardt, John, and Larry Spears, "Servant-Leadership and Philanthropic Institutions," in *Focus on Leadership*, edited by Larry C. Spears and Michele Lawrence, New York: John Wiley & Sons, Inc., 2002.

"Business Ethics," www.bsr.org/resourcecenter/topic_output.gep?topicID=192.

Campbell, Joseph, The *Hero with a Thousand Faces*, Princeton, New Jersey: Princeton University Press, 1973.

Campbell, Susan, *The Couple's Journey: Intimacy as a Path to Wholeness*, New York: Impact Publishers, 1980.

Capra, Fritjof, *Hidden Connections*, New York: Doubleday, 2000.

Cashman, Kevin, *Leading from the Inside Out*, Provo, Utah: Executive Excellence Publishing, 1998.

The Center for Conflict Resolution, *Building United Judgment: A Handbook of Consensus Decision Making*, Madison, Wi.: The Center, [xxxx].

The College Board and Educational Testing Service, Algebridge Program, New York: McGraw-Hill, 1990; see also, http://www.sra4kids.com/everydaylearning/about/glencoe.html#.

Covey, Steven, *Principle-Centered Leadership*, New York: Simon & Schuster, 1991.

Darwin, Charles, *The Descent of Man*, New York: D. Appleton, 1909.

DePree, Max, *Leadership Is an Art*, New York: Doubleday, 1988.

_____, "Servant-Leadership: Three Things Necessary," in *Focus on Leadership*, edited by Larry C. Spears and Michele Lawrence, New York: John Wiley & Sons, Inc., 2002.

Dillard, Annie, *Pilgrim at Tinker Creek*, New York: Bantam Books, 1974.

Drucker, Peter, *On the Profession of Management*, Boston: A Harvard Business Review Book, 1998.

Druskat, Vanessa Urch, and Steven B. Wolff, "Building the Emotional Intelligence of Groups," *Harvard Business Review*, March 2001.

Edel, Abraham, *Ethical Judgment*, New York: The Free Press of Glencoe, 1955.

Education Leadership Tool Kit, A project of the National School Boards Foundation implemented by NSBA's Institute for the Transfer of Technology to Education with a grant from the National Science Foundation. http://www.nsba.org/sbot/toolkit.

Elkind, David, *The Hurried Child: Growing Up too Fast too Soon*, Reading, Mass.: Addison-Wesley, 1981.

"Ethics, Compliance & Responsibility: Nature of the Responsible Business Enterprise," Washington, D.C.: EPIC, http://www.ethicaledge.com/quest_4.html

Ethics, Leadership & Organizational Integrity: Six Styles and Five Modes of Ethical Leader, http://www.ethicaledge.com/quest_4.html.

Ethics Today Online, 1, 4, December 2002, http://www.ethics.org/today/et_current.html.

Farren, Caela, and Beverly L. Kaye, "New Skills for New Leadership Roles," in *The Leader of the Future*, edited by Frances Hesselbein, Marshall Goldsmith, and Richard Beckhard, The Drucker Foundation Future Series, San Francisco: Jossey-Bass Publishers, 1996.

Frankena, William K., "Recent Conceptions of Morality," in *Morality and the Language of Conduct*, edited by Hector-Neri Castaneda and George Nakhnikian, Detroit: Wayne State University Press, 1965.

Frick, Don M., and Larry C. Spears, editors, *On Becoming a Servant Leader: The Private Writings of Robert K. Greenleaf*, San Francisco: Jossey-Bass, 1996.

Fry, Art, "Creativity, Invention and Innovation: A Corporate Inventor's Perspective," *Communique*, XIII, Fall 2002.

Gardner, John, "The Anti-Leadership Vaccine," *Annual Report of the Carnegie Corporation of New York*, New York: The Corporation, [XXXX].

Gilligan, Carol, *In a Different Voice: Psychological Theory and Women's Development*, Cambridge: Harvard University Press, 1982.

Giuliani, Rudolph W., *Leadership*, New York: Talk Nilramax Books, Hyperion, 2002.

Green, Ron, Jr., "Sources: Leak Picks Florida," *The Charlotte (N.C.) Observer*, January 5, 2003, F1.

Greenleaf, Robert K., *Servant Leadership*, New York: Paulist Press, 1977.

Havener, Cliff, *Meaning*, Edina, Minn.: Beaver's Pond Press, Inc., 1999.

Helgesen, Sally, "Leading from the Grass Roots," in *The Leader of the Future*, edited by Frances Hesselbein, Marshall Goldsmith, and Richard Beckhard. San Francisco: Jossey-Bass Publishers, 1996.

Herbert, Bob, "Remarkable School in N.C. Quietly Succeeds," *New York Times*, quoted in *The Charlotte (N.C.) Observer*, December 18, 2002, 17A. See also: http://www.kipp.org /our_focus/history.html.

Hester, Joseph P., *Bridges: Building Relationships and Resolving Conflicts*, Chapel Hill, N.C.: New View Publications, 1995.

_____, *Teaching for Thinking*, Durham, N.C.: Carolina Academic Press, 1994.

Hester Joseph P., and Patricia J. Hester, "Brain Research and the Middle School Curriculum," *National Middle School Journal*, November 1983.

_____, and Philip F. Vincent, *Philosophy for Young Thinkers* series, Monroe, N.Y.: Trillium Press, 1983, 1989.

Hinman, Lawrence M., *Ethics,* New York: Harcourt Brace College Publishers, 1998.
Hodgkinson, Christopher, *Educational Leadership, the Moral Art,* Albany: State University of N.Y. Press, 1991.
Hoenig, Christopher, *The Problem Solving Journey,* Cambridge, Mass.: Perseus Publishing, 2000.
Holzer, Sunita, "In-House Networks Help Employees Develop," *The Charlotte (N.C.) Observer,* October 14, 2002, 18D.
Jaworski, Joseph, *Synchronicity,* San Francisco: Berrett-Koehler Publishers, 1996.
Johnson, David W., and Frank P. Johnson, *Joining Together: Group Theory and Group Skills,* second edition, Englewood Cliffs, N.J.: Prentice-Hall, Inc., 1982.
Joseph, James A., "Leadership and the Changing Role of Ethics in Public Life," Austin: Center for Ethical Leadership, Lyndon B. Johnson School of Public Affairs, The University of Texas at Austin. http://www.utexas.edu/lbj/research/leadership/publications/conference1/LeadershipChangingRoleofEthics.html.
Kohn, Alfie, *The Brighter Side of Human Nature: Altruism and Empathy in Everyday Life,* New York: Basic Books, 1990.
Kotter, John P., "What Leaders Really Do," *Harvard Business Review on Leadership,* Boston: Harvard Business Review Paperback, 1998.
Kushner, Harold S., *Living a Life That Matters,* New York: Alfred A. Knopf, 2001.
Lapham, Lewis H., "Notebook," *Harper's Magazine,* Fall 2001.
Lappe, Frances Moore, *Rediscovering America's Values,* New York: Ballantine Books, 1989.
Larrabee, Mary Jeanne, editor, *An Ethic of Care: Feminist and Interdisciplinary Perspectives,* New York: Routledge, 1993.
Lawrence-Lightfoot, Sara, *Respect,* Reading, Mass.: Perseus Books, 1999.
Leiberman, M. A., "Group Methods," in *Helping People Change,* edited by F. Kanfer and A. Goldstein, New York: Pergamon Press, 1980.
Levoy, Gregg, *Callings,* New York: Three Rivers Press, 1997.
Lezotte, Larry, "Distortions and Misconceptions of the Effective Schools Movement," http://www.effectiveschools.com/defend.html, a response to Donald Thomas and William Branbridge's "The Contamination of the Effective Schools Movement," *The School Administrator* 58, 3 (March 2001): 55.
Maccoby, Michael, *The Leader: A New Face for American Management,* New York: Ballantine Publishing, 1983.
Maxwell, John C., *The 21 Irrefutable Laws of Leadership,* Nashville, Tenn.: Thomas Nelson Publishers, 1998.
McSpadden, Kay, "School Dreams Won't Be Built without Money," *The Charlotte (N.C.) Observer,* October 5, 2002, 11A.
Mehler, Mark, "Who Are You?" *Priority,* October/November 2002.
Moxley, Russ S., *Leadership and Spirit,* San Francisco: Jossey-Bass, 2000.
Navran, Frank, "Seven Steps for Changing the Ethical Culture of an Organization," Ethics Resource Center, 2003, http://www.ethics.org/resources/article_detail.cfm?ID=785.
Neilson, Gary L., Bruce A. Pasternack, and Albert J. Viscio, "The Seven Dimensions of the E. Organization," *Strategy & Business,* 18, First Quarter 2000.
Niebuhr, H. Richard, *The Responsible Self,* New York: Harper and Row, 1978.
Noer, David M., "A Recipe for Glue," *The Leader of the Future,* edited by Frances Hesselbein, Marshall Goldsmith, and Richard Beckhard, The Drucker Foundation Future Series, San Francisco: Jossey-Bass Publishers, 1996.
Patterson, Jerry L., et al., *Productive School Systems for a Nonrational World,* Alexandria, Va.: ASCD, 1986.
Peck, M. Scott, *The Different Drum: Community Making and Peace,* New York: Simon & Schuster, 1987.
Pilsuk, Mark, and Susan Parks Hillier, *The Healing Web: Social Networks and Human Survival,* Boston: University Press of New England, 1986.

Rasberry, William, *Washington Post* Writers Group, *The Charlotte (N.C.) Observer,* December 14, 2002, 13A.

Ratner, Gary, "Needed: Education Roadmap," *Special to the Baltimore Sun,* January 16, 2003, http://www.sunspot.net/news/opinion/oped/bal-op.education16jan16.story.

Rauhauser, William, *America's Schools,* Chapel Hill, N.C.: New View Publishers, 1995.

Rawls, John, *Lectures on the History of Moral Philosophy,* Cambridge: Harvard University Press, 2000.

Rorty, Richard, *Achieving Our Country,* Cambridge: Harvard University Press, 1998.

Royce, Joseph R., *The Encapsulated Man,* Princeton, N.J.: Van Nostrand Company, Inc., 1964.

SAS Institute, http://www.sas.com

Schlechty, Philip C., *Schools for the 21st Century: Leadership Imperatives for Educational Reform,* San Francisco: Jossey Bass, 1990.

Schrage, Michael, "Playing Around with Brainstorming," *Harvard Business Review,* March 2001.

Scriven, Michael, *Primary Philosophy,* New York: McGraw-Hill Book Company, 1966.

Selznick, Philip, *The Moral Commonwealth,* Los Angelus: The University of California Press, 1992.

Senge, Peter M., *The Fifth Discipline,* New York: Doubleday, 1990.

_____, "Leading Learning Organizations," in *The Leader of the Future,* edited by Frances Hesselbein, Marshall Goldsmith, and Richard Beckhard. San Francisco: Jossey-Bass Publishers, 1996.

"Servant Leadership: A Model That Can Pay Great Dividends," *Dallas Business Journal,* August 31, 1998, http://dallas.bizjournals.com/dallas/stories/1998/08/31/smallb4.html?t=printable.

Shaffer, Carolyn R., and Kristin Anundsen, *Creating Community Anywhere,* New York: The Putnam Publishing Group, 1993.

Soras, George, *Open Society,* New York: Public Affairs, 2000.

Sowell, Thomas, *The Vision of the Anointed,* New York: Basic Books, 1995.

Spears, Larry C., and Michele Lawrence, editors, *Focus on Leadership,* New York: John Wiley & Sons, Inc., 2002.

Thornton, Bruce S., *Plagues of the Mind: The New Epidemic of False Knowledge,* Wilmington, Del.: ISI Books, 1999.

Toffler, Alvin, and Heidi Toffler, "Supercivilization and Its Discontents," *Civilization* 7, 1, February, 2000.

Torrance, E. Paul, *Education and the Creative Potential,* Minneapolis: University of Minnesota Press, 1963.

_____, and Garnet Millar, *Manifesto for Adults,* Athens, Ga.: The Torrance Center for Creative Studies, 2001.

_____, editor, *On the Edge and Keeping on the Edge,* Westport, Conn.: Publications in Creativity Research, 2000.

Traill, Leanna. *Highlight My Strengths,* Crystal Lake, Ill.: Rigby, 1993.

Turiel, Elliot, *The Culture of Morality,* Cambridge, U.K.: Cambridge University Press, 2002.

Ulrich, Dave, "Credibility x Capability," *The Leader of the Future,* edited by Frances Hesselbein, Marshall Goldsmith, and Richard Beckhard, The Drucker Foundation Future Series, San Francisco: Jossey-Bass Publishers, 1996.

Watts, Alan, *On the Taboo against Knowing Who You Are,* New York: Vintage Books, 1972.

"What's Right in North Carolina: Thoughts on Leadership, Compassion, Discovery, Hope, Talent, Innovation, and Conversation," *Our State: Down Home in North Carolina,* January 2003.

Wheatley, Margaret J., *Leadership and the New Science,* San Francisco: Berrett-Koehler, 1994.

Whyte, William, *The Organizational Man,* New York: Anchor Books, 1957.

Work, John W., "Leading a Diverse Workplace," in *The Leader of the Future,* edited by Frances Hesselbein, Marshall Goldsmith, and Richard Beckhard. San Francisco: Jossey-Bass Publishers, 1996.

Young, H. Darrell, *Leadership under Construction: Bridge to the Next Century: A Training Manual Focusing on Unity of Vision, Transformance of the Workplace, and Developing Leadership*, Marietta, Ga., 2000.

Zander, Rosamund Stone, and Benjamin Zander, *The Art of Possibility*, Boston: Harvard Business School Press, 2000.

Zohar, D., and Ian Marshall, *The Quantum Society*, New York: William Morrow, 1994.

Index